DISCOVERING MEDIAEVAL ART

DISCOVERING
MEDIAEVAL ART

by
G. M. DURANT

LONDON
G. BELL & SONS, LTD
MCMLX

First published 1960

Printed in Great Britain by
The Camelot Press Ltd., London and Southampton

FOREWORD

~~~~~~~~~~~~~~~~~~~~~~~~~~~~~~~~~~~~

THIS book is not an exhaustive history. It is an *introduction* to the art of the Middle Ages. It does not pretend to say all there is to be said on the subject; it could not possibly, within the limits of a volume this size, deal fully, much less exhaustively, with the many types of mediaeval art with which it has concerned itself. But it does try to present the subject as something worth studying in more detail after interest has been aroused; and its chief aim is to kindle that interest through better understanding. The art of the Middle Ages had its origins in a mentality so different from ours that it cannot be immediately understood. Moreover, it has too often been treated merely as matter for dissection, tabulation, dry speculation and arid argument, so that in the end one cannot see the wood for the trees, and what should be a living flower bringing delight to the senses becomes only a botanical specimen in a laboratory.

The aim of this book is to present the living flower, not the dissected laboratory specimen. It sets out first, to kindle delight in what was once an art that formed a part of all men's lives; secondly, to give a keener edge to that delight by accompanying it with knowledge; just enough knowledge to set the wanderer in the realms of Mediaeval Art on his way.

If the present volume has served its purpose that wanderer will do the rest for himself. If it awakens in him a love for this long bygone art which both directs him towards more detailed works, and better still — far better — urges him literally to journey to see the products of the mediaeval artists for himself it will not have been written in vain.

G.M.D.

v

ACKNOWLEDGEMENTS

ACKNOWLEDGEMENTS are made for permission to reproduce the following: Plates I (Lindisfarne Gospels), II (New Minster Charter and Codex Aureus), III (St. Omer Psalter, St. John the Baptist and Boating Party), to the Trustees of the British Museum; Plate I (Book of Kells), to the Board of Trinity College, Dublin; Plate II (Madonna and Child), to the Bodleian Library; Plate IV (Christ Pantocrator) Anderson, Rome; Plates IV (Entry into Jerusalem) and V (Calling of St. Peter and St. Andrew) Iris Verlag, Berne; Plate V (Mosaic in San Vitale) The Mansell Collection; Plate VI (The Purgatorial Ladder) National Buildings Record; Plates VI (Guardian Angels Chapel) and VII (Holy Infancy Scenes), the Courtauld Institute; Plate VII (Wheel of the Five Senses) Crown Copyright, H.M. Ministry of Works; Plate VIII (Kilpeck Church) the Author; Plate VIII (Abbey Dore) the Royal Commission on Historical Monuments, from Vol. I of the Royal Commission's Herefordshire Inventory, by permission of the Controller of H.M. Stationery Office; Plate IX (Crosses at Middleton-by-Pickering) Thames & Hudson Ltd., publishers of *English Parish Churches*, by Graham Hutton and Edwin Smith, from a photograph by the latter; Plate IX (Anglian Cross Shaft) the Controller of H.M. Stationery Office – Crown Copyright; Plate IX (Cross Shaft from Easby Abbey) by courtesy of the Director of the Victoria and Albert Museum; Plate X (Canterbury Cathedral Capitals) Alec Tiranti Ltd., from *English Romanesque Sculpture* 1066-1140 by G. Zarnecki; Plate X (Wells Cathedral Capitals) Phillips City Studio, Wells; Plates XI and XII (Statues at Chartres) Mr. Charles Stainer; Plate XII (Malmesbury Apostles) from *English Sculpture of the Twelfth Century* by Dr. Saxl, published by Faber and Faber, the Warburg Institute; Plate XIII (Statues of Wells Cathedral) from *Mediaeval Sculpture*, C.U.P., Mr. Arthur Gardner; Plate XIII (West Front of Exeter Cathedral) Raphael Tuck & Sons, reproduced by permission of the Dean and Chapter; Plate XIV, (Prior's Doorway Norwich) the Courtauld Institute; Plate XIV (William the Conqueror) from *Mediaeval Sculpture* as above; Plate XIV (St. Matthew) the Gernsheim Collection, by permission of Mr. H. Gernsheim; Plate XV (the 'Prykke of Conscience' window) Miss M. Deas; Plate XVI (The Magi) Messrs. B. & W. Fisk-Moore, reproduced by permission of the Friends of Canterbury Cathedral; Plate XVI (Window at Christ Church, Oxford) the National Buildings Record.

CONTENTS

LIST OF PLATES

(between pp. 120–21)

1

THE ENCHANTED WORLD
OF ILLUMINATION

I REMEMBER distinctly when the first glimmering of realization began to dawn over my mind, though I little guessed then what a journey lay before me. All around were threats of major war. It was March, and the rain-clouds were like yellow fog over London. The present was drab and featureless, the future promised only violent extermination. All existence, leading but to this, seemed as purposeless as the life of flowers blooming unseen in unfrequented places, propagating their kind – to what end? Why propagate, since that which was propagated had no reason for existence except to propagate reasonless life again?

In those days, just before the Second World War, even the young in years cried, 'What is the sense of it all, what is the use of anything, when war will come and utterly destroy everything?' The consciousness of impermanence haunted like a nightmare. The present was shifting sand, the future a dark void. All that remained was the past, which had been, and now could never not-be. Partly to shelter from the rain, partly to cling to that ineradicable past – as I happened to be near it at that moment – I went into the British Museum.

I did not much care, or even notice much, whether I

went straight on or turned left or right. As it happened –
or was there a purpose in it all? – I turned right. Drab
gloom and a long, cloud-darkened manuscript saloon lay
before me, and a number of blind display cases – for over
each was drawn a curtain, hiding what lay beneath. An
invitation to pull back the curtains prompted me to look
at what they were protecting. Out upon the grey day
flashed gold and blue and ruby-red: I stood transfixed,
and stared.

Such was my introduction to the enchanted world of
mediaeval illuminated manuscripts.

There it was, visible at the drawing of those curtains,
gleaming upon the sight as the treasures of Mycenae rich
in gold gleamed upon the eyes of Schliemann when he
unearthed the buried wealth from the shaft graves of pre-
historic Achaean kings. Through the gloom they shone,
and nothing could dim their shining. Some glittered with
gold; the crimson of some was as vivid and deep as the
poppies which grow among the tumbled stones of the
Greek islands. Their lapis-lazuli blue – the blue of far-
away ages, of Mesopotamian palaces and pharaonic
temples – was achingly intense, like the blue of anchusa,
or such gentians as only Alpine slopes know; their greens
thrilled like the emerald of sunlit forest trees at the spring's
returning. Cloudy white and purplish pink were the foils to
these colours, in case they should prove too piercingly bright.

Something awoke in me as I stared and moved on to the
next case and stared again, and so again and again; and
I knew I had found that for which I had been craving. I
came a second time, and a third, I came whenever I had
the opportunity. And when war crashed at last upon the
world, and I could come no more; when that glory of colour
was hidden away where the forces of destruction might not
rend it to pieces, then I sought out in a world impoverished
of all but the stark essentials of living every shop-soiled,
second-hand, years-old reproduction of those illuminations
I could find, over which to pore.

At that time I hardly noticed what pictures it was which these colours were 'lighting up'. These illuminated manuscripts were then no more than just that: manuscripts 'illuminated', 'lit up' by colour to a glory I did not think of analysing. But presently it was not enough for only my eyes to see. My mind began to pierce below the superficial wonder of colour to that which lay beneath.

I had not recognized till now that what lay beneath was so varied and so diverse. Not only the human form in various guises was represented, but flowers, trees, birds, animals and insects, cities and towers, mountains of the real world and of the fantastical, the horses and oxen and carts of the farm and the nets of the hunters, the tournaments of knights, the sports of the field and the toil of the kitchen.

Here was Christ in Majesty, elongated and sombre, seated upon a rainbow; here a female saint in scarlet robe and voluminous grey mantle reading a book on a grass plat beside a castle tower. Under twin pointed arches a tall angel with crooked wings pointed a long finger at a blue-mantled Virgin, over whose head hovered the dove of the Holy Spirit. In the capital E of the word *Exultet* sat a tiny figure striking energetically at the bells hanging from the curve of the E. Two equally tiny monks sang lustily from one shared choir book, and a crowned king of similar dimensions knelt with hands upraised in prayer in the D of *Domine*. I saw queer shapes such as never were on land or sea: bearded heads of men with tube-like bodies ending in horses' hindquarters, or manikins

Above: Playing the Chime-bells
Below: King Praying
13th. century MS. illumination

with tails, with one foot, or with their eyes in their
bellies. There were monkeys roasting pigs on the spit
or stealing babies from their cradles, or turning somer-
saults on the backs of blue and white horses. The sullen
ploughman too, was there, in his slouch hat, guiding the
clumsy plough drawn by four extraordinary oxen, two dark
grey, two brown; and horses of strange, unequine colours
leaping uphill as they dragged behind them a two-wheeled
cart laden with hay.

I left these rural scenes and entered other realms, where
writers dressed like Roman senators sat upon thrones before
looped curtains, with strange lions, or bulls, or eagles above
their heads; where men hooked exaggerated fingers at
each other, and stared with solemn or baleful eyes against
a background of sheet-gold; where sheep – presumably
they were sheep – with grotesquely articulated joints and
long, shrivelled necks cropped huge tufts of grass on hills
like gigantic, sea-washed pebbles.

Again the scene changed, and I was walking towards an
enchanted forest, with a steepled church at the edge of it
and a track bending mysteriously into deep green glooms
and to hilly glades where archers and spearmen attacked
fleeing deer and snarling black wild boars. Or a stream
was flowing beside me, rising, no doubt, in the ethereally
blue mountains in the remote distance; close at hand the
grass was starred with flowers, and a little wooden bridge
crossed the stream to a fairy castle, a very cloud-castle of
white towers shining against the sky. Would such a dream
bridge bear the weight of humankind upon it? Yes, the
weight of humankind such as dwelt in these lands of long
ago: lords and ladies of supple grace, clad in robes apparently made of cobwebs taken when the frosty dew of late
autumn had turned them to silver.

Then that world too would fade, and all around would
be humpbacked, taper-toed, large-eyed, hook-nosed little
men, gesticulating, capering, leaping. Their every action
was staccato, the ground beneath them heaved like a

tumult of crested waves, the clouds were scratchy lines in a blank sky. Mountains reared up suddenly to pointed summits where stood the Lord God beckoning with enormous fingers and dealing destruction to the ungodly. Then, strangest of all, I saw no mountains or streams or intelligible landscape anywhere, no men recognizable as such; only maze upon maze, coil upon coil, of twisted, interlacing lines, and birds and serpents, lacertine creatures and creatures for which there is no name, twining interminably in and out of each other, with their own tails, having accomplished a long and tortuous journey, returned back to them and in their mouths; or other creatures woven into a tapestry of ordered line and colour where I lost all sense of direction as I wove my way in and out and out and in, and round and round and up and down, bewilderingly, endlessly.

Yet, as these mazes *had* order; as I could, when I would, trace those convolutions from the head to the tail of one indivisible beast, so, I thought, it should be possible for me, if I cared to do so, to thread my way through all this apparent disorder of diversity from the head to the tail and find it one indivisible development. Why should I see on this side these delicate, fantastical dream figures of men and women swaying affectedly, and on that earthy beings, in plumed hats and wide-skirted tunics, with hawks on wrist and cumbrous horses treading heavily through a solid countryside? Why here taper-toed, elfish creatures with agitated clothes, and there static figures of unearthly aloofness staring ahead as into eternity? How was it that in one place there were charming little men clambering up among leafy tendrils and in another ill-proportioned, ungainly travesties of humankind, with enormous hands and anatomy all awry and heads too big for their elongated bodies? Why these figures of classic calm dressed in Roman togas, and then no human figures at all – only writhing coils and whirls and spirals and savage beasts of preternatural length tearing and biting one another?

This questioning was the beginning of a journey without end. Now I realized that the tapestry of colour which had adorned the Middle Ages and which subsequent centuries had rolled up and cast aside was still in existence for those who cared to look for it. So I set out to find it, along paths that led me far away, much further than I had ever dreamt, travelling through the world of Mediaeval Art on a journey as fascinating to me as Marco Polo's was to him, when he left Venice for the lands of Kublai Khan behind the sunrise.

2

BACK THROUGH THE CENTURIES
WITH THE ILLUMINATORS

∞∞∞∞∞∞∞∞∞∞∞∞∞∞∞∞∞

AT the beginning, as I stepped out of the modern world
into the nearer past, the paths were clear, with no
wonderment over them, no quagmires of questioning
encroaching upon them, wherein one might sink and be
lost. Anyone, untutored and unguided, could have understood and delighted in these first scenes. I found myself,
for instance, in December in a farmyard where a stocky
peasant in a green tunic was killing a pig, while his wife,
white apron over pink skirt, phlegmatically, without a trace
of sentiment, held a long-handled pan under the beast's
throat to catch the blood, and farmhands in the background, male and female, brought in kindling and bread;
birds perched on the thatched roofs to pick up what they
could find, and a woman in an open room near by had
rolled up her sleeves and was kneading in a trough. Or I
could join a boating party in May, stocky figurcs again
passing under a bridge with a battlemented gate leading
to the spires and stepped gables and narrow streets of a
mediaeval city. Or I could watch the reaping with hand-
sickles in August, while the weary, barelegged harvester sat
with his wife on the edge of the cornfield, waiting with
outstretched bowl for the ministrations of the peasant
woman with a basket on her head, and the hot summer light

threw reflections of the thick foliage of the trees into the waters of the river near by. At such times I was in fifteenth-century Flanders, in the midst of the rural life of the Books of Hours of Simon Bening of Bruges and his disciples, while they painted the Labours of the Months as the eternal agricultural year unfolded itself season by season from January to December.

Or I might cross to fifteenth-century France, and contemplate the courtly life of *Les Très Riches Heures* of the Duke of Berry, Peer of France, son of one French king and brother and uncle of two others. In this '*roi des manuscrits*', '*l'un des plus complets chef-d'œuvre que nous ait laissés le Moyen-Age*'* there are peasants; but here also are lords and ladies sumptuously arrayed, making love or riding to the hunt; here too is the great Duke himself, feasting in the

15th. century figures

month of January, with his dogs walking upon the table among his gold plate, his brilliantly arrayed servants in attendance. The wall is hung with a tapestry depicting a battle of armoured knights among castle-towers and green hills; in a riot of glorious colour, deep blues and verdant emeralds and rich reds his chamberlain cries, '*Approche, approche*' to a hesitating visitor, his words turning to Gothic letters of gold upon the air. But though the scene is resplendent, like all the other scenes in this masterpiece, and the artistry of the illuminators (we know their names — the brothers Limbourg) is supreme in its delicacy and grace, the scenes of *Les Très Riches Heures* share certain characteristics with the Flemish farmyards and harvest

* Waagen.

fields, the Magi travelling to Christ, the Virgin suckling the Holy Child, the crowds watching a tournament, St. Christopher stepping through a river full of fish to set down his sacred burden on the opposite bank. They all illustrate, if not real scenes, scenes which easily could be real. They all depict, whether it be courtier or peasant, earthly people, and depict them realistically, without exaggeration or grotesqueness.

They all – yes, even the ethereally beautiful *Très Riches Heures* – are more concerned with material values than spiritual. If they are not all earthy, they are all worldly, materialistic. It is opulent figures they depict, worldly beyond measure, smacking of the great international fairs, of trade and the market-place, of the Hanseatic League and Wool Staples, prosperous towns, merchants and shop-keepers, asserting their will and building great churches. It is the last century of the waning Middle Ages – the fifteenth century, heyday of the towns and the bourgeoisie.

And yet, behind the velvet and the plumes, the furred gowns and gold chains of mayoral office, the worldly goods, the riches and material prosperity, a shadow glided; a cold wind seemed to rise in the heart of those forests where the turrets of the lordly castles rose, and go sweeping past, and a whisper trailed wraith-like in its rear, sighing the one word, '*Mortality. . . .*' In the forests, among the trees all decked with red and gold apples, there were three kings riding to the hunt, crowned, jewel-decked, their robes embroidered in silver and gold, hawks upon their wrists, the bloom of health upon their cheeks. But their eyes stared ahead in horror: facing them were three beckoning skeletons, grimacing, worm-riddled and horrible. This was the vision of *Les Trois Vifs et les Trois Morts* – the Three Quick and the Three Dead – and it reminded men constantly of their inevitable doom. 'As you are, so I was; as I am, so will you be'; 'The sword of Damocles hangs over us'; '*Memento mori*' – give thought to death; 'Vanity of vanities, saith the preacher, all is vanity'.

Is it the spirit of a dying era – the fading of an epoch – the last agony of the departing Middle Ages? Perhaps; for even when the protagonists of an age do not realize the end of an era they seem to feel the spirit of its dying stirring around them. *Fin de siècle,* we say, a weariness of all things as they are, disillusionment, maybe, a sense that the world is too much with us. Yet, long ages before this fifteenth century, men had thought of dying, and had rejoiced at the thought, for had not Christ conquered Death, and was it not *Mors ianua vitae* – Death, the gate of life? How else could the noble army of martyrs have gone so triumphantly to their end?

There is a change here. Worldliness cannot walk hand in hand with spiritual sublimity. There is nothing sublime, nothing sublimated, no sense of it in the fifteenth century. The men of the fifteenth century, and of the fourteenth, had had ample opportunities of looking in the face of Death and finding it hideous – when incessant wars spread corpses in so many hundreds over the land that they could not be buried before they rotted, and when the sudden swift stroke of the enemy that walked in darkness – plague – struck home like a whizzing arrow. These were the centuries which saw the Hundred Years' War and the Black Death; and neither passed without leaving its ineffaceable mark upon the minds and imaginations of men.

Behind the worldly glitter of this life's material prosperity crept the cold shadow, and I drew back out of the orbit of its sinister influence, farther backwards into an earlier age. I was in the fourteenth century now. As worldly as ever were all things around me, but the bourgeoisie had gone. It was for the most part a land of courtiers. Slender, graceful, but oh, how finicking! Their figures were S-bends; they affectedly threw out their hands; even Mary at the foot of the Cross, her head bowed in grief, displayed the S-bend; the blessed John's fingers, as they clutched his chin, aristocratic fingers, tapering and boneless, expressed self-conscious and somewhat overwrought mourning.

14th. century figures: the S-bend,
male and female

Even the ploughman of the *Luttrell Psalter*, with the peasant behind the harrow, scaring birds with slingstones, bent like the letter S, and postured, and pointed the tapering toe of his right shoe as if he had been an eighteenth-century dancing master.

This crowned queen in long robes hanging in such graceful folds about her, waving a gracious finger and bending affectedly in the inimitable *Queen Mary's Psalter* (the fourteenth century is the great age for psalters, as the fifteenth is for Books of Hours) is the Virgin Mary, a gentle and lovely figure, but so aristocratic it is difficult to know how one could ever approach her. The saints and the prophets bend like the letter S, so do the hunters with hawk on wrist, so do the trumpeters with long instruments at their disdainful lips; the man who, with his tunic girt above his knees, strikes at the bear and the lady who, with uplifted hand, shrinks from the beast; the mailed knight drawing his sword, and King Solomon giving directions to the builders of the Temple; the angel offering Adam and Eve garments to cover their nakedness, and St. Margaret disputing with the Prefect, to all appearances a mediaeval king: they all display the S-bend, they all point uplifted admonitory fingers at each other; the folds of their robes ripple to the ground as if they were waterfalls, they mince, they pirouette, they affectedly gesticulate. Their affectation sometimes passes all bounds, but their elegant grace is undeniable.

Sometimes they stand in niches with architectural canopies soaring above their heads, forests of finial upon finial, crocket upon crocket, spirelet behind spirelet leaning crookedly sideways with their own extravagant height, architectural absurdity piled upon architectural absurdity. Only the grotesques lumbering through this land of courtly elegance do not finick and contort themselves, do not point their toes and sway as it were in some wind. They could not even if they would, for some of them have tails for feet, some are armless, some have two heads growing from one neck, or the forequarters of a beast turned backwards to face the hindquarters – possessing four clumsy legs and hoofs altogether.

These grotesques, starting harmlessly and divertingly

many years before, with little humorous, fantastic, birds and beasts and half-human figures of charming quaintness, developed overmuch in the fourteenth century – the century which exaggerated many things – and in the *Luttrell Psalter* I stumbled upon a nightmare world one day. There the horrors that walked the great pages could have been only the creations of a disordered mind. Small wonder if Sir Geoffrey Luttrell really did refuse to pay for the book when it was finished, as has been surmised. Better the affectations of the swaying saints and soldiers, pages and peasants, lords and ladies hunting and dancing, than this travesty of illumination. So I hurry past this psalter's latter pages

A 14th. century 'grotesque' (from the *Luttrell Psalter*)

to the *Belleville Breviary*, to the *Psalter of Robert de Lisle*, a beautiful blue-coloured psalter, but in it we get a fourteenth-century representation of that sinister Three Quick and the Three Dead; to *La Lumière au Lais*, and the *Gorleston* and *St. Omer* psalters, where the tall, slim figures appear again, clad in their blue and green robes with the waterfall folds, walking or standing daintily amid lines of Gothic blackletter text where each capital letter is a jewel of ruby or sapphire, each line-space is filled with colour, and the margins are decorated with curving stems or leaves which, lit up with red and gold, twine along top and bottom of the text; where the proportion of blackletter text to Gothic illustration is at last perfectly adjusted.

So I looked behind the affected swaying, the exaggerated spreading out of hands, the posturing and posing, to an innate refinement and delicate grace, and I wondered if the delicacy and grace had been there first, and had developed as the century had worn on into this posturing and affectation. If so, whence had it come?

Searching for its origin, I went farther back still into the world of illumination of the thirteenth century.

Here the air was still and tranquil; the music of pipe and tabor, the rush of the dance, the noise of the hunt and the clashing of the tournament had died. A holy hush enfolded these realms, for that rustle of angels' wings, that harmonious throb of the music of the heavenly Jerusalem was not a sound to break the silence, but a pervasive presence, the same presence which was filling this little illuminated kingdom with light. 'Behold the handmaid of the Lord,' murmurs Mary, bowing her head before Gabriel; 'Peace on earth, goodwill towards men', sings the multitude of the heavenly host in the dark blue, starry sky above the wonder-stricken shepherds. The Spirit of God is close at hand.

With humility mankind bows low before the Almighty; with simple faith men lift up their hands, triangles of ecstatic prayer. On a background of burnished gold,

13th. century illumination. King David (from the *Psalter of Isabelle of France*)

before a line of steep gables standing beneath a trefoil-headed arcade in the *Psalter of Isabelle of France*, the Ark of the Lord is reverently borne to the diminutive mediaeval gates of a city, where a church with lancet windows is conspicuous; King David himself, in a simple, flowing robe, plucking with spidery fingers at his harp, precedes this outward sign and symbol of the Covenant God made with the Children of Israel. He prays also, on another folio, to an image of God in curly clouds – below, two monks sing lustily. Christ, with sad tenderness, gazes at those who buffet Him; two martyrs, with the same other-worldly sadness, kneel in the letter D beneath the executioners' swords.

In the *Durham Psalter* too they kneel, or play the chimebells, or from the great choir-books opened upon a lectern sing with expressions of childlike naïveté, delicate little figures, clad in gowns that fall in graceful simplicity to their feet; yet, small as they are, they are giants to the castellated cities they enter, the altars before which they kneel, the tufted trees they pass on their way.

Here, in a French psalter of the thirteenth century, is Christ entering Jerusalem. The walls of the city are a deep blue; upon its battlements stand curly-haired figures with disproportionate hands, welcoming the holy Rider upon the uncouth ass. Figures of men and women nearly as tall as the round tower near by completely fill a gateway; the little man and his companions looking down upon the scene from an adjacent, unreal tree are out of all proportion to the tree itself, the city gates and the personages below; Christ and His disciples are boneless, over-tall, narrow-shouldered and ungainly.   Here are Gabriel and Mary again, each beneath a steep gable and a three-lobed arch, standing in front of that same sheet-gold background, which cuts them off from the ordinary world; here is depicted the birth of Christ under similar arches (only now a sanctuary lamp hangs in each one) again with the blank gold background, and St. Joseph, between looped curtains, watching Mary as she lies stretched upon her bed.   The steep gables, the three-lobed arches, the sanctuary lamps and the gold background appear once more as the Christ Child, sitting upright and alert, is presented in the Temple to a Simeon who receives Him with hands veiled in a white cloth.

Yet none of the inconsistencies of proportion and anatomy of men or beasts disturbs me: I see these last of all.   What I first see – eventually it is the only thing I see – is the dreaming spirituality of this age, the purity of its faith, a sad gazing-forward as if from the sorrows of this world to the vision of a better, and over everything a gentleness, which fills with graciousness everything which it enfolds.

For this luminous and lovely world of thirteenth-century art had known St. Francis, God's 'little poor man', the *Poverello* from Assisi; the gentle saint, the imitator of Christ, had walked the rough stones of life, and where he had walked the flowers of lovingkindness and mercy had blossomed.   Even to-day white doves nest in the arms of his statue in the cloister of Santa Maria degli Angeli – that ornate church which he would have hated, standing in all its worldly pride on the Plain of Spoleto; in the lamplit gloom of the Chapel of the Portziuncula one may still feel the Christlike humility of this lover of the most lowly of God's creatures, or in the crypt of the lower Church at

Assisi stand before the iron grille of the saint's tomb, while
flickering candles light the subterranean darkness and a
young Franciscan murmurs St. Francis' prayer:

> Where there is hatred, let me sow love,
> Where there is injury, pardon,
> Where there is darkness, light,
> Where there is sorrow, joy,
> Where there is doubt, faith,
> And where there is despair, hope;

and while doing so one may realize why the passing of St.
Francis across the early years of the thirteenth century
changed the tenor of the age.   And not in the attitude to
life only, but also to death.   Here are no grinning, worm-
riddled skeletons confronting mankind, nor the gruesome
face of Death the Destroyer: 'Praised be Thou, my Lord,
for our brother Death,' cries Francis in his *Canticle of
Brother Sun*; 'Blessed those who are found in Thy most holy
will, to them the second death will bring no ill.'

The Cellarer

St. Francis had a sense of
humour too, and that was
not missing from thirteenth-
century illumination, for this
century had its lighter side.
Performing bears and mon-
keys at their tricks are here;
grotesques, not yet grown to
nightmare hideousness; and
I well remember the sly picture of a monkish cellarer in
his loose brown habit standing against a dull gold background in a capital letter
of a Franco-Flemish manu-
script.   He is drawing some
alcoholic liquid from a bar-
rel into a baluster-jug which he holds in his left hand, while

his right, with the cellar-keys still dangling from the fingers thereof, balances a bowl from which he is drinking with evident enjoyment, his eye meanwhile cocked in a sideways glance to make sure he is unobserved.

But there were some things which puzzled me in this same thirteenth century. That airless, other-worldly gold background, for instance; those veiled hands; those curtains looped round the frail and impossibly slender shafts supporting the steep-gabled arches: why were they so constantly repeated? Were they a passing fashion, or had they some significance? On I went, farther back still into the past, to find the answer to my question.

The golden luminousness of that gentle Franciscan light faded as I left the thirteenth century behind and went farther back into the twelfth. A different sort of radiance surrounded me now: the awful, still, white radiance of eternity. Presences greater than my finite mind could encompass stirred about me; I stood now in the presence of forms of praeternatural majesty. These elongated figures with the brooding eyes, gazing through and beyond me – was it these the romantic mysticism of St. Francis banished from illuminated Bible and Gospel, Psalter and Breviary and Troper? There is no grace here, no meek or simple faith, no light of dreaming spirituality. This is spirituality of a different kind: lofty and austere, as far removed from the fashions and foibles and frailities of this world as are the ice-caps of Everest among the everlasting snows from the villages in the valleys far below. They transcend all earthly things. The light of eternity is in those brooding eyes. They do not see what is, but all that ever has been and all that ever shall be.

I see Mary, destined Mother of God, visiting Elizabeth, the mother-to-be of John, the Voice-that-crieth-in-the-wilderness; but this is not a picture of two cousins greeting each other with tidings of glad pregnancy. This is the Mother of Sorrows foreseeing the inevitable end even while the Christ Child lies in her womb; her eyes are fixed upon

the vision of the Crucifixion as Elizabeth's are upon the
severed head on the charger. Not two women: two
symbols, rather, of the sorrows of women.

This same Mary, when the Angel of the Annunciation
appeared to her, was no young girl with the grace of youth
shining like light around her; she was a stern-faced symbol;
no mother, only the vessel destined to bear the Son of God,
the Pantocrator, the Almighty, the Ancient of Days, the
Ruler and Judge of the world in the Day of Doom.   These
three kings, these Magi, do not bring their gifts and kneel
to a little child, a prince of peace: they gaze upon the great
God made manifest on earth, the Incarnate Logos: a sight
so awful and holy their tongues are dumb, their senses
paralysed.

Here, in a Commentary upon the Psalms, I see that
Incarnate Logos again in the arms of His Mother.   No
humble mother this, whose Son was born in a stable; no
baby this, nestling against his mother's breast.   Upright,
aloof, gazing ahead, a book in His left hand, His right
upraised in blessing, sits the Maker of the world between
the Virgin's outspread knees; and she, without tenderness,
greater than human, as the pagans of Greece and Rome
had represented their deities, erect and unbending upon
her throne, sits crowned, a sceptre held between two
fingers, gazing, not at her Child, but ahead, into the unfathomable mysteries of life and creation, meeting, for she
is among the few who may, the gaze of Him whose spirit
moved in the void upon the face of the waters and set the
universe in motion.

These are the vastly conceived, elevated figures of
Romanesque art. Deeply moved, yet often chilled,
sometimes even repelled and yet at the same time fascinated
by their brooding austerity, small and insignificant in their
greater-than-human presence I move among them. Their
robes cling to their bodies curiously, in what is called the
'damp fold' style, making double-outlined ovals around
their knees or shoulders or across their breasts, sometimes

curving, sinuous ridges, from knee to foot, or from neck to waist. They sit, like giants of old legend upon pre-historic mountain-tops, their knees wide apart, their feet drawn to gether, their garments covered with harmonious, sweeping lines; they raise great hands to heaven, or hook enormous fingers at each other. Sometimes they violently contort themselves, godly men or sinners larger than life struggling with beasts or demons.

I see, for instance, in the *Winchester Bible* (the twelfth century is the age of the great Bibles, as the four-teenth was to be of psalters, and the fifteenth of Books of Hours) the prophet Jeremiah leaping back as God lays His fingers upon his lips,

Romanesque figure with 'damp fold' (from the *Winchester Bible*)

crying (the words are written on a waving scroll), '*Ecce, dedi verba mea*' – behold, I have given thee my words; Jeremiah's mantle is a hollow of ridged V-folds, his robe clings in 'damp-fold' lines to his back-thrust right leg. Elisha, his head fallen back at right angles to his body, receives the mantle of Elijah, his right foot thrust far down the stem of an initial P, his upraised left leg bare, his robe sweeping downward in dynamic ovoid folds. Doeg, his upper half bent back to form a V with his back-thrust legs, his clinging robe a pattern of ovoid shapes, slays the priest in a great letter Q. In the same style, in the *Winchester Bible*, the young man kills the Amalekite, David rends the jaws of the lion, the Egyptian smites the Hebrew and Moses smites the Egyptian, and the risen Christ thrusts His lance into the mouth of hell.

Only rarely do I see that gracious gentleness which I left behind in the thirteenth century, and that is when the illuminators are drawing near the thirteenth century again. All around in the earlier twelfth century, in this Romanesque age, are sternness and austerity, souls removed from human weaknesses, indifferent to this mortal world and mortal life, concerned only with the eternal realities. With these monkish figures one cannot laugh, one dare not even smile; here is no trifling, no mood for trivialities, all the world is the Devil's gin and snare for the unwary. Does a man beset with continuous foes, seen and unseen, smile when he is bent only on saving his soul alive?

And yet there is greatness in this illuminated world of Romanesque art — the greatness of the superhuman, the transcendent, the infinite. Unapproachable, vast, unfathomable, with the impersonality of the motions of the Cosmos, the rhythms of the invisible spheres in its sweeping lines, this monkish art soars upwards as the peaks of mountains soar against the illimitable sky. It is great as mountains are great. It knows no human tenderness, it stoops to no human weakness, but rises aloft to the heights of heaven and places the offerings of its austere faith upon the throne of Almighty God.

Such is Romanesque art of twelfth-century illumination. But far from answering my questions it has posed more of its own, to send me journeying still. Whence came these elongated, severe figures, with their gaze fixed upon the Eternal? And here, too are those sheet-gold backgrounds which shut out all the features of the natural world of mountain and valley, tree and forest, city and river and countryside, and enclose the onlooker in a world withdrawn into itself, concentrated upon infinity. Here once more are the veiled hands, the looped curtains, and often a frontal, rigid pose which I have not noticed before. Were these characteristics a fashion, only starting in the twelfth century, or am I to seek their origin even farther back?

Even farther back, it seems — but not in the eleventh century: I realize that as soon as I cross its threshold. There is no answer to my question in these Evangelists

seated beside their lectern-like desks with their eyes uplifted to the sky as if seeking inspiration, and above their
heads an angel, or a lion, a bull or an eagle. These are
the 'evangelical symbols' according to the vision of the
prophet Ezekiel among the captives by the river of Chebar,
when the heavens were opened and out of the midst of fire
came the likeness of four living creatures; a winged Man,
a Lion, a Bull and an Eagle. So the Man was taken to
symbolize St. Matthew, because he began his Gospel with
the human genealogy of Christ; the Lion St. Mark, whose
Gospel opened with the voice of one crying in the wilderness, the habitation of lions; the Bull St. Luke, because he
stressed the sacrificial nature of Christ's Passion; and the
Eagle St. John, because as the eagle alone of birds could
look unblinded straight into the glory of the sun, so St.
John alone of men could see the heavens opened and gaze
upon the 'seven lamps of fire burning before the throne,
which are the seven Spirits of God'.*

The knees of the Evangelists are wide apart, as were the
figures of those I passed in the twelfth century, but here I
am in a different world altogether, light, airy, rapid and
alive. The rapidity of it, indeed, increases sometimes to a
whirl of frenzied hurrying. The fine and flowing folds of
the Evangelists' robes are innumerable, flicking up at the
hems like little tongues of flame; the looped curtains
flutter as in a strong wind behind their thrones. Only the
heavy borders of conventionalized leaves twining in and
out of two supporting poles, sometimes with great floriated
corners and medallions containing tiny figures, restrain the
nervous energy that seems like a fire devouring the restless
creatures within. So, in the *Grimbald Gospels*, written in
the early eleventh century at Winchester, appear St. Luke
and St. John; so too King Edgar, in a swirling tunic, with
both hands upraised to a whirl of angels above him,
offering the New Minster Charter to Christ seated aloft on
a rainbow in a mandorla; so too, Gabriel and Mary in an

* Revelation iv. 5.

Annunciation in the *Benedictional of St. Ethelwold*, where, on another folio, she dies under a great foliated arch supported on capitals impossibly composed of similar stylized leaves, while the apostles crowd below.

Here, in a psalter from Croyland, or perhaps Ely, is Christ triumphant, tall, delicately drawn, with His right hand touching rather than clasping a thin sceptre; the fingers of His left are curved upon an open book. He leaps forward with His right foot as if He were striding up a mountain, but actually He is treading upon two beasts. The folds – or swirls, rather – of His robe twist and twine with no consideration for the form of the body they cover; a scarf-like appendage blows out to the side, the edges of His garments flutter and waft about as if His progress were sending a breeze through them. Here too, are the heavy borders; but here the foliage twining around them flutters almost as breezily as Christ's robe. Or I come upon a Crucifixion where the very Cross is restless, the edge of the Saviour's loincloth is a jagged zigzag, and John and Mary are in violent, dramatic action.

Sometimes, especially in certain psalters, there are not even any restraining borders – there is nothing static whatever. Everything is in motion in a world of linear surface pattern where the drawing is exquisite but the painting is reduced to a pale and partial colour wash. The action becomes more dramatic, the hems flutter more, the ground surges up in more violent motion, the farther back into the past I go. At Monte Cassino and at Reichenau, at Canterbury and at Cologne, at Newminster (which is Winchester) and at Hildesheim it is the same, until on the threshold of the tenth century I come into a strange land of hills like clouds and trees like feathers, where angels fly on flickering wings, their garments streaming like water in the violently agitated air. The earth heaves, gales blow through every tree, the mountains swirl upwards to impossible peaks, and spiky-legged men rush up them on tiptoe; the wicked, in a writhing mass, are put to rout by the spears – like darts of wind – of the righteous, and the Lord of Hosts sits in a breezy sky in wind-tossed attire, extending a hand to the earth.

Swift, scratchy strokes of the pen have produced these airy figures enacting scenes which literally illustrate the psalmist's not always literal utterances. Nervous energy is wearing them out in a world of perpetual motion where nothing ever rests, nothing is still. We rush up hills and flee down them again, we shoot arrow after arrow or aim unceasing spears, we fall headlong, we prostrate ourselves, we grovel or we stretch hands of praise to heaven. Sometimes, our feet tapering to nothing, our shoulders hunched, our heads thrown back, we scythe the heaving fields among hills which are swirling pen-strokes; we sow the seed in sweeping gestures, our fingers sticking out like spikes, the clouds behind us like mounting and turning waves; or we prune trees in the margin of a psalter calendar, trees which are but coiling arabesques growing out of ground resembling the edge of a cumulus cloud; and we ourselves, on taper toes, chinless and humpbacked, wield the scimitar curve of our knives as if we were dancing with them.

This is strange indeed, all this swirling, nervous line, this *drawing*, this linear representation of everything; it seems that in seeking the origin of Romanesque I have again found no answer but only another question still: Whence came *this* style?

My road has led me now into those centuries before the Norman Conquest, improperly called 'The Dark Ages': days before Danish marauders brought flames and slaughter to the land, sacked shrines and destroyed monasteries; when St. Edmund of East Anglia suffered at their hands the fate of St. Sebastian; and when, while monks and people fled before the storm of fire and destruction brought by the invaders, the cry of the litany went up to God: 'From the fury of the Northmen, good Lord deliver us.' In a word, I am back in the seventh century, when St. Columba – Colum Cille – brought Christianity out of the dim Celtic world of Eire to Iona, and sent thence his missionary, the gentle St. Aidan, to convert the heathen of Northumbria. Soon after that, the northern parts of Britain, in the misty seventh-century years, were full of saints. There was St. Cuthbert, he who longed in vain to live a recluse on Lindisfarne, whose spirit, they say, haunted that holy island, the cradle of British Christianity, long after his death, over whose bones, centuries later, monks raised the mighty Durham Cathedral, towering majestically on its rock above the Wear. There was St. Wilfrid, both righteous and quarrelsome, who built of Roman stones filched from the ruined town of Corstopitum two miles south of Hadrian's Wall the tiny Saxon crypt which still stands intact beneath Hexham Abbey; there was St. Oswald, king of Northumbria, the friend of St. Aidan, who sent out the meats of his own feast on a great silver dish to the starving poor at the gates; and there was also St. Hilda, abbess of Whitby, she who encouraged the swineherd Caedmon, the first English poet, 'by heaven and not a master taught',* when the angel of his vision bade him, all unlettered as he was, sing the song of Creation.

In this far-off mist-hung world are several treasures of illumination. Some of them belong to a later century than the seventh, many of them must have been burnt to ashes by marauding Danes; but still there exist the *Lichfield Gospels*, *The Book of Durrow*, The Book of Colum Cille (usually called the *Book of Kells*), and the *Durham Book*, which is the same as the *Lindisfarne Gospels*.

The strange, remote poetry of these treasures filled me with that emotion one experiences in looking out at night upon the hosts of the stars, or in hearing the music of bird-song in the forest. For the poetry of this so-called Hiberno-Saxon art is the unheard poetry of sweeping, rhythmic line, curving and coiling and winding out and in and in and out in perpetual motion, to form a miracle of the most intricate abstract design the world of art has

* Pope.

ever known. Spirals, coils, whorls dynamically spinning like planets in outer space, trumpet patterns and fretted interlaces, jewel-like circles, mazes of delicate interwoven lines, form disciplined design within the sweeping curves of capital letters; and when one looks more closely, one sees lacertine creatures and elongated bird and animal forms twining in serpentine profusion, biting and clawing one another, reminiscent of old Scandinavian tales of snakes and dragons and all the monstrous creatures of Norse mythology.

The *Book of Durrow* goes right back, perhaps, to the end of the sixth century, with its interlacing ribbons and writhings and twistings of long-bodied creatures disporting themselves in them. Did any of those who made the book see, perhaps, among the ruins of Roman cities in Britain, the mosaic pavements of a Mediterranean people? For the Romans had these interlaced borders, although they were never so imaginative, so wildly, intricately fantastic, as these products of Hiberno-Saxon artists. But when my eye falls upon the symbol of John the Evangelist I can have no doubt about whence its inspiration came. This is a painted version of a metal eagle, enamelled in bright colours as the Celts enamelled their brooches and torques and shields, even in the days of the Roman occupation.

The patterns of the *Book of Durrow* seem complicated enough, until I come to the *Lindisfarne Gospels* and the *Book of Kells*; then, by comparison, they are simplicity itself. This *Book of Kells*, the Book of Colum Cille, written in honour of St. Columba, first amazes, then captivates me by its 'weird and commanding beauty, its subdued and goldless colouring'.* Here I walk through a starlit night of dim and mystic loveliness. I stand in astonishment before the magnificent, sweeping curves, the unfathomable diversity and complexity of the great sombre capital X of the Greek form of '*Christi*'; once again I see all four evangelical symbols in medallions resembling blue and yellow

* Sir Edward Sullivan, *The Book of Kells*.

C

and dark purple enamelled Celtic brooches; I lose myself in the incredible mazes of the opening words of St. Mark's Gospel: *Initium Evangelii Jesu Christi*, all solemn reds and dark blues and browns and yellows. Then, just as I begin to feel a sort of loneliness creeping upon me in the midst of all this impersonal, un-human beauty of abstract art I suddenly come upon an unexpected sight: a little Irish warrior of long ago, with tousled yellow hair and big eyes, dressed in green as befits a man of Erin, sitting with his spear and buckler on the end of a line of text. A quaint little, white-faced, large-nosed figure: I later come upon one or two similar quaint humans in Colum Cille's book, and upon a couple of realistic rats nibbling the eucharistic wafer while an equally recognizable cat looks on, at the bottom of the aforementioned capital X.

Yet the little Kells warrior and his kind are exceptional. Most of the curly headed figures with twisted lips which stare not unkindly out of the *Book of Kells* are not realistic representations of men. They are part of the general design, and if they are not regarded as such they might mistakenly be called grotesque caricatures. I see what purports to be St. John, with his Gospel: his enlarged nimbus is a glorious piece of pattern, its outer circle, intersected by large discs, encloses a band of intricately interlaced animal forms, the inner circle is filled with enamel-like inlay and design suggesting mosaic. His hair, his beard, his very features are stylized symmetry; his raiment, with sublime disregard for the folds into which a garment on a human body can and cannot fall, curves and loops and twists to make a pattern. St. John is as much pattern as the interlacings in the border around him and the designs on his halo are pattern.

So with the figure of Christ being arrested in the Garden of Gethsemane: His very hair is interwoven pattern, as well as His robes; so with what is called the 'doubtful portrait', and most of the figures of people in the *Book of Kells*, and even more so in the *Lichfield Gospels*, written in

The Human Figure as pattern: St. Luke
(*The Lichfield Gospels*)

honour of the kindly St. Chad, patron saint of all healing wells. In this manuscript St. Luke appears with his crossed sceptres, one in each hand, a mere rectangle of arabesques, circles and S-curves arranged as an enameller on metal would have arranged them, with two more or less human feet dangling from the bottom of the rectangle and an expressionless, stylized face framed in symmetrically arranged tubes (representing hair) projecting from the top.

St. Matthew and the Virgin in the *Book of Kells* are in similar case. A strange figure, the Virgin, and stranger still the Child, in this sombre design of green and dark purple and pallid yellow – if they are taken as representations of the human figure (as they were never meant to be) and not as pattern (as they were).

Or I look at the *Lindisfarne Gospels*, written 'in honour of

God and St. Cuthbert and all the saints in common who
are on the island [of Lindisfarne]' either at the very end of
the seventh century or in the opening years of the eighth, and
kept at Lindisfarne till, at the coming of the Danish
destroyers, the monks fled with it, in 875 or thereabouts,
and, carrying the body of St. Cuthbert also, started the
wanderings which ended at the rock above the Wear.
Here there are not even those pattern figures, the curly-
headed, stiff angels with paper-like hands, the big-eyed,
sorrowing faces which appear in the *Book of Kells*; only
magnificent whole-page and capital designs in solemn
green and red and purple intermixed with dull yellow
and black and outlined with tracings of red dots which are
almost a hallmark of these ages – they are to be seen also
in the *Book of Kells*. The interwoven pattern is so marvellously fine its artistry can only be fully appreciated when it
is studied under a magnifying glass. The whole pages of
abstract ornament are once again clearly influenced by
metalwork – perhaps the metalwork, set with precious and
symbolic stones, which once decorated the bindings of
these great Gospel books, for yellow circles like metal studs
appear, and the outline of the Cross as if it were in metal
standing out upon the background of the windings of the
lacertine creatures which twist and twine symmetrically
behind it. Or again there are patterns reminiscent of
Roman mosaic pavements – surely there is an echo of the
past here, an influence reaching out across three or four or
five centuries?

Then suddenly, in the midst of all this purely non-
representational artistry I come upon the figures of the
Evangelists again. They are still sitting, as in the *Book of
Kells*, writing their gospels, but now the looped curtains of
later centuries have appeared, and though their faces and
attitudes are stiff and mannered, and their clothes like
rubber pipes bound round them, they are no longer mere
pattern, they are, more or less, men.

Here is St. Matthew, with his angel symbol above his

head, St. Mark, underneath his somewhat heraldic lion, sitting in the attitude of a man, with the proportions of a man, and with the folds of his garments taking almost natural lines; St. Luke with his weird-faced bull, and a scroll across his knees (I take note of the scroll – writing in the eighth century was not done on scrolls) and St. John with his eagle.   Behind each is the word HAGIOS.   Not the Saxon *haelig*, holy, or even the Latin *sanctus*, but hagios. Hagios is Greek.   The names of the Evangelists are in Latin: MATTHEUS, MARCUS, LUCUS, IOHANNES.   There are cross currents here: in the midst of the abstract, non-representational art of the barbaric north, which reduced everything, even the horse and chariot on the gold staters of Alexander the Great, to pattern, I find Greek and Latin words, classical scrolls such as had been used long before in the Mediterranean world, and Roman togas – for such, with some elaboration, are the garments these Evangelists wear.

3

LIGHT IN THE WORLD OF
LATE ANTIQUITY

HERE I am on the threshold of the ninth century – A.D. 800. On Christmas Day in this year Charlemagne, the Frankish king, greatest of the barbarians who had destroyed the ancient Roman Empire, was crowned 'Emperor of the Romans' by Pope Leo III at Rome, in that basilica of St. Peter which, in the fourth century, Constantine the Great had raised over the venerated shrine which was believed to contain the Apostle's mortal remains. Charlemagne had a nostalgic ideal: to revive the glories of the mighty empire of the past which his ancestors had brought to ruin: not least its learning and its art. So I look around upon the era of the 'Carolingian Renaissance'; and in the illuminated manuscripts I find other things besides traces of the old barbaric (here called Merovingian) art. I see St. Mark once more, in the *Gospel Book of Ada* (a legendary sister of Charlemagne), dipping his reed pen in the inkpot, wearing a brick-red toga with jerky hems over a long, purple tunic – there is no pattern here, in the barbaric manner, but a human figure in the classical one, rather too bulky in the waist, perhaps, but soft in outline, with a gentle face. This is representational, Mediterranean, classical art, not the abstract art of the North.

Or here is the Emperor Lothair, in a miniature from his

Gospel Book, sitting like a high Roman dignitary, swathed
in the voluminous folds of his toga, on his high-backed,
curtained throne with his guard behind him.   Again, in
the *Gospel Book of Charlemagne* the Evangelists appear at their
desks, in sandals and Roman-style tunics.   In the Bible
which was presented to Charles the Bald by Abbot Vivian
about the middle of the ninth century there appear, in
horizontal bands across the pages, scenes from the life of
St. Jerome, he who translated the Bible into the Latin
version called the Vulgate; and immediately memories
arise of an illustration in a Virgil manuscript now in the
Vatican, which is arranged in this same horizontal manner,
with figures in a line and a building or two in the background: the gardener instructing his workmen, as Virgil
describes him in one of the *Georgics*.   For a moment I am
back in the Roman world – and then my eye is caught by
something else, quite different: what appears to be the
praising of the Lord upon the organ, the praising of Him
upon the trumpet, from a psalter written about A.D. 832 at
Hautvillers, near Rheims, and now called the *Utrecht Psalter*.

Here is revelation.   It is now apparent whence came
those illustrations in English psalters, with their rapid,
scratchy, nervous pen-strokes, their heaving ground, their
cloud-like mountains, their tiny, taper-toed figures in fluttering, wind-swept clothes.   They are from the *Utrecht Psalter*, of
the so-called 'Rheims School' of the Carolingian Renaissance.

But ultimately . . . ?   This is obviously not the end of the
journey.   Men at the court of Charlemagne did not wear
togas – nor, for that matter, did they speak Greek, and call
their saints *hagios*.   Nor is the journey so straightforward
as I had imagined it would be.   Charlemagne's 'Renaissance' was an attempt at a revival of the dead Roman
Empire, and I see that to understand these Carolingian
Evangelists I must go back to the art of ancient Rome; but
the *Utrecht Psalter* cannot be thus explained.   Ancient
Roman authors did have pictures of themselves writing
their works affixed to their books, and out of these the

The *Utrecht Psalter* style

Evangelist portraits have obviously come, but no Roman ever drew in the rapid, swirling, wind-blown fashion of the Rheims school and its line of imitators – particularly English imitators.

How far the journey has brought me – back to the empire of ancient Rome!   I am walking now under the light of the dawn of Christianity, in the first centuries of the Roman Empire.   Here are the temples of the pagan gods around me, incense is curling heavenward from pagan altars, up goes the cry of *Io triumphe!* as the victorious Roman general rides, purple-cloaked, behind his soldiers and his captives, along the Sacred Way to make sacrifice upon the Capitoline Hill to Jupiter Greatest and Best.   There is a clash of cymbals, the wild riot of the bacchanals in Dionysiac orgies; I see the sacrifice of black bulls to Hecate, queen of the dead, consort of the king of the Underworld.   The sybil falls raving at the coming of the god, chthonic powers rumble at my feet, shake the fast-rooted trees, and split the rocks asunder as the earthquake comes.   I see men bow down to strange foreign gods, to Asiatic Cybele the all-powerful Earth Mother, demanding obscene rites; to Mithras, Persian Lord of Light, who wrings from his initiated devotees the torture of the pit, he who caught the blood of the Bull he had slain in the World Cave, whose attendants are Darkness and Light, who is accompanied by the winds which blow souls down to earth, then up to heaven again. I hear the tinkling music as in solemn processions there pass by the shaven priests of Isis, serene, Egyptian Isis, the beneficent queen of nature, adored in stately ritual.

On promontories and on hilltops stand temples of shining marble, in sacred groves are holy shrines. The great god Pan, ruler of the mysterious forests and all wild creatures that dwell therein, keeps the goats secure and helps the herdsmen, he is found in every wood, he haunts all country places. Men pray to him, and to the female spirit Pales; they adore the gods of the stream, the Dryads of the forests, the kindly deities of healing springs.

They take delight in the beauty of man's body, and think it no crime to enjoy the world around them. The philosophers are divided: the Stoics believe in the immortality of the soul, the Epicureans deny its existence; they deny, too, that there are any gods who care for mortal man; they are

> . . . the gods who haunt
> The lucid interspace of world and world
> Where never creeps a cloud or moves a wind,
> Nor ever falls the least white star of snow,
> Nor ever lowest roll of thunder moans,
> Nor sound of human sorrow mounts to mar
> Their sacred, everlasting calm. . . .*

There is unease; an era is dying, the world of Late Antiquity is passing, but perhaps all the more lustily for that does that pagan world enjoy its pagan pleasures, pagan love, pagan revelry, pagan ideas.

Into this world of superficially joyous yet at heart unsatisfied paganism Christianity was born.

Paganism is all around the new faith. This Graeco-Roman world is all pagan; it knows no other life, understands no other. Those who would convert it to Christianity must take account of this. Can a man change overnight

* Tennyson: *Lucretius*.

an outlook on life which has been with him since he was born? The austere early Christians would wipe the whole of every land clean of pagan classicism, but this would be dragging a rose by its roots from its customary soil and transplanting it into the sands of the desert, expecting it to flourish there. Instead, therefore, they effect a gradual and subtle transformation.

Therefore I see paganism in all its familiar forms being moulded to other purposes. The apostles of Christianity take into the service of their faith the pleasant beauties of that pagan art to which their converts have been so long accustomed, they pass them through the fires of Christianity, and turn them out transmuted gold, offering them thus to those who find it difficult to be attracted to an image-less, eastern religion which gives them no familiar statues to worship, but only the written or spoken word, the strange, abstract conception of the Three-in-One and One-in-Three, and the God who is pure Spirit.

So saints are depicted in Roman togas – they are dignified Roman senators. The ancient philosophers of Greece and Rome, by an easy transition, become the Hebrew prophets, Isaiah, Ezekiel, Jeremiah. Loves and cupids, those fat little winged *putti* who busy themselves in the frescoes on the walls of the House of the Vettii at Pompeii, turn into heavenly cherubs. The winged Victories upon Greek and Roman monuments are metamorphosed into the angels, the messengers of God. The half-goat god, Pan, or Faunus, because the country people cling obstinately to his worship and he therefore appears as the arch-enemy of Christianity, becomes the horned, cloven-hoofed Devil, the Evil One of the Middle Ages. River gods still preside over the waters of their ancient streams, and the god of the Jordan watches the Baptism of Christ. And Christ Himself is represented in a guise that all the world could understand and reverence – never as the Crucified, for the death of the cross signifies to pagans only one thing – the death of a slave or criminal upon a shameful gallows – but first, as the youthful Apollo, god of all light, beauty, healing, and prophecy, triumphant and heroic; and secondly, through eastern, chiefly Syrian, influence, as the remote and bearded figure, the Zeus Omnipotent, the Father of gods and men of the age that was dying.

Now at last I might think that I have reached my journey's end. I have gone back through the centuries and found myself beside the Mediterranean, in the world of Greece and Rome. To understand illuminated manuscripts I have found it necessary to study Late Antique, and even classical Greek and Roman art, for out of that art did Mediaeval Art develop . . . with a difference, springing from two sources.

My travels so far have made it easy for me to understand one source. It was at the court of Charlemagne, the lover of the dead Roman Empire, who tried to resurrect it and did, indeed, resurrect its pale ghost, that two streams of diverse origin met and ran together: the representational art of the Greeks and Romans, who loved the human form, made man the measure of all things and rejoiced in the features of the physical world, picturing all creatures as they are, realistically; and the abstract art of the dynamic, vigorous, barbarian North, which saw everything as whirling, coiling pattern and interwoven design. The waters of both mingled and flowed on as one river into the Middle Ages.

The other difference went deeper. I looked upon Classical art: it was as if I were looking upon cold marble. I looked upon Late Antique art, when the classical world was dying, and it was as if the Spirit of God, that same Spirit which moved upon the face of the waters and created life in the darkness of Chaos and Old Night, breathed upon it, and gradually, slowly but surely, something entered into it which it had lacked before: Mysticism. Pagan Greek art, with its crystal clear reasonableness, and pagan Roman art, full of majestic splendour, is without mysticism; Antique art becomes Mediaeval when it becomes transcendental: that is, when it ceases to represent only the outer physical form, and concerns itself also with the spirit within.

4

THE SOMBRE GLORY OF
THE MYSTIC EAST

~~~~~~~~~~~~~~~~~~~~~~~~

B^UT whence came that transcendentalism? Not from the North, for classical art did not meet the art of the North till the days of Charlemagne, in the late eighth century. It came when Christianity came. Christianity brought it from the East, the home of meditative mysticism. It seems that to understand further I should go East. To Greece? No, even farther east, to the Eastern Roman Empire, which lived on for nearly 1,000 years after the Empire in the West had fallen to the barbarians, and which had its capital at Constantinople.

All around now, in this Eastern Roman Empire, classicism is disintegrating as new elements flow into it from the Orient. The Hellenic civilization of Periclean Athens has long since passed away, merging into the Alexandrian Hellenistic of Alexandria itself, of Antioch, Ephesus and Pergamum; and now, as Rome is tottering beneath the blows of the barbarians closing in upon her, power is passing to Constantinople, that city on the Golden Horn which had been founded nearly 700 years before the birth of Christ by Byzas, a Greek of Megara, and which has been refounded by Constantine the Great three centuries after Christ. So it has been renamed the 'City of Constantine'; but Byzas held his own in the end. 'Constantinople' has vanished in favour of 'Istanbul', but we still call the ancient culture of the city, from the fourth century of our era till its fall to Mahomet the Conqueror and his janisseries in 1453, Byzantine, after the city's first name, Byzantium.

Now, in the days of Constantine, the first Christian Roman emperor, the gods of the antique world have had their little day and are no more. The temples of the Olympians still stand, but the fires upon their altars are dead and cold:

> The lonely mountains o'er
> And the resounding shore
> A voice of weeping heard, and loud lament;
> From haunted spring and dale
> Edged with poplar pale
> The parting Genius is with sighing sent;
> With flower-inwoven tresses torn
> The nymphs in twilight shade of tangled thickets mourn.

> In consecrated earth
> And on the holy hearth
> The Lars and Lemures moan with midnight plaint;
> In urns and altars round
> A drear and dying sound
> Affrights the Flamens at their service quaint;
> And the chill marble seems to sweat,
> While each peculiar Power forgoes his wonted seat.*

A new God has come out of Judaea, out of the spiritual East; Christ, the Anointed One, the initial letters of whose Greek name, *Christos*, Constantine ordered to be placed on all his standards and the shields of his bodyguards, the Chi-Rho sign; Christ, whose Nature the theologians of Greece and Asia Minor, in Nicaea, and Antioch, Caesarea and Heraclea, Myra and Alexandria and Nicomedia, are now disputing, 'splitting the world for one iota'. Was he *Homoousios*, of the *same* substance with the Father, or *Homoiousios*, of *like* substance? And so the Council of

* Milton: *Ode on the Morning of Christ's Nativity.*

Nicaea in 325 pronounces: 'That which had been incarnate at Bethlehem in the reign of Augustus Caesar, suffered under Pontius Pilate, and risen from death in the last days of Tiberius was neither deified man nor angel, nor demi-god nor any created being however exalted, but Very God of Very God, co-equal and co-eternal with the Father.'

In the streets, in the market-place, even, so they say, in barbers' shops, ordinary men and women, artisans, fishmongers, all and sundry, in short, are theology-mad, and are discussing the doctrines and eternal verities of Christianity as we in our age might discuss the weather. 'If you ask a

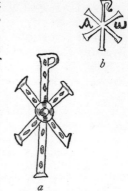

The Chi-Rho: *a*. from the shield of Justinian's bodyguard *b*. from an Early-Christian tomb

man to judge a piece of silver,' someone says, 'he informs you wherein the Son differs from the Father; or if you inquire whether the bath is ready, the answer is, "The Son was not made out of nothing".' This is truly a different world from the pagan Roman one of the earlier Caesars.

One vain attempt to bring back the pagan gods was made by Julian the Apostate, but it was short-lived. Nevertheless, classicism – the classicism of Pompeii and Alexandria – lingered in the illuminated manuscripts. But the sort of classicism which hangs over them – more poetic, late-Greek than practical Roman – is like the romantic, Gothicized classicism of an eighteenth-century 'folly'. The serene, balanced, emotionless figures of true, Hellenic classicism seem remote and distant as I look, for instance, at the pictures of the *Joshua Rotulus*. This roll was actually illustrated in the Eastern Empire not earlier than the eighth century A.D.,* but it faithfully copies prototypes

* The date is disputed. Some authorities put it later, and the text is certainly later than the illustrations. It is now in the Vatican Library, and divided into fifteen membranes.

Alexandrian 'Romantic' Landscape (from the *Joshua Rotulus*)

dating back to Alexandrian times, so the actual date, in this context, does not matter. Here its very form – a long, frieze-like scroll, originally thirty-five feet in length – is a reminiscence of the storied spiral friezes winding up the Roman triumphal columns – of Trajan, for example, or Marcus Aurelius. It tells, as they do, the story of a war: the tale of Joshua's invasion of Canaan. The soldiers are dressed in Roman uniforms, those who carry the Ark of the Covenant wear Roman togas. There are high, flat-roofed houses with upper pergola-like storeys of the type found in Pompeii, there are sacred trees in holy precincts, classical stelae, personifications of Tyche, the spirit of cities, floating above the heads of the protagonists, the city of Ai is personified in a figure which seems to be copied directly from a Roman tomb. There are pagan-style altars, classical towers in groves, and reclining river and mountain gods. All these in an illustration of events according to the *Septuagint*, the Greek translation of the Hebrew *Old Testament*!

And over it all there is that same faint atmosphere of a romantic past, of the long-ago-and-far-away, of a never never land of the imagination. The trees are the dim trees of dreams, the towers among the trees belong to ages half forgotten, the armies are hosts of the warriors of legend. The pictures in the *Joshua Rotulus* stir vague memories of the mist-hung, enchanted life of dreams, a life curtained with fantasy and poetic imagination. The Hellenic classicism of the Parthenon and Pheidias never had this dreamlike, romantic atmosphere; it comes from Alexandria.

Meanwhile, something else has caught my attention in the *Joshua Rotulus*: the fineness of the drawing, the vivid movement in some of the scenes, the sketchy, impressionistic technique. These things begin to remind me – of what? Of the *Utrecht Psalter*. I search for such earlier prototypes of the *Joshua Rotulus* as still exist, and find Greek psalters and illustrated Greek Bibles; either they have a large picture illustrating each psalm, or they have figures scattered about their margins. Some are uncoloured drawings, their expressive outlines brought out by the pen, and faces indicated by only a few quick strokes; a few pen-strokes also create a landscape – hills with trees in the valleys, turreted houses in gardens – or an army on the march amid a forest of spears. Here, then, I see what I have been looking for – the origin of that curious, *Utrecht Psalter* style.

There was evidently something in these sketchy Alexandrian miniatures which appealed to the North – to England especially, which always excelled in linear representation and outline drawing – when these Greek and Byzantine illustrations were passed into the Western Empire and so later inherited by the Carolingian court artists in the days of the Carolingian Renaissance; whence through the *Utrecht Psalter* they came to England, growing more vigorous, more sketchy, more violently contorted, and losing their dreamlike Alexandrian quality in a pointed, almost bristling sharpness on their way.

But now, having arrived in the far-off world of the Byzantine Empire, in Constantinople, I hear that the Emperors, the heirs of Constantine the Great, are considered to be divinely appointed to their office by God; they are God's representatives on earth. They are 'Friends of Christ'; they are surrounded with ceremonial that is religious, almost liturgical. In art they are depicted with the nimbus about their heads; their palace is the *Domus divina*, the sacred house.

From the days of Constantine this Greek colony on the Bosphorus, open to every Oriental influence, has been growing less and less pure Greek, while at the same time it was never pure Oriental. The Greek and the Oriental elements are fusing, and now, in the sixth century, when Justinian is ruling by the Golden Horn, the civilization of the city is neither Greek nor Oriental, it is Byzantine – Greek impregnated with the mystic spiritualism of the East.

'Glory be to God who made me worthy to surpass even thee, O Solomon!' So exclaimed Justinian, boasting, on the twenty-seventh of December in the year A.D. 537 at the inauguration of the second Church of the Holy Wisdom – Sancta Sophia – in Constantinople. One cannot now see Justinian's Sancta Sophia as the sixth century saw it, when the great dome 'swam in gold, radiating light', and the whole interior glittered and shone with mosaic decoration; when its 107 columns of porphyry and 'emerald green from Sparta' and 'many coloured marbles from the Phrygian range in which a rosy blush mingles with the white stone from Lydia and products of the Celtic crags'* adorned it. Earthquakes and the coming of the Turk as well as the passage of Time have dimmed some of its glories and wiped away others for ever. Paradoxically, the centre of the Byzantine Empire is not the best place in which to study Byzantine art. Not even that most Byzantine art of all, which has now caught my attention, for as I see it for the first time I have the answer to another of my questions:

* Paul the Silentiary.

D

whence came the austere, elongated, other-worldly figures
of Romanesque manuscripts? The reply is: from Byzantium; especially from Byzantine mosaics.

Here they are, the sheet-gold backgrounds, the frontally
placed, staring figures, remote and aloof. In the tenth
century the Byzantine princess Theophano married the
German prince Otto II, and going from the Golden Horn to
the Rhine (no doubt taking manuscripts and other Byzantine art treasures with her) she was one of the channels
through which Byzantine influence penetrated to the
northern world.

Byzantine mosaics! Nothing quite like them had been
known before. The Romans had taken cubes of various
naturally coloured stones or tiles and had set them into a
cement bed in geometrical patterns or medallion or lozenge
pictures depicting the Seasons personified, or Orpheus
taming the beasts with the music of his lyre, or scenes from
the hunt, or from Greek legend; these had decorated the
floors of their more important rooms, and were called
mosaic pavements. But Byzantine mosaics are not of this
kind.

Byzantine mosaicists took tiny cubes of coloured stone or
glass – smaller cubes than the Romans had ever used – or
cubes of bottle-glass covered with real gold-leaf coated in
its turn with transparent glass; occasionally, for certain
exceptional details, as for instance the ornaments of
Justinian and Theodora at Ravenna, they even used
mother-of-pearl. Then these highly skilled craftsmen
would press the tesserae one by one into a layer of still wet
plaster, keeping meticulously to the boundaries of the
design before them. So they lined walls and domes and
semi-spherical apses and vaults and pendentives, completely covering the interiors of buildings, leaving nothing
exposed, not even columns or string-courses or corner
angles: every architectural accent was muted. Thus they
took away from these interiors their earthly skeletons, so
to speak, that which visibly propped them up and kept them

standing firmly upon earth, and made them appear things as unsubstantial as the vault of heaven; and as the tiny glittering cubes were pressed irregularly into the plaster, and their surfaces consequently did not lie in the same plane, they did not reflect the light uniformly. As the spectator moved, he would see one gleam while another went dead, and then a moment after the dead one would flash out while the gleaming one sank into

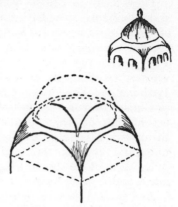

The principle of the Pendentive

shadow.   And as he looked he would slowly feel as if he had left the finite world for one of pure spirit where mortal values no longer had a meaning.

So I saw them, the stiff, staring, frontal figures on their gold backgrounds: impersonal, unemotional, austere and ineffably aloof. 'Men were convinced,' says Peter Meyer,* 'that the Nature of the Divine Being transcended all powers of human imagining, that it could not be described or expressed in the form of earthly reality, but merely hinted at. . . . Byzantine mosaics are neither representations nor idealizations – they are allusions, sacred emblems . . . sacred ideograms with conventional signs.' I realized as I looked upon them how much Eastern mysticism, Eastern solemnity, Eastern ceremonial reverence for Godhead had entered into their making.   It is true that the technique of mosaic involves rigid adherence to the outline of a design, with a consequent stiffness in the work produced, accentuated, of course, by the hardness of the medium; but the rigidity of the earlier Byzantine mosaics is not all due to the technique.

* *Byzantine Mosaics.*

These forms of Christ's vicars on earth, these sanctified, apostolic forms, these Divine Forms of God and the Mother of God are set apart from mortal men: they are limitless, ageless, timeless, one with the unfathomable Eternal. They do not move or gesture, or weep or laugh or suffer warring emotions as mortals do – they are not mortals. Justinian and Theodora are not represented as mortals but as Christ's instruments and representatives on earth. The accent falls on their divinely appointed office, not on themselves. Their stiff, frontal pose, their staring gaze are unnatural because they are supra-natural. We do not judge them as we should judge creatures of like habits and needs and frailties as ourselves.

As I studied mosaics more and more closely and thereby grew to understand them more I could not but feel how great a change the influence of the East upon the Greek world had brought to the antique pagan joy in life, its humanity, and its reiterated belief, proud, almost arrogant, that man was the measure of all things. Nowhere in the pre-Christian Greek or Roman world had I found the human body treated with this rigidity, this lack of soft naturalness, this impersonal formality and Oriental, ceremonial solemnity. As for those poetic fantasies, those romantic Alexandrian landscapes behind the actors in the scenes of the *Joshua Rotulus* – those hills with trees in their valleys, turreted houses in gardens, sacred trees in holy precincts – where are they in these earlier mosaics? All gone; blotted out by the glimmering, abstract, other-worldly gold backgrounds which eliminate all sense of temporal space. 'Ageless, timeless, one with the un-fathomable Eternal': these words recur as I stand in dim Byzantine churches where the mosaics are creating above and around me a sombre, subdued glory of shifting, shimmering light.

Everywhere now I study mosaics: those of Sancta Sophia, the Church of the Holy Wisdom, and the Church of the Kahrieh Djami in Constantinople itself; those of St.

Demetrios in Salonika, of Santa Pudenziana and Santa
Maria Maggiore in Rome; of Sant' Aquilino in Milan.
Sicilian and Venetian mosaics; and above all, the mosaics
of Ravenna: of San Vitale, Sant' Apollinare Nuovo, and
Sant' Apollinare in Classe, a few miles outside the town,
the only surviving building of the Port of Ravenna made
at the close of the first century B.C. by Augustus.

The earliest existing wall and vault mosaic with a
Christian theme is in a strange place: in the buried street
of pagan tombs beneath St. Peter's basilica. The fascinating story of the excavation of this ancient cemetery in
the search for the bones of St. Peter under the High Altar
of the great basilica is outside the scope of my journey
and may be read elsewhere;* but let us glance at the
photographs of this mosaic on the ceiling of the tomb of
the Julii.

Here, in the midst of an octagonal space formed by a
brilliant green vine (did not Christ say, 'I am the true
vine', and was not the pagan symbol of Dionysos taken by
the new faith as the symbol of Christ?) is a beardless figure
with rays shooting outwards from his nimbus: a charioteer,
though of his equipage only his two white galloping horses,
their red harness, and a tiny wheel among their hooves
remain. The style is pagan and classical. I should at
once have exclaimed, 'The charioteer of the Sun – Apollo!'
on seeing this picture, had it not been for the fact that it is
surrounded by indubitable Christian themes: Jonah
tumbling headlong into the jaws of the whale, an angler –
a Fisher of Souls – casting his line, and the head of the
Good Shepherd, with a sheep laid across His shoulders.
This is therefore not Apollo, but *Christos Helios*, Christ the
Sol Invictus, the Unconquered Sun – an early symbol of
the Ascension, of Christ's victory over Death. This, like the
Vine, wafts me back to the early days of Christian art,
when it was taking the forms of paganism and converting
them to its own use; in this fragmentary mosaic is 'a

* J. Toynbee and J. Ward Perkins: *The Shrine of St. Peter.*

microcosm of the whole dramatic history of Christ's peaceful penetration of the pagan empire'.*

In Santa Costanza in Rome I pass from the third to the fourth century, but I do not pass out of the sphere of classical Roman influence. In one of the apses of the church St. Peter receives the Law from the hand of Christ. The influence here goes deeper than the Roman togas and the Apollo-like appearance of the yellow-haired, beardless and youthful Christ. The whole scene is reminiscent of imperial Roman administration. As the Roman emperor gave audience to one of his legates on the eve of his departure to the province he was to govern in the emperor's name, and as he handed over to him, written on a scroll, his official commission, so Christ, Lord of the whole world, entrusts to his faithful apostle Peter the scroll of the Law. St. Paul, like a bearded philosopher of the ancient world, stands on Christ's other side and the sheep at the feet of our Lord are perhaps symbolical of other apostles. The figures are Roman too, pre-Byzantine in that they have weight and rounded substance, and have not stiffened into those hieratic, frontal, staring figures I shall meet elsewhere; in that their colours are dull, they have not the luminosity of Byzantine mosaics, and the spiritualism of the East has not touched them.

There are evidences of the birth of this other-worldly, transcendental spirit, however, in Sant' Ambrogio in Milan, where the saints Ambrosius and Protasius stand robed in white togas before a deep blue background 'fastening their gaze on what remains immutable for ever'.† It stands out even more plainly in the mosaics of the apse of the Cappella di Sant' Aquilino in San Lorenzo, where, against a gold background, Christ, youthful and beardless, sits in the midst of his white toga'd disciples, who gaze far away into eternity, ordinary men no longer, but dedicated souls raised from martyrdom to sit at Christ's side on high.

* *The Shrine of St. Peter*, p. 117.   † Eusebius.

In Rome, in the church of Santa Pudenziana, there are
fifth-century mosaics in the apse. Here too, Christ is
teaching in the midst of His disciples, but He sits on a
lordly throne at the foot of the Cross, and here He is
bearded, with flowing hair – no longer a youthful Apollo,
rather a majestic Zeus, Father of gods and men, Jupiter
Greatest and Best. Perhaps the rather grandiloquent
majesty of this enthroned figure was a counter-blast to the
upsurge of resurrected paganism under Julian the Apostate
in the years A.D. 360 to 363. But the figure which is most
attractive here, which takes one back to the world of late
antiquity and early Christian Rome is that female one
which symbolizes the *Ecclesia ex gentibus* – the Church of
the Gentiles. Appropriately she stands behind the Apostle
of the Gentiles, St. Paul. Her head is veiled like the heads of
those about to make sacrifice in classical days; she slightly
inclines it as she gazes with thoughtful sadness at the scene
before her. Far removed from things of earth, she looks
down the centuries to come, as if she were indeed, what she
so resembles, a sybil of old, such a prophetess as guided
Aeneas to the realms of the dead and the Elysian Fields,
where secrets usually hidden from mortal minds were
revealed to him with the vision of all that was yet to be.

I am passing rapidly now from the antique world of solid
reality, and concrete materialism, to a different realm,
where values have changed, the concrete is melting into
mists of irreality, and a light from within glows over every
scene. Here is the world of men to whom prayer meant
not, as it had done before, a bargain-making with a deity
who must be appeased lest he did them a mischief, but a
communion with God, an entrance into God's presence, a
touching of the hand of God. In Santa Maria Maggiore
I am no longer in the city of the Caesars, but in the still
and silent presence of all who have gone before, testifying
to the nearness and reality of God.

Here the mosaics, instead of confining themselves to
vaults and apses, are extending over all the walls of the

church. They cover the nave, and appear on the triumphal arch which gives entrance to the sanctuary.   On
one side of the nave they tell the story of the Old Testament
Patriarchs, on the other they depict the exploits of the
Hebrew leader-heroes, Moses and Joshua; while on the
arch is the Annunciation to Mary of Christ's birth,
the Adoration of the Magi, and the presentation of the
Holy Child in the Temple.

In the nave Abraham first greets, then entertains the
three angels in the Plains of Mamre; running from his tent
in the heat of the day he recognized one of them – represented here in an all-enveloping aureole like shining
crystal – and bowed down and said, 'My Lord, pass not
away, I pray Thee, from Thy servant.'*   A light seems to
radiate from the Three like a spiritual radiance shining
through them; they do not tread upon earth, but upon
clouds.   Already it seems that the three angels have
become a symbol of the Trinity, as they are often hereafter
to be found in the art of the Orthodox Church.   Gold
backgrounds, with their sense of infinity, are now becoming
more frequent.   There is one behind Melchizedek, 'King
of Salem, priest of the Most High God', bringing his offering to Abraham.   It gives way only to the blue and grey
and fiery red of the firmament where heaven opens and
reveals the Figure of God clad in a cerulean robe which
sweeps out like a cloud behind Him, accepting the sacrifice.
Even in the violent scenes of battle, where the narrative is
more important than symbolism – the destruction of the
hosts of Pharaoh in the Crossing of the Red Sea, Joshua's
victory over the kings of the Amorites – there is that remote
atmosphere of 'old unhappy far-off things, and battles
long ago'.

But on the triumphal arch of the sanctuary there is no
mistaking the new spirit of deep and mystic symbolism
impregnating the scenes depicted there.   At the Annunciation angels attend Mary, as, robed in gold, she sits spinning;

* Genesis xviii. 3.

an angel and the Dove of the Holy Spirit hover in a sky shot through with gleams of fiery red above her. Below, the Wise Men, in curious costumes, bring their gifts to the Lord of the World garbed like a little Roman philosopher, but gold-nimbed, and seated upon a throne watched by luminous white angels in the rear, while the whole scene is backed by the glory of timeless gold.   Seated beside Him is an enigmatic, dark-robed figure with veiled head, her right hand pensively supporting her chin.   Who she is no one now knows.   Perhaps she is a sybil, a prophetess of the ancient world of the Gentiles.   She is represented with the coming of the Magi at the season of Epiphany, when the light of the star shone over the heathen and called them to the stable where the Christ Child was; it is therefore very likely that she stands for the expectation of the Gentiles, a prophetess of the pagan world bowing her head in silent meditation before the Incarnation that was to dissolve the cold philosophy of the ancients in the glowing fires of spiritual ecstasy of Christianity.

5

'THE SILENT CITY OF THE ADRIATIC'

~~~~~~~~~~~~~~~~~~~~~~~~~~~~~~~

AFTER Santa Maria Maggiore I come at last to Ravenna. Ravenna! What echoes the very name awakens down the long colonnades of history! Ravenna, first the capital of the fugitive emperors from fallen Rome, then the city of the conquering Ostrogoths, then the seat of the exarchs of the Byzantine Empire, in the days of the sixth century A.D. when Justinian – or Belisarius his general, acting for Justinian – reconquered for a while the Roman Empire of the West. The exarchs were Justinian's viceroys, sent from Constantinople to govern the reconquered part of the Western Empire until, 200 years later, it fell again, this time to the Lombards. Now it is 'the silent city of the Adriatic', by-passed by commerce and industry and all the strident clamour of the twentieth century; but it keeps a large part of its treasures inviolate still. In Ravenna rather than anywhere else are mosaics redolent of the true Byzantine spirit, the greatest and most perfectly preserved Byzantine mosaics of all.

I go first, because the earliest ones are there, to that exquisite jewel-house of mosaics, the so-called Mausoleum of Galla Placidia, the sister of the Roman emperor of the West, Honorius, who in A.D. 410 sent the famous message to Britain, far northern outpost, in those days, of the

Roman Empire, telling her that she must 'look to her own defences', for all Roman legions were now needed at home. In that very year, 410, the Eternal City was sacked by the Goths. Honorius fled to Ravenna, and set up his court there; and the earliest Ravenna mosaics date from shortly after this period.

A great stone sarcophagus of heavy Roman build stands in the dim little cruciform mausoleum; above rise vaulted roofs diapered with mosaic patterns of white stars, crosses, and little roses with white centres on a vibrant, glorious blue background; shafts of muted light penetrating the alabaster windows strike through the dim interior and make the stars shine out and the values of the deep blue shift and change so that it seems to scintillate with inner fire. In the centre rises the dome of the cupola, and here, above the symbols of the four Evangelists, is a night sky full of golden stars, and in the midst, a golden Latin cross.

Like ghosts in the dim light there appear on the lunettes under the dome the white shapes of toga'd apostles, with an arm extended, like philosophers of the Graeco-Roman world. Between each couple are doves drinking from a calyx. There they stand, spectral against the dark blue, gesturing everlastingly into the empyrean, witnesses through fifteen centuries of the Christian faith. Among green arabesques of foliage tipped with gold, there are also two deer approaching the fountain of life, an illustration of the psalm, 'As the hart panteth after the water brooks, so panteth my soul after Thee, O God';* and here, in the lunette over the entrance, the Good Shepherd sits among his sheep in a rocky landscape tufted with trees and backed by a sky of limitless blue – a Roman feature, this, untouched, in these fifth-century mosaics, by the airless infinitude of Byzantine gold. Yet even so there is a remoteness about the scene which sets it above the world of mortality in the deathless realms of the spirit. All these mosaics in the mausoleum of Galla Placidia are, as one would have

* Psalm xlii. 1-2.

expected, Roman inspired with no admixture yet of the Oriental.

Indeed, in the Arian baptistry I feel that I might be standing in the pagan world, although I am looking up, in the central dome, at so christian a subject as the Baptism of Christ. For there, while the white Dove of the Holy Spirit descends upon the head of a youthful, almost boyish Christ standing naked in the waters of Jordan and gazing profoundly ahead, and while a bearded figure like some antique hero – John the Baptist – stands upon a rock and baptizes Him, the horned river-god of the Jordan sits in the manner of a classic deity, full-bodied and muscular, his robe falling in ample folds over his lap and knees to the ground, watching and apparently approving the scene. So long did it take paganism to die – if it ever did die, and did not rather, submerged beneath the waters, sleep until the men of the Italian Renaissance roused it again.

In passing from the mausoleum to the Arian baptistry I have stepped forward through the fifth century to a time, long after Honorius' death, when Theodoric, King of the Ostrogoths, ruled in Ravenna in place of the conquered Roman emperors, and the fifth century was passing into the sixth. Theodoric, who was an Arian Christian,* built he Arian baptistry, and he built the basilica beside his palace, the church of Sant' Apollinare Nuovo.

Here, in this church, there are, above the nave arcade, mosaics for which Theodoric was responsible. Both on the right hand and on the left, high up between the windows and the roof, there are rectangular panels holding scenes from the life of Christ. I see Him with outstretched arm, young, beautiful, gazing ahead as if beyond the vision of Calvary to the Infinite, performing the miracle of the loaves and fishes; or (though here He is bearded) with His disciples reclining, Roman fashion, at a semi-circular table

---

* Arians held that there was only one true God – the Father; and that the Son and the Holy Ghost were created beings of similar but not identical substance (cf. the modern Unitarians).

at the Last Supper; or in the Garden of Gethsemane, His apostles on one side and the soldiers on the other, and the traitor in the centre betraying Him with a kiss. Again He appears before Pilate, when the Roman 'took water, and washed his hands before the multitude, saying, "I am innocent of the blood of this just person; see ye to it" ';* the three Marys appear at a classical circular tomb like a miniature temple of Vesta – a great angel with drooping wings is seated beside it. In all these scenes Christ wears the ancient world's insignia of dignity and rank: the purple robe and the nimbus. But best of all He appears, a tall figure with one hand raised in a gesture of command, calling the fishermen Peter and Andrew; again He is clad in a purple garment draped toga-wise, and the cross nimbus stands behind His head. He stands almost frontally, His eyes fixed afar; He does not look at the fishermen in the boat, but they gaze at Him as if their eyes could never leave Him. Behind them the world does not exist; it is shut out by an unearthly expanse of gold. The gold background does not allow the onlooker's eyes to rove beyond the forms which stand before it – it is a barrier shutting out the world of men and enclosing in a luminous light this transcendental world of the eternal.

A little lower, in the gold spaces between the windows, there are white figures carrying prophetic scrolls; and below these the rhythmic march of two white-robed processions one on the right, the other on the left, moving eastwards. They seem to emerge on the one hand from the palace of Theodoric and to move towards the Saviour on His throne, on the other to come out of the port of Classe and to make their way, preceded by the Wise Men, to the Virgin with the Child upon her knee. Theodoric had the palace and the Saviour, Classe and the Virgin and Child executed; but when the Ostrogoths were conquered by Belisarius, and Ravenna became the city of the Byzantine exarchs under the patronage of Justinian, the *Damnatio memoriae* of the

* Matthew xxvii. 24.

Arian Ostrogothic king was destroyed with the destruction of whatever lay between these extremities, and the processions of male martyrs on the right hand, the line of virgin martyrs on the left were substituted. Everlastingly they move in the dignity of spiritual exaltation on their way, the male martyrs to lay their crowns at the feet of Christ enthroned, the Holy Virgins to place theirs before the static, outward staring Mother of God with, upon her knee, not a baby child, but the solemn, sacrificial Emmanuel, God-with-us. The gold backgrounds glitter behind them; facing frontally, although they are moving forward, the male martyrs clad in white Roman togas, the virgins in garments embroidered in red and green and gold, their bodies paper-thin, without substance, they float rather than walk, each separated from his neighbour by a stylized palm-tree, symbol of victory.

Mosaic Static, 6th. century
(Ravenna)

As I gaze upon them from the centre of the nave the long processions, caught up in a *moto perpetuo* of rhythm, seem actually to be moving towards their goals, spirits in corporeal form gliding onwards to their God; in their eyes stands the vision of the regions of the blest where all the mystery of life and of life's purpose shall at last be known. A transcendental light surrounds them, glittering from that unearthly gold behind them; and silence stands over and about them, the inscrutable silence of those who have looked upon things no mortal man may know and learnt secrets no finite mind can comprehend.

I have now reached the second quarter of the sixth century, the days of Justinian, emperor of the Eastern Roman Empire; I enter the octagonal church of San Vitale, and beyond the great arch which divides the body of the church from the choir, see all San Vitale's mosaics shining, completely covering choir walls and dome and apse beyond.

As I enter the choir and look upon them they seem at first Roman rather than Byzantine. Here are 'white forms clad in the stately garments of Antiquity',* the shadows falling greyish-blue upon their togas, naturalistic enough in the Roman manner, with rounded bodily form showing beneath their draperies. In a great lunette on the left-hand wall of the choir Abraham, in a green landscape flecked with the red of small flowers in the foreground and of fiery clouds in the heaven above entertains the white-robed angels who sit, their golden haloes gleaming, under a tree in a green meadow, brown, blue and white outlines of rocks being vaguely suggested in the background. Further on, the patriarch is shown again raising his hand to strike Isaac, the sacrificial offering demanded by God, while the hand of the Almighty is stretched forth from the red-streaked clouds to stay his stroke. In the spandrel above Moses, in a white toga shadowed with blue, receives the tables of the Law from similar fiery clouds burning above the variegated browns, blues, greens and shades of gold of the jagged, fantastic rocks upon which the Hebrew leader stands.

On a similar lunette opposite, Melchizedek the priest-king and the poor shepherd Abel carrying his lamb bring their offerings to a large table-altar. Again Moses appears in the spandrel among those precipitous, many-hued rocks, watching Jethro's sheep at the foot of them, and up on their heights taking off his sandal at the bidding of the Lord. Up near the windows the four Evangelists, once more white-robed figures of classical philosophers, wait with their

* Grabar: *Byzantine Painting*.

writing materials beside them till the breath of inspiration
from God shall bid them start their Gospels, their offering
to Christ.   And far above, in the dome of the choir, amid
a glory of brilliant red and green and gold arabesques
touched with blue, four soaring angels on blue globes hold
up a garland of flowers and fruit, the offerings of every
season, and in the midst of it, on a blue background
spangled with stars, appears the mystic white Lamb of God,
the centre of the firmament of heaven, the Being to whom
all below – Evangelists, prophets, angels, patriarchs, kings,
leaders and poor shepherds, are bringing their meed of
adoration, their offerings of every kind.

I approach the apse. Immediately the Roman falls
behind me.   Here, in the apse, hovers the spirit of the
mystic East, which thought its God so holy, so incorporeal,
it both shrank from presenting Him and had no forms in
which to body Him forth till the Greek mind supplied it –
but a Greek mind touched now with that reverence which
forbade a pagan Jupiter, muscular and voluptuous, or a
pagan Apollo of purely physical beauty to represent God.
God was greater than any creature He had made.   A mind
filled with thoughts of this world could not approach Him;
for him who would contemplate God, or even His saints,
the world must be blotted out, he must rise above and
beyond the world.   God, His saints and the Holy Virgin,
and the Emperor who was Christ's Vicar on earth, did not
move in the realms of ordinary men.   In a rarefied world
of the spirit, in austere aloofness and awful majesty, they
had no dealings with the mundane and the temporal, but
fixed their far-seeing gaze upon eternity.

Here is that Emperor, Justinian, and on the opposite wall
his Empress, Theodora, bringing their offerings likewise to
Christ, as the holy martyrs and Virgins in Sant' Apollinare
Nuovo brought their crowns to cast them before Him.
Gone now is the naturalism of the mosaics of the choir.
Against a background of glittering gold shutting out the
finite world Justinian and Theodora, with their richly

attired retinues, move in ceremonial pomp in processions
that seem never to have had a beginning as they will never
have an end.   Their paper-thin, weightless, unsubstantial
bodies appear not to be walking, but floating in a void
with a slow, majestic rhythm that includes all — priests
and generals, bodyguard and emperor, attendants, ladies
and empress – in the sweep of one unified ritual action.
Though they move to the side, they are placed frontally,
and stare out straight ahead; and they glide as ghosts do,
with no glance at where they are going, wafted irresistibly
by an unseen force towards their bourne.   Justinian and
Theodora wear the gold nimbus of imperial dignity, the
imperial purple, which is repeated in the purple stripes of
the court dignitaries, old symbol of the Roman senators,
and jewelled crowns; they bear golden vessels in their
hands to offer to the Most High.   They come like the
kings of the East who opened their treasures at the manger :
for were not the Byzantine rulers the new Magi, bidden
not only to bring their offerings of gold to Christ, but to
follow the light of the word that had been revealed to the
Gentiles and to establish it in the Eastern Church?   So
upon the brilliant and beautiful green and gold shield of
Justinian's bodyguard appears in gold the Chi-Rho
monogram, acknowledgement to all the world of the
Emperor's faith; so on his left hand stand the white-robed
priests of the Church of the new faith of Christ, with Archbishop Maximianus carrying the gold Cross, his companions a golden codex and a censer; so on the hem of
Theodora's robe is embroidered the theme of the Three
Magi of the East, bearing, as the Byzantine rulers are
doing, their gifts to Christ.   In the hush of supernatural
silence she draws near the Holy of Holies, and beside her
a solemn, gold-robed attendant lifts the looped curtain to
let her through.

Then, in the semi-dome of the apse just above there
shines out that to which all that has gone before has been
tending.   Aloft upon the deep blue sphere of the Cosmos,

E

clad in purple and nimbed in gold, sits in majesty Christ
the Redeemer, youthful and triumphant, gazing down
through apse and choir and out across the ages. A white
archangel stands on either side of Him; with His right hand
He takes the martyr's crown of precious stones from San
Vitale, who offers it as a dignitary of the Byzantine court
would have offered a gift to his master and his king, with
his hands veiled. On the other side is Bishop Ecclesius, in
purple tunic and pallium, holding a model of this church
which he had founded. At the feet of men and archangels
are the rocks and flowers of a green garden of Paradise.
The ethereal, weightless, rhythmic figures are clearly
manifestations in a world of the spirit, shut off from
terrestrial materialism by the glittering infinity of the gold
background, intensified by the unearthly streaks of red and
white cloud above the Saviour's head.

On the flat land three miles away, long since deserted by
the waters of the Adriatic which made the port of Classe in
the days of the first emperor, Augustus, stands the only
complete surviving building of that vanished port – the
church of Sant' Apollinare in Classe, saved when all
around it sank, by the circumstance of its having been built
on rising ground. This is a basilical church, and all its
remaining mosaics are in the apse at the far eastern end: a
shining vision of bright green with the orant figure of Sant'
Apollinare in the midst.

A closer inspection shows, of course, that there is much
more than this. The great vault, indeed, displays a complex symbolical design. Above the saint, standing in the
ancient classical attitude of prayer, in a rocky meadow of
vivid green, there gleams out, in a circle sewn with precious
stones, a huge Cross upon a background of innumerable
stars; because, in the clouds above it the white half-figures
of Moses and Elias appear, and the hand of God emerging
from the streaks of red in the golden sky, pointing down to
it, it is clear that this is a symbolical representation of the

Transfiguration of Christ on the 'high mountain apart', when the voice of God spoke out of the cloud saying, 'This is my beloved Son in whom I am well pleased: hear ye him.' The three sheep below, looking up at the Cross, are Peter, James and John his brother, witnesses of the event. Below the brown and greenish rocks outlined in white and the flowers of various kinds planted between, below the green meadow where Apollinare stands, a procession of lambs, six each side, approach him. These are the faithful Apostles of Christ; and there they are again in another procession, on the triumphal arch of the apse, where the head of Christ in a medallion appears in a cloudy sky from which issue stormily the eagle, the angel, the tawny-winged lion and the white-winged bull: the four evangelical symbols.

The daylight is fading. They have flooded the apse with such artificial illumination as the artists of that mosaic Transfiguration never knew, and it is shining in glory as I cast a final look at it from the end of the shadowy nave. Brilliant above all shines the gold Cross upon its background of stars; in endless prayer the saint beneath stands raising his hands to the vision above him. Then the light vanishes. Saint and Cross are one with the darkness of coming night. The silent City of the Adriatic has closed its early-Christian treasure chest, and has sunk once more into its twentieth-century sleep.

6

AFTER ICONOCLASM

~~~~~~~~~~~~~~~~~~~~~~~~~~~~~

UPON Constantinople, capital of the Eastern Empire, headquarters of the consecrated Basileus who was God's mandatory on earth, and fountain-head because of imperial patronage, of that subtle mingling of the Greek and the Oriental in art which we call Byzantine, there fell, in the year A.D. 726 an artistic catastrophe: Iconoclasm.* In that year the depiction of the saintly or divine form in painting, mosaic, or any other artistic medium was forbidden by imperial decree throughout the Empire of the East, and many such representations already in existence were destroyed. Therefore, when one looks to Constantinople for Byzantine mosaics one is faced with the situation that the city which was the source of Byzantine inspiration has fewer Byzantine works to show than almost any other city of the former Roman Empire; and even those that exist date almost without exception from the years after A.D. 843, when iconoclasm came to an end. The exceptions include the crosses on a gold ground which Justinian ordained should be put there when he rebuilt the Church of Christ Holy Wisdom between the years 537 and 562.

The hatred of images of the conquering Turks in the fifteenth century did not extend to their destruction; the conquerors merely obliterated them with whitewash, which

* 'The breaking of images.'

can be, and in many cases has subsequently been, removed. Therefore in Sancta Sophia, many of those post-
iconoclastic mosaics which were made when the ban on
images was removed may still be seen. High up, between
the windows of the side walls under the dome, rigidly
frontal, and standing in white shadowed with blue before a
background of gold, is the figure of that most famous bishop
of Constantinople, St. John Chrysostom; and on the
threshold of the nave, above the main entrance, Christ sits
enthroned with the Emperor Leo VI prostrate at His feet
and a medallion on either side of Him, from one of which
the Virgin looks out upon the world, and from the other the
angel Gabriel. Leo, the 'philosopher basileus', crowned
and nimbed and richly attired as the vicegerent of Christ on
earth, is receiving from the hands of the Lord that supreme
and holy wisdom to which the whole church, four centuries
earlier, had been consecrated. The mosaic is dark and
subdued in colour. Against a sombre gold background the
white and grey-green robes of both Emperor and the
Omniscient Christ stand out dimly, and on His throne
Christ sits with a grave, almost stern expression, in an
attitude both hieratic and judicial, his gaze directed not at
the kneeling Emperor, but afar over all the world.

Above the south entrance, in similar frontal pose and
impersonal majesty, appears the blue robed, solemn-eyed
Virgin, holding upon her knee Christ the incarnate Logos
with the knowledge of all the ages of earth and of the
infinity of heaven in His unwavering gaze. On her left
stands the Emperor Constantine the Great, inclining his
head in reverence over the model of the city he founded,
which he holds in his hands; on her right, similarly inclining
his head over a model of the church of Sancta Sophia,
stands Justinian. These are no portraits. These mosaic
Emperors resemble each other as the originals were far
from doing; and both are preternaturally grave, hollow-
cheeked, careworn and ascetic looking. The hand of some
monastically inspired artist seems to have created them: the

monks of the Eastern Orthodox Church loved gauntness
and the ascetic look.

The mosaics in the south gallery are not so easily to be
approached and seen, but there are excellent reproductions
of the most beautiful of them:* a fragmentary twelfth-
century Deesis, that is, a representation of Christ with Mary
and John the Baptist. The Christ has been destroyed, but
the head and one shoulder of the Virgin is preserved, and
the upper part of St. John the Baptist. I realize here how
far I have travelled from the Ravenna days. They are in
three-quarter view, with gravely inclined heads, still static,
though not now emotionless. Both express a pitying
sorrow, an outlook upon tragedy which is even yet,
however, divine rather than human. The colouring, apart
from the gold background, is sombre, the outlines very fine,
perhaps almost too fine and delicate. I have now moved
out of the old hieratic, formal world. It is the end of the
twelfth century, and the Ravenna mosaics are already more
than 600 years old.

Yet once more, before I leave the stern aloofness and
awful majesty of the early Byzantine world for good, I go
back into the eleventh century as I enter the small cruciform church of Daphni near Athens and Eleusis, the
ancient centre of the Eleusinian mysteries. Here, from the
crown of the dome, a vast and awe-inspiring Christ Pantocrator, bearded and grim, frowns sternly down: not the
gentle Christ of 'Suffer the little children to come unto me',
or 'Let him who is without sin among you cast the first
stone', but the dread Arbiter of the day when the Last
Trump shall sound and all shall be called to account at the
final Judgement.

The mosaics of the nave are rather less alarming, and
more pleasing. Pleasing – but they have lost the solemn
majesty, the spiritual exaltation of the Byzantine mosaics
of pre-iconoclast days. The colours are bright, the figures

* Grabar: *Byzantine Painting*, pp. 104-5; Weidlé: *Mosaici Paleocristiani
e Bizantini*, Pl. XVIII and pp. 141, 142.

actively on the move. Angels bend and gesticulate over the manger where the infant Christ lies swaddled, Mary reclines gracefully, the folds of her deep blue gown falling over her legs for all the world like the true classical folds of the so-called 'Three Fates' from the east pediment of the Parthenon; gentle beasts drink at the stream, and Joseph rests a pensive head upon a classically drawn hand. In the scene of Christ's Baptism the Saviour's naked figure is modelled almost as it might have been by an Hellenic sculptor of the age of Pheidias. A new era is dawning. These mosaics are very early twelfth century, but they already show signs of that classical revival which in Italy we associate with the Renaissance.

When I pass westwards to Sicily I find all these tendencies increasing. At Cefalù, at the Cappella Palatina, at Martorana in Palermo and at Monreale, lightness, elegance and delicacy have ousted the remote grandeur of the impersonal majesty of the earlier Byzantine mosaics. These churches were all built in the twelfth century by the Norman kings of Sicily or by their great admiral, George of Antioch, and decorated with mosaics at their behest by Byzantine artists.

Northwards of the Adriatic, too, in Venice and Torcello, there is the same type of mosaic decoration. In the vault mosaics of the atrium of the basilica of St. Mark in Venice, Noah leans from the open window of the ark with quite human anxiety as he catches a plump returning dove in his hand, and the blue, green and white waves of the flood coil and twist in stylized pattern below. The builders of the infamous Tower of Babel are actively engaged in their tasks, carrying bricks aloft, shouting instructions, wielding pickaxes, bending, stretching, kneeling, their tunics falling in natural folds around their hips; the blue-robed angel with the magnificent drooping wings of brown, yellow-gold and fire inclines forward, with gentle grace that matches the mild solemnity of his expression. God creates the world and the whirling constellations, the sun and moon, the night

Mosaic Realistic: Noah receiving back the
dove (St. Mark's Venice)

and the day, in a wonderful colour harmony of blues and
greens wherein birds and fishes in effortless grace twist and
turn and leap and fly.   At Torcello, only a few miles away,
meanwhile, the angels of the Last Judgement, with very
vigorous gestures, drive souls to a hell of blue-grey demons;
their eyes are fixed determinedly upon what they are
doing, they do not any longer gaze out into Eternity.   How
much lighter, more worldly, more *superficial*, is all this than
that which had gone before!

So, at Sicilian Monreale, Lot and his daughters flee from
the fiery destruction and toppling towers of Sodom and the
pillar of salt which was Lot's wife at a good racing run, the
hems of their garments rippling as they go, Lot's cloak
fluttering behind him.   There is the same rapid movement,
in a swirl and flutter of light robes and cloaks, as Jacob
wrestles with the angel – another being with magnificent
outspread wings – in a stylized landscape of rock and trees.
Amid a skurry of many-hued wings at La Martorana the
angels proclaim the birth of the infant Jesus to genuinely
astonished shepherds, while a blue-robed Virgin of meek

aspect reclines in the mouth
of a cave, her hands upon
the Babe, swathed in swaddling bands like a tiny
mummy. The maids pre-
paring the bath to wash
the holy Child provide a
homely touch which would
have been inconceivable to
the earlier Byzantine artists.

And so it is with all these
Sicilian mosaics, wrought
when the Normans ruled
the island. In the Cappella
Palatina, built by King
Roger II about A.D. 1132,
bright, light colours – red,

Mosaic Mobile 12th. century
(Sicily)

green, blue, golden brown – and the little figures in
the foreground, running to strew their garments before
Him whom they greeted with 'Hosanna! Hosanna!' en-
liven the scene of the Entry into Jerusalem. The Christ
Pantocrator, the Ancient of Days, filling the whole semi-
dome of the apse of the Cathedral at Cefalù, above the
Virgin in the classical 'orant' attitude of prayer, adored by
archangels with outspread wings and with all the Apostles
below her, has a far milder aspect than the great Judge of
dreadful majesty at Daphni. Like St. Mark's at Venice,
like the cathedral at Torcello, these Sicilian churches
glitter with colour and shine with light, they flutter with
movement; they also pulse with drama, as when the uplifted hand of the flying messenger from God stays Abraham
in the act of lifting his knife to kill Isaac, as when Cain
heaves his axe above his head to smite Abel, or as when the
Child Jesus leans from His mother's arms and stretches out
across the arch of the sanctuary to a hastening Simeon who
lifts veiled hands to receive Him.

Yet, among all these twelfth-century mosaics I feel the

ghostly influence of the Byzantinism of the long-past fifth and sixth centuries still hovering. However much landscape there is of rock and tree and turreted town and palace, in the background stretches, not Nature's open sky of cloud and light and air, but that closed curtain of glittering, airless gold; however swiftly the events of Old and New Testaments may move, and the garments of the actors in them flutter and swirl, there is always some saint standing near by, aloof, austere, frontally staring in unapproachable solemnity; however sweet may be the expression of the Virgin in one place, as her hands rest upon the manger which cradles her newly-born Son, in another there will be a representation of her as she stands in the semi-dome of the apse at Torcello, her background a sheet of unrelieved gold, she herself elongated, stern, rigidly frontal, with the characteristic Byzantine large eyes, long, narrow nose and tiny mouth, the characteristic boneless, long-fingered hands, holding not a child, but the Timeless One, the incarnate Logos, in her arms.

And now, as one returning to a house where the feasting is over and the lights are burning dim I go for the last time to Constantinople, to the church of Kahrieh Djami, not far from the mighty Theodosian walls of the City of the Golden Horn. It is now the fourteenth century, 900 years since Justinian cried as he looked upon Sancta Sophia, 'Glory be to God, who made me worthy to surpass even thee, O Solomon!' and 200 years have passed since the mosaics of Venetia and Norman Sicily first shone out upon the world. But still, in Kahrieh Djami, Mary rides to Bethlehem on a light-limbed, prancing horse before the tall towers of a city with trees of blue and green spiring up among them; preceded by a Joseph in silvery, grey-blue garments with refined and silky folds whose feet move over the ground in almost a dancing measure. Cloaks flutter and the hems of garments ripple in a pleasing rainbow world of gay, bright colour.

The picturesque telling of a story or presentation of a

character is now the artist's chief concern. The scene in the outer narthex of the church, picturing the Enrolment for Taxation before the governor Cyrenius has been made not for edification, not to symbolize the eternal truths of the Christian faith, but to satisfy the spectator's sensual pleasure in colour, design and minor details. The governor, in his deep blue robe and crimson cloak, sitting like a mediaeval king upon a throne, the crowded Roman officials and soldiers beside Mary and Joseph, with their ornaments and weapons, their plumes and phalerae and elaborate costumes, the subtle harmonies of the blues and gold-browns, the reds and the whites, the shimmering gold background behind the queer trees and architectural features: all these make a charming picture, but they no longer thrill with a sense of the ineffable, the eternal Divine. Or the young fair-haired martyr saint in his richly embroidered, delicate garments of pink and white and gold and blue, holding his ceremonial sword and a cross like a frail, bejewelled ornament rather than a symbol of the supreme Sacrifice: does he not more greatly resemble a gently nurtured page learning the ways of chivalry than one who has borne fire and torment for his faith?

All is delicacy and subtle charm. As the lordly peacock struts before a narrow, round-headed doorway at Kahrieh Djami near two blue steps leading mysteriously under another round-headed doorway into what can only be a land of magic and enchantment, where that proud peacock of vivid blue and green will unfold the glories of his irridescent tail, I think no more of the incarnate Logos and the Day of Doom. Of what *do* I think? Of revelry and material pleasures? Yes . . . the material pleasures of the Decameron Nights in the house at Fiesole, while the horror of deadly plague brooded over Florence below.

Less than 100 years after these carefree, charming mosaics had been set in their beds of plaster the Sultan Mahomet II the Conqueror was hammering at the gates of Constantinople, and on a May night in 1453 the lights of his camp could be seen in Galata on the Bosphorus. On Whit-Monday, May 28th, Mahomet said to his troops, 'I give you to-day a grand and populous city, the capital of the ancient Romans, the very summit of splendour and glory, which has become, so to say, the centre of the world: I give it over for you to pillage.'*

On that same day Constantine XI, last of the long line of Eastern Roman emperors, heard the liturgy celebrated for the last time in Sancta Sophia, there for the last time he did penance and received the Holy Communion. Just after dawn on the morning of the 29th the cry went up, "Εάλω ἡ πόλις" – the city is taken; and Mahomet the Conqueror and his janisseries stormed into the streets and in Justinian's Sancta Sophia thanks were given to Allah, and the 'Great Church' of Christ-Holy-Wisdom became a Mohammedan mosque. So fell the capital of the Eastern Roman Empire inaugurated by Constantine the Great on May 11th 1,123 years before; so finally fell the once mighty Roman Power which had embraced the whole known world; so snapped the link which had bound together Oriental mysticism and the high intelligence of the Greek, and produced Byzantine art.

* Critobulus, quoted by Liddell, *Byzantium and Istanbul*.

7

THE HUMBLER ART

~~~~~~~~~~~~~~~~~~~~~~

Bᴜᴛ now Byzantinism was everywhere. It had started on the Golden Horn, it spread through the Isles of Greece, and into Greece itself, it crossed the Ionian and the Adriatic, it came to Ravenna and Venice and Torcello, it penetrated to Sicily, it crossed the Alps to the cold afforested lands of the northern barbarians. It was plain to me now that this was no end of my journey. I must pursue those Byzantine influences, and not in mosaics only.

In Monreale, the Capella Palatina, the Martorana, Cefalù, the walls were covered with mosaics because these buildings were the foundations of kings, princes, admirals. In lesser, poorer churches there could be no such lordly and expensive decoration. Mosaics were the gifts of emperors and high dignitaries; less wealthy donors adorned the walls of their foundations with frescoes. In following Byzantine art onwards in its course I inevitably found Byzantine frescoes.

My journey therefore led me now through a land of painted walls. Some of the decorations were true frescoes, painted on priming when it was wet, others are best described as wall-paintings merely, or murals, since the colours were laid on a dry ground. The chief difference, as far as I was concerned, was that for technical reasons connected with the chemical action of pigments laid on wet plaster or on dry, the true frescoes were in a better state of preservation than the murals.

In the Old Stone Age, 40,000 years before Christ, in the caves and rock shelters of Altamira, Lascaux, Font-de-Gaume, La Madeleine and the Dordogne, in northern Spain and south-west France, Aurignacian and Magdalenian man had painted pictures of the bison, mammoths, stags and wild horses which he wanted to kill in the hunt.

Cave Paintings at Lascaux:
Stone Age Art

Millenia later, the Etruscans in Central Italy had painted the walls of their half subterranean tombs. At Tarquinii and Chiusi, at Orvieto, Vulci, Caere and Veii these paintings brighten the funerary walls to this day. Here Achilles in ambush waits at the fountain to do to death the Trojan prince Troilus as he rides through the forest to water his long-legged horse; dancers in bright blue and brick red gesticulate in the dance, lightly clad men and women leap in spirited motion. There is music everywhere; a player with large limbs and huge, clumsy hands, dressed in a short yellow cloak with a terracotta and blue striped border, plays upon the double pipes; there is also a lyre player supplying music for a female whirling like an eddy of wind in the dance, while at Vulci the winged goddess of destiny, Vanth, and the blue-grey, livid demon Charu, fantastic inhabitants of the Etruscan underworld, attend the sacrifice of the Trojan captives at the tomb of Patrocles.

The Romans also painted walls. I saw them at Pompeii, Herculaneum, Stabiae, the buried cities of the eruption of Vesuvius in A.D. 79, maidens picking flowers in a green meadow, an impressionistic picture of Trojans drawing the wooden horse inside the vaguely outlined battlements of Troy, a painting full of streaks of light and half-lit shade, with an overall atmosphere of shadowed doom; and even scenes of everyday life: the baker's shop and the market-place, and still-lifes with eggs and pitchers and bowls of fruit. But all these are true, humanistic, classical art, with no trace of mediaevalism in them. I found the first trace of mediaevalism in the paintings on the walls of the catacombs beneath the streets of Rome.

Here again were classical themes adapted to Christian uses, as in the illuminated manuscripts, pagan deities metamorphosed into Christian saints, or into Christ Himself, all with that far-looking,

Etruscan Tomb Painting: a dancer

searching gaze with which mysticism entered into art, when Christianity adopted it for its purposes, and the influence of the East impregnated the old Hellenic forms. In the catacombs Hermes, the country god, and the guardian of the flocks, has become Christ the Good Shepherd, bearing a lamb over His shoulders; the saints — except for that look in their eyes — are Roman citizens in Roman togas. But most of the paintings tell Old Testament stories, and most illustrate the theme of the Resurrection. All are symbolic, perhaps so that only the elect might understand their meaning.

Here are Abraham and Isaac, standing with their arms outstretched in prayer, giving thanks to God for the deliverance hinted at by the presence of the ram beside a tree which represents a thicket. Jonah is being cast from a ship and swallowed by a sea-monster, to be afterwards disgorged by it, an allegory of the Resurrection. Moses is striking the rock whence gushes the stream of water for the thirsty Israelites: all these scenes are symbols of salvation. Or the celebration of the Eucharist is represented, which at first

a. Moses striking the rock
b. Communion   *c*. Sacrifice
of Isaac
Catacomb Paintings

glance might be taken for a pagan sacrifice upon a pagan tripod. The colours, dim in the flickering candle or lamp-light, are reddish brown and green with flecks of blue on a creamy background, subdued but decorative; the execution is usually sketchy and crude — they were not the best artists who decorated these shrines of the new and despised Faith.

But after Constantine's Edict of Toleration, and as the years rolled by to the Peace of the Church, the Christians came up from worship at their underground shrines and built churches above ground. Then because kings and popes now favoured them, and paid artists — usually Byzantine artists — to decorate these houses of God, a different style of fresco appears.

Among the ruins of the Roman Forum, over against the remnants of the ages-old shrine of the pagan deity Juturna, goddess of salutary waters, there stands the ancient sixth-century church of Santa Maria Antiqua. No one knows quite how old some of the fast fading frescoes here are, but the best preserved seem to be eighth or ninth century. On the crumbling plaster of the wall of the northern aisle Joseph is being taken from the well and sold by his brethren to the Ishmaelites; he then appears with Potiphar; and there are other scenes of his life, disappearing, after 1,000 years of hidden existence, into faded incomprehensibility now they have been exposed to the Italian light. Also, on this same wall, is Christ enthroned, in the act of blessing; the doctors of the Greek and Latin Churches stand on either side. This is a cross-haloed, stern and frontal Christ, in a rigid Byzantine attitude, staring ahead; the doctors of the Church are as stiff and frontal, with books held upright in their left hands, with formal priestly robes, feet splayed outwards, bodies without substance, deep-brooding expressions, and grim, unsmiling faces; these frescoes belong to the same world as the older Byzantine mosaics.

Under an arch of Roman bricks I pass into the chapel of Saints Julith and Quiricus, and here are more Byzantine saints. Below them, in the lowest zone of decoration, there is a painted similitude of hanging draperies. These hangings on the lowest zone of fresco decoration are destined to travel far – across the Alps, through France, and into England – fading vestiges of them appear in English parish churches.

In this same chapel there is also the oldest known representation in fresco of the Crucifixion. It is a forceful scene. Christ, the largest figure because He is the most important one is shown on the Cross in the Eastern, Syrian fashion, not naked, but clad in a long, straight blue robe known as the *colobium*; His arms are extended in a straight, unbending line, and He shows no sign of suffering. He is not a human being, enduring the agonies of a cruel death, but a symbol of the redemption of mankind after the primeval Fall in the Garden of Eden. Below Him, smaller in scale, are Mary dressed in blue, her eyes full of grief, and St. John, one hand rolled in the folds of his brown robe, the other holding upright, like the doctors on the wall of the north aisle, a jewelled book; and two smaller, minor characters appear in the rocky background: Longinus, piercing the Saviour's side with his lance, and the soldier in a brown tunic offering the sponge soaked in vinegar. Over the Cross, in the deep midnight blue sky, the sun has disappeared and the light of the moon is almost extinguished.

It is not only, however, in Italy but in Greece and the Balkans that I find wall-painting influenced by Byzantinism. Sometimes the Hellenic element is predominant, sometimes the rigid, hieratic spirit of the Orient. In the frescoes of that part of the Balkans which we now call Yugoslavia – at St. Sophia at Ochrid, at Neresi, Milesevo, Gracanica and Sopoćani – it is the classical element that has triumphed. In these frescoes are broad, sweeping lines, wide, rounded curves. The Roman toga lives on here, falling in baggy folds not always related to the anatomy of the body underneath, but in the classical way there *is* a body underneath, and rippling muscles. Men with domed bald heads appear, or with thick, curly hair and beards, usually grey. Women are swathed in voluminous long-sleeved robes with mantles which twist from the shoulders over the head to make what is almost a wimple, unless they are maidservants, when their long arms are bare, and the articulation of the shoulder joint is particularly distorted; their heads are uncovered.

Gone are the sheet-gold, airless Byzantine backgrounds. Architectural elements enclose the scene, pillars and tiled roofs and rather Italianate arcaded walls, and baldachinoes over what are apparently open-air altars against a background now almost dark grey. Stern faces gaze heavenward, grief-stricken apostles mourn with heads aslant, hands buried deep in their huge, Roman-style garments as Christ receives the soul of the dead Virgin, like a little, swaddled child, to bear to heaven; the Virgin herself lies like the dead St. Clare whose mummified body may still be seen, in her nun's habit, in the church of Santa Chiara at Assisi.

All the lines of these Yugoslavian frescoes curve in majestic harmony, or sweep in dramatic movement. The soft pinks and greens and pale blues and yellowish browns which their artists favoured merge in a symphony of colour. Yet the Byzantine influence is there. It breathes in the solemnity, the austerity always lurking in the wake of a greater tenderness than the original Byzantine art ever knew; it shows in the swarthiness of the faces, with their long noses, small mouths and sad, brooding eyes; it is

apparent in the elongation of the figures, and even in such
details as the ceremonially veiled hands.

Just beyond the ruins of ancient Sparta, climbing a steep
spur of Mount Taygetos, there is the mediaeval ghost city of
Mystra. To-day, 'its houses crumble back into the Greek
earth, and ivy swallows up the ramparts';* its narrow,
corkscrew streets are piles of stones, the castle of the Despots
of the Morea crowning its hilltop is silent and deserted.
But several Byzantine churches of the thirteenth, fourteenth
and fifteenth centuries still stand, their domes and multiple
apses clustering picturesquely as they cling to the hillside,
and still, though no one knows for how much longer, the
frescoes of the nunnery of the Pantanassa and the church of
Peribleptos are visible, but perishing fast. In the Peribleptos Mary, clothed in black, solemn, with Byzantine
features, reclines, head on hand, in the mouth of a rugged
cave, her Son lying swaddled in a manger behind; the
three kings ride amongst the rocks in the rear, and angels,
against a background of dark blue midnight sky, surround
the scene. In faded colours below the maids wash the
Child (who in mediaeval wise appears again in the same
picture) and Joseph sits by, meditating. This is the same
scene as in the mosaics – Byzantine to the core. It belongs
to the fourteenth century. In the Pantanassa there is a
fifteenth-century representation of the Raising of Lazarus,
cracked and peeling and in places obliterated. There is a
great difference between these Greek frescoes and those of
Yugoslavia. Though the domed heads and vast, curly
beards are still in evidence the lines of all the figures are
less sweeping, less boldly dramatic, less exuberant. There
is a delicacy and a finesse about these paintings of the
Peloponnesus, a minuteness, almost, and over attention
to detail which reminds me again of that world whence –
so long ago it now seems – I set out: the world of illuminated
manuscripts.

Now, as I follow these Byzantine influences, my road is

* A. G. Keller: *Mystra under the Despots*, History Today.

winding northwards, over the Alps. First, into France, where the wall-paintings of Le Puy, Tavant, Berzé-la-Ville, Vicq, Montoire, Saint-Savin and the rest, are no longer called Byzantine, but *Romanesque*. These solemn, almost gloomy figures, stern, elongated, statuesque, closely resemble not only early Byzantine figures but those manuscript illuminations which had first sent me on this journey into ever widening vistas. Indeed, in one way they resemble them more than they resemble their ultimate Byzantine prototypes; it is for this reason that one is called Byzantine, the other Romanesque. The Romanesque paintings are linear, flat upon their backgrounds, whereas even the most hieratic of the Byzantine frescoes, made by artists who always remembered, because they always had around them, products of the art which had been inspired by classical ideals, have kept so much of that spirit that they never fail to show something of the rounded human form beneath the garments – the bulge of a thigh, or of the upper arm. In Byzantine frescoes, too, there is a depth in which stand city walls, the turrets of houses, and fantastically rocky heights; they are always three-dimensional.

There is nothing of this in these French Romanesque wall-paintings. At St. Savin the sons of Noah (in short mediaeval tunics with rippling hems and ovoid folds outlined doubly, as if by a pipe) cover their father's nakedness under a tumbled array of turrets innocent of perspective in the same plane as that in which they stand; there is no depth to the picture – it is two-dimensional only. And when I look at the three angels of the New Jerusalem, bending over in sweeping curves, rhythmic and unreal, it is the linear disposition of the three which tells me the mural is Romanesque, and not a Yugoslavian-Byzantine fresco.

Then there is the Christ in Majesty of Berzé-la-Ville. Here, in a mandorla, is a Byzantine Christ, elongated, bearded, solemn and frontal, with deep brooding eyes and an infinity of space about Him: this is the oriental fused with the classical Greek, but both metamorphosed into

Romanesque by the passion for linear pattern of the once barbaric North.

For there it is clearly apparent: the continuing conflict between the realistic representation of the classical Graeco-Roman world and the urge to abstract, linear pattern of the Teutonic and Viking lands of the North; only in these frescoes the classical world is not the Greek and Roman world of Pericles and the Scipios, or even of Alexander the Great and Augustus, but the world of Justinian and Byzantinism, impregnated with influences from the East. There is something else, too, in these austere Christs in Majesty of Berzé-la-Ville or Montoire, in these stern-faced, unyielding Vices of Tavant, these gaunt, unbending, gloomy figures of Christ washing Peter's feet, Judas giving the kiss of betrayal, and of the Annunciation and Joseph reproaching Mary, which are at Vicq: an asceticism which is not Byzantine, a dark gloom which is not Byzantine, a morbid austerity almost frightening and certainly depressing, which was not present in Byzantine art.

When I found this same dark gloom in England, in the Sussex churches at Hardham and Clayton, both within the orbit of Lewes, where one may still see, beside the railway on the edge of the town, a few poor ruins of the once great Cluniac Priory of St. Pancras, I realized the source of all this organized gloom. Cluniac priories were all dependent on the mother house at Cluny, between the Saône and the Loire, once the greatest church of mediaeval Christendom, now hardly existing, even in ruin. The Cluniacs were a reformed monastic order of great strictness. The fires of damnation burnt very brightly before the imaginations of the monks of Cluny; the awful Day when the Last Trump should sound and the Judgement of Souls should begin was very real to them. Life was stern, life was earnest, life was nothing but a preparation for the world to come. The joys of the earth, the songs of the birds, the glory of the changing seasons, the majesty of the eternal hills, the shimmer of moonlight on the sea or the rainbow flash of the dew upon the grass at sunrise were, if they heard and saw them at all, not beauties, but snares of the devil to enmesh their souls, leading them from the unwavering contemplation of God along the primrose path of dalliance to that hell which awaits the triflers, the sensuous, the seekers after the vain jewels of this evil and transitory world.   The pictures those monks painted or caused to be painted on the walls of the tiny churches at Hardham and Clayton in the early twelfth century were not meant as decoration.   They were intended to instruct the illiterate congregations gathered therein.   At Clayton, nestling unobtrusively at the foot of the South Downs not far from where the London to Brighton trains clatter into the tunnel at Hassocks, the theme of the paintings is the Judgement of the world by Our Lord. At Hardham, just beyond Pulborough, on the Littlehampton road, there is added to this theme scenes from the fall of Man and the life of Christ, all intended to present vividly to those who could not read the great truths of the Christian faith.

These faded, half obliterated paintings still have, for those who will take the trouble to understand them, compelling power.   One summer morning while the heedless traffic of the twentieth century roared by outside on its way to the coast I stood in Hardham church and looked at the solemn, aloof Virgin and Child staring ahead, no glance directed by either at the faint traces of the worshipping Magi at the Virgin's knees; on the north nave wall was the now featureless figure of St. George on his spectral horse coming to the aid of the Christians at the Battle of Antioch in the last years of the eleventh century; a censing angel was painted above the ancient chancel arch, over which his wing drooped majestically.   Near him was the Byzantinesque figure of a Madonna Annunciate – no soft and yielding woman, no expectant mother soon to be filled with tender love for her Child, but the elevated vessel of the Divine Will, the aloof and awful one who was destined to carry God in her womb.   The strangely drawn, naked bodies of Adam and Eve, as they received the forbidden fruit from the serpent, were in the chancel; above the altar were the three elders of the Apocalyptic Vision of the Revelation of St. John, and a seraph enfolded in his own wings. As I looked, the centuries seemed to fall away; such evocative power had those 800-year-old, faded brown paintings that for an instant of time I felt what those who looked upon them in their gleaming youth must have felt – a sense of awe and reverence, of something far greater than myself, a power and a presence.

I felt, too, what our ancestors worshipping there could not have felt, the majesty of tradition and antiquity; the sense of a long line of influences stretching away back into the depths of centuries long since dead and gone. And when a kindly September sun lit up the small, humble interior of Clayton church, where the Apocalyptic horseman rode amid the souls of those awaiting their fate, and on the south wall four angels carried the great Cross while another bent forward, holding the scales of Judgement in which so many were weighed and found wanting; when I saw Christ in a mandorla above the chancel arch, cross-haloed, sitting in unbending, austere majesty with His right hand raised in blessing, all these sensations were renewed in me; I saw in that Christ the Christ of Berzé-la Ville again, and behind the two of them the dignity and majesty of the mosaic Christs of Ravenna and Constantinople.

Sometimes, as I sought out twelfth-century wall paintings in England, I came upon interesting aberrations – if paintings which do not seem to conform to any style commonly found in this country may be so described. Two of these are worthy of special note. The first was high up on the apsidal wall of St. Anselm's chapel, on the south side of Canterbury cathedral. A buttress was built across this apse in the thirteenth century, blocking it when it was less than 100 years old; the buttress was not removed for six centuries,* and consequently the little painted panel is to

* It was removed in 1888.

this day resplendent in practically all the pristine splendour of its vivid blue background, green border and brown-cloaked figure with white robe shaded in blue. Fully revealed in twentieth-century light is a representation of St. Paul, when, shipwrecked on Melita,* he had 'gathered a bundle of sticks, and laid them on the fire [and] there came a viper out of the heat and fastened on his hand . . . and he shook off the beast into the fire and felt no harm'.† The viper is now very difficult to distinguish, but everything else stands out boldly. There was St. Paul, with a high, domed forehead, inclining to baldness; on his cloak were the customary Romanesque ovoid folds with their 'pipe' outlines and curious fine, delicate lines in the shape of a manifold S to indicate highlights. His cloak swept in a noble curve from his neck over his shoulder to his right foot; but what made the painting seem unique in the Romanesque world was its classical feeling for, and evident delight in, plastic form, its indication of a rounded body beneath the clinging draperies. In this it seemed to have some kinship with Yugoslavian frescoes, although no one could have mistaken it for Yugoslavian work.

The second lone outpost in this twelfth century was the wall painting of a purgatorial ladder on the west wall of the tiny village church at Chaldon, not far from Redhill in Surrey. This is not a noble work of art, but is noteworthy because it is in an excellent state of preservation and because it depicts a subject rare in this form – or at any rate a subject which has not in this form otherwise survived. Here, on a deep red ochre background‡ is a curious scene – or rather, four scenes. The Purgatorial Ladder, rising from the lower zone of Hell to the upper zone of Purgatory, cuts the picture in half; it is thronged with the leaping, joyful souls of the Saved, represented, as are all the souls in the painting, as diminutive, nude figures. On the left, in Purgatory, St. Michael weighs the vices of souls against their virtues in scales which a foul demon tries to pull down

* Malta.   † Acts xxviii. 3, 5.   ‡ Repainted in modern times.

on the vices' side; on the right, on the other side of the central ladder, Christ drives the vexillum into the gaping jaws of prostrate Death – a scene known as the 'Harrowing of Hell' – and leads the souls of the saved out of Limbo; He has by the hand Adam and Eve, in the forefront of the rescued. Christ is pictured again, a half-figure in a medallion, bearing a cross in His left hand, in the centre of a wavy-outline semicircle representing heaven, at the top of the ladder. But at its foot, among the flames of Hell, are the torments of the Damned, and the hideous forms of the Seven Deadly Sins – Sloth, Gluttony, Pride, Anger, Luxury, Avarice, and Envy – which had brought them to their doom.

I did not, in my journeyings, find any other painting which had any kinship whatever in style with this curious and unique mural.

8

THE PAGEANT OF THE
PAINTED WALLS

~~~~~~~~~~~~~~~~~~~~~~

THE road now stretched onwards through the fading
world of English wall-paintings; and as I passed from
the twelfth century into the thirteenth, from the
thirteenth to the fourteenth, thence to the fifteenth, I met
all those characteristics which I had noted before as I
travelled through the brightly coloured fields of manuscript
illumination. Here I was, back again out of the austere
dignity and the gloom, in the light of thirteenth-century
tenderness and grace: the century of the lovely roundel in
the chapel of the Bishop's Palace at Chichester, representing the Virgin and Child. No austere figure of unapproachable majesty is here; only a gentle, girlish mother bending
her head till her cheek nearly touches her Child's, only an
adorable little Child reaching up to clasp His mother's
neck, and raising His face to kiss, or be kissed by her. The
silver of the censers of the worshipping angels on each side
has oxydised with the passing of 700 years and made dark
blotches on the painting, but they hardly matter. The
faded pinks and blues, the subdued gold, are like the
fragrance of an old-world rose. Humanity enfolded in
wild rose petals; all the dreaming spiritual loveliness of
the thirteenth century in a quatrefoil enclosed in a medallion less than three feet in diameter!

And what of the chapel of the Guardian Angels in Winchester Cathedral? The winged busts of those divine messengers, in green and pink and blue, with great eyes and gentle lips and wings drooping behind their shoulders are enclosed in medallions in the vaulting of the chapel, more than a dozen of them, twined about with exquisite coils of conventional foliage and daisy-like flowers interspersed with six-pointed stars, so that the chapel seems canopied with a starry heaven crossed by the filigree of tree-tendrils, full of the rustle of angels' wings, the tranquillity and repose of angels' protecting presence. And there is none of the austerity of the Christ of Clayton and Berzé-la-Ville about the thirteenth-century Christ in Majesty sitting in the upper half of a quatrefoil in the chapel of the Holy Sepulchre at Winchester. Below Him on this same wall the faces of St. John and of Nicodemus, gazing upon their Lord as His body is lowered from the Cross are full of pitiful sorrow. Most moving of all, perhaps, is the face of the dead Christ.

They passed as in a pageant of dim and muted glory before me, mural after mural, faded and fragmentary. There were the tall, aristocratic figures of Christ and the doubting St. Thomas putting his hand to his Master's wounded side, and, in a canopied niche beside this, the giant St. Christopher bearing the Christ Child, painted seven centuries ago in the south transept of Westminster Abbey by some court painter – perhaps the 'beloved Master William' of Henry III, that lover of artists who had rebuilt in the French taste the eastern parts of this, Edward the Confessor's foundation at Westminster. In the same aristocratic style was the crowned head with the gentle features and large, staring eyes just outside royal St. George's Chapel at Windsor Castle; its colours glowed as softly as an autumnal wood irradiated with the setting sun. There were the undersized, charmingly ill-proportioned saints with the innocent faces – St. Matthew, St. Peter, St. John the Divine and St. Paul, with their proper attributes of keys, swords and scrolls – in medallions of the vaulting of Christ Church Cathedral at Oxford, St. Paul with one forelock on the bald front of his head, as he had been pictured as he shook off the viper at Canterbury, and with a magnificent sword nearly as long as himself.

Then came the murals of the country church at Brook, not far from Ashford, in Kent; only a little aisleless Norman church, but with a mass of thirteenth-century wall-paintings on the east and south walls of the chancel, done in contiguous medallions with the spaces between their circles filled with eight-petalled flowers. Holy Infancy and Passion scenes filled the medallions, and scenes from the life of the Virgin. Details were mostly gone, and often the pictures were now mere silhouettes upon a black background alternating with white, but one may make out the ochre details of the journey into Egypt, where Mary was riding on a realistic, patient looking donkey, preceded by Joseph carrying a large carpenter's T-square, and the horned, animal-like figure of an idol toppling headlong from its pedestal as the Holy Family approaches. There was another realistic donkey in the Entry into Jerusalem, and another medallion shows Christ bearing the Cross, preceded by an executioner carrying a very distinct and workmanlike hammer.

One perfectly preserved half of the Wheel of Fortune exists in the choir of Rochester cathedral. The impassive figure of Fortune, 'the fickle jade', crowned and clad in long, loose yellow robes, turns the wheel and some struggle on the spokes and one, richly dressed, sits proudly aloft on the rim, looking down on those who have fallen as the wheel turns inexorably (though this half of the painting no longer exists, one can guess what it pictured).* There are hectic spots on the cheeks of all, and the colour of the mural resembles that of an old, embrowned parchment whereof the hues have intensified with age to the glowing red of

* See Sydney W. Wheatley, *Rochester Cathedral – notes on its Wall-Paintings*.

russet pears; all the faces have
a fragile, aristocratic, far-away
look, not untouched by a gentle,
poetic melancholy.

A line of paintings comes next
in the procession, green, red,
black with a little greyish blue,
enclosed in a continuous painted
arcade formed of wide, trefoil-
headed arches with slender
shafts upholding them, on the
nave arcade of the church hidden away in rural Sussex lanes
at West Chiltington; there,
amongst other scenes too faded
and defaced for decipherment,
was Christ riding into Jerusalem, Christ bound to the pillar,
and carrying His Cross; there
also was the Crucifixion with
Mary and St. John standing on
each side of the Cross. On an-

The Wheel of Fortune,
Rochester Cathedral

other wall of this church are the Annunciation, the Visitation, the Nativity. Other Crucifixions and Annunciations
in gentle, faded colours are painted on the austere Norman
piers of the nave of St. Alban's Abbey – they would have
been reredoses for altars which have long since vanished.

At Little Missenden, another rural church, this time in
Buckinghamshire, I saw, facing the south door, a great St.
Christopher with a forked beard and a long, aristocratic
nose treading among the fishes of the ford with his long
staff planted before him and on his left arm an exceedingly
solemn-faced Christ Child holding in His hand the orb of
the world. Near by, on this same wall, were scenes from
the life of St. Catherine. There was the Roman Emperor
Maximinus, crowned with a distinctly mediaeval crown,
and with the hideous face of a demon, and there were

several St. Catherines, one disputing with the philosophers, who were all tonsured as if they were mediaeval monks, before Maximinus, who this time had an angry glare as he held a huge and menacing sword while St. Catherine stood undismayed, with arms uplifted. She appeared once more, her hair falling over her shoulders, an angelic figure in a long, loose pink robe, while fragments of the wheel upon which she had been condemned to be broken, but which had been destroyed by a just visible angel, flew in all directions and struck the executioners, whose heads lay with closed eyes in a heap below.

So I saw them pass before me, these and others too numerous even to mention; some mere ghosts, some flaking fragments, some sere and withered as the leaves of a summer dead long ago, but all full of that spiritual grace, many pregnant with that wistful poetic melancholy which breathes over all the wall-paintings of every kind of the thirteenth century.

Sometimes, of course, as I travelled from this place to that, from cathedral city to market town, from market town to village, to buried country lanes or deserted marshland where the tide of the lives of men had ebbed as the centuries had passed, I came out of that thirteenth century and found myself in the fourteenth or fifteenth. The wall-paintings then still echoed the themes and recalled the atmosphere of the illuminated manuscripts of those centuries. The first fourteenth-century mural I ever saw was that series of pitiable fragments in the British Museum, salvaged from St. Stephen's Chapel at Westminster when the old Houses of Parliament were burnt down in 1834. These show the Destruction of Job's Children by the fall of the roof while they were feasting, when 'there came a great wind from the wilderness, and smote the four corners of the house, and it fell upon the young men', and the appearance to Job of the Messengers of Misfortune, coming one after the other while the former was 'yet speaking'.*   I saw

* Job i. 18.

in these fragments Job's sons and daughters sitting at a table on which were silver cups and spoons; in front of them was an elegant arcade of three taper-thin shafts rising to Gothic arches; above them the Demon of the Storm was pushing the beams downward upon the heads of the feasters. The colours were pure and delicate, a lovely rose-pink, blue, green, red and gold – apparently unfaded. Though the fragments were so broken and the sum-total of all that was saved so small, a vivid realization came to me as I looked of the appearance of a mediaeval interior in the days when men were not afraid to paint stone, or to be riotously gay in the material surroundings in which they passed their lives.

Entering the Chapter House of Westminster Abbey one day I caught sight there, in the eastern bay, of late fourteenth-century wall-paintings in five arched compartments. Dim and damaged as they were I could distinguish Christ enthroned with a globe at His feet; He wore a crimson robe, and had behind His head a gold cruciform nimbus. This was evidently a Last Judgement scene, although it was now incomplete; the face of Christ was solemn and dignified, and the whole scheme was quite free of the mannered affectation usually to the fore in fourteenth-century work; there was something about it which lifted it nearer the spiritual realms reminiscent of early Byzantine frescoes. Under the arcading of other bays of the Chapter House walls were portions of another scheme, this time illustrating the Apocalyptic Vision of St. John and a few episodes from his life, and below them were depicted attractive animals and birds-in-trees: the Lyon, Reynder, Wilde Asse, Ostrych, Kameyl, among others, creatures as quaint as the mediaeval spelling of their names. These had nothing to do with the Apocalypse. They were painted nearly 100 years, perhaps, later.

Angels danced in the fourteenth century – I saw them on the vaulting of the south choir aisle in Christ Church, Oxford. They played clumsy fiddles like vegetable marrows, with bent bows; they gesticulated, and looked happy. St. Edmund, King and Martyr, appeared on the east wall of Sanderstead church in Surrey, holding a sheaf of the arrows which slew him, the long, pointed toes of his fourteenth-century shoes curling over the pedestal on which he stood. St. Christopher showed himself once more, on the north wall and facing the south door of the church at Paston in Norfolk. (They say that this saint was so frequently depicted in this position because if you caught a glimpse of him in the morning you would not meet death that day; so it needed only a church door ajar and your path to lie past it, and there you were.) This St. Christopher was quite twelve feet high, outlined in black, with black and red ochre body colour; the Christ Child, holding the orb of the world as before, was so tiny as to be able to sit on the giant's left hand. The saint was bearded and cloaked like some rich fourteenth-century merchant, and had his breeches tucked up above his knees; he was a much more worldly figure than the thirteenth-century saint at Little Missenden, as was to be expected. Here too, at Paston, I saw a little farther along the same wall a representation of that morality, that 'memento mori' which I had seen in the manuscripts of the later Middle Ages – the Three Quick and the Three Dead. One red ochre skeleton was complete, and there were fragments of two others, all jigging in the wind; to the east of these apparitions were the kings, elegant, with forked beards and curled hair and wearing crowns. One of the three was defaced, but the others were clear enough, together with an attendant, apparently blowing a bugle for the hunt.

Not very long afterwards I came upon the Three Quick and the Three Dead again, in Surrey, at Charlwood Church, alongside three tiers of only half distinguishable incidents in the life of St. Margaret on the one hand, and an outsize representation of the martyrdom of St. Edmund (which had practically obliterated St. Nicholas and his doings, painted a couple of decades or so earlier) on the other. Both the story of St. Margaret and the Three Quick and the Three Dead must originally have been very richly coloured in ochre and dark green, blue and red, for vivid traces of these colours still survived. In this painting of the morality the horses of the three crowned kings seemed galloping towards the three horrible corpses which to this day stand out in gruesome distinctness.

I had not by any means done yet with the Three Quick and the Three Dead. I was to meet them again in the fifteenth century. The representation of this theme seems to have been extremely popular in these times; it has been said* that there are twenty-six paintings of the subject in English churches, and no one knows how many more there may be lying hidden under layers of puritanic whitewash.

I found, not without relief, a different, though seemingly almost as popular a morality on the west wall at Trotton, a humble little country church in West Sussex. The west walls of churches were usually given over to blood-curdling representations of the Last Judgement and the torments of the damned, but at Trotton there was, instead, the nude figure of the Evil Man surrounded by the Seven Deadly Sins, and balancing him, the Good Man, clothed, encircled in like manner by the Seven Works of Mercy. Once upon a time Christ sat on the top of the wall over the west door of the church, with an angel on each side and Moses and the Tables of the Law below, but the traces of these are now fading away, along with the Seven Deadly Sins. In the summer morning in 1947 when I saw the murals, however, Gluttony was still quite clear, drinking from a leather bombard with his head thrown back, and there too was Avarice, plainly sitting upon his treasure chest. At that time the Good Man was a lovely figure, with beard and curly hair, dressed in a long, voluminous girdled gown, clasping his hands in prayer with a gentle, spiritual expression. Around him the naked were being clothed, the hungry fed, strangers received

* Dr. Storck.

hospitality, the sick and the prisoners were being visited.

Only once did I have an opportunity of seeing that very rare thing — fourteenth-century wall-paintings in a *secular* building. This was at Longthorpe Tower, about one and a half miles out of Peterborough. The tower is a low, squat, clumsy building with a pyramidal roof, and its exterior gives no indication of the wealth of fourteenth-century painting within. In the great chamber on the first floor there were mediaeval paintings not only all round but also in the vaulted ceiling above. On the north wall, among other scenes, one can make out a Nativity, with the Virgin suckling the holy Child, closely wrapped in swaddling bands and resembling, as He often does in mediaeval art, a tiny mummy, while Joseph sits looking on. Above, in a sort of arc, were the Seven Ages of Man, from *Infans*, a child in a cradle, to *Decrepitus*, an ancient in a hood, bearded, and hobbling along on crutches.

On the west wall were the Apostles, each holding a wavy scroll upon which was written that sentence which, according to legend, each contributed to the Creed. Near by, there were personages wearing broad-brimmed hats, who are considered to have been, on the strength of the hats (I do not know why) classical philosophers. The Three Quick and the Three Dead make yet another appearance in a recess by the door. All the overpainting of the three corpses has decayed, and they now appear as three bogeys, being deep black. A less grim spectacle was the musicians between the ribs of the vaulting of the ceiling. There was David playing the harp, and other unidentifiable figures making a cheerful noise unto the Lord upon the bagpipes, psaltery, viol and portative organ. On the west wall also that favourite manuscript theme of the Labours of the Months reappeared, in scenes reminiscent of the *Luttrell Psalter*.

But the best scene of all was on the east wall, where an unusual subject stood out in remarkable distinctness in red and yellow ochre; the Wheel of the Five Senses. The

Senses were represented, rather arbitrarily, as creatures on the circumference of the Wheel: there was the Spider for touch, the Boar for hearing, the Cock for sight, while the Monkey and the Eagle stood respectively for taste and smell. Behind the wheel, and apparently turning it, swayed a tall, elegant figure of aristocratic aspect, drawn in the mannered style characteristic of the fourteenth century. The black smudges which appeared on parts of his face and garments – the underpainting showing where the flesh tints above had decayed – did not seem to detract from the beauty of his contemplative face and the melancholy gaze of his steady grey eyes. His beard was thick and curly, his yellow waving hair flowed over his shoulders, upon his head was a typically mediaeval crown. This was Crowned Reason: the only representation of such a personification that I have ever met in mediaeval art.

I had to go forward into the fifteenth century to find another mural in a secular building – to the Byward Tower at the entrance to William the Conqueror's Tower of London. Here, in pale green and faded rose-pink, near a beam painted green with a gilt fleur-de-lys on it, was a Virgin half disappearing into a mystical dimness. Her flesh tints were deep rose, her eyes blue, her nimbus was edged with vermilion, her cloak was a light blue edged with dull red. She was, it seems, part of a Crucifixion scene; the building of a Tudor chimney breast has destroyed the Christ and St. John on the other side of the Cross. There still remains, however, part of the figure of St. Michael, presumably weighing souls; and one carries away from the Byward Tower a lasting memory of the muted glory of his outspread wing, shaded from pale to deep pink, and from that through rose to crimson.

As I look around in the fifteenth century I see several familiar subjects: many St. Christophers, all facing the south door, and here, for instance, at Raunds in Northamptonshire, which has a large and imposing church, appear again the three crowned kings walking in all the pomp and splendour of fifteenth-century attire (which could be exceedingly splendid) confronted in a grim and rocky landscape by the grotesque, grinning corpses of the Three Dead, gesticulating with their skeletal fingers. But there are, too, scenes less familiar in wall-paintings. One strange one, many times repeated, is the so-called *Christ of the Trades*. He appears, for instance, in the splay of a window at that rural church I visited before, for the thirteenth-century Passion scenes – West Chiltington in Sussex. Here was a figure painted rather crudely, in red ochre and yellow, nimbed and wearing only a loose loin-cloth, with arms upraised and hands extended to show the Crucifixion Wounds, standing on a fragment of a wheel. They say there used to be visible around the Figure a scattering of painted workmen's tools: a shuttle, a hatchet, a knife – but these are now largely indistinguishable.

At Breage Church in Cornwall the Christ is more distinct, but just as uncouth in appearance. This time, though His Body is covered completely with wounds, or rather the drops of blood springing therefrom, and He wears only the loin-cloth, He is crowned, points to the wound of Longinus' spear in His Side, but does not show those in His hands. Behind Him is a thick conglomeration of tools.

These are only two examples among more than a dozen still existing in English churches of this curious subject, which has been described as 'art by the people for the people'. It never appears before the latter part of the fourteenth century and is most common in the fifteenth; it is therefore supposed that it is connected with that Middle English political poem, William Langland's *Vision of Piers Plowman*. We all know how Langland, while he slept, 'weary of wandering on Malvern Hills', dreamed that he saw a 'field full of folk' – all the folk of fourteenth-century England, most of whom, especially the rich, and out-outstandingly the ecclesiastical rich, he satirizes with bitter venom. But amongst the others he saw Christ, in the person of Piers Plowman, a poor workman labouring and

suffering among his fellows.   Thus the dreamer preaches
the socialist doctrine of the sanctity of labour, and thus he
is the precursor of John Ball, socialist priest of the people,
who sped forth the message.

> When Adam delved and Eve span
> Who was then the gentleman?

thus he gave a voice to the growing discontent of the
peasantry, which surged up and broke bounds in the
Peasants' Revolt of 1382.   The idea of Christ as a labourer
like themselves, His suffering (shown by His scarred body)
and Crucifixion (by His five wounds) analogous to their
own lives of toil and hardship was obviously very popular
with the common people, in the southern and south-western
counties and East Anglia particularly.   But the workmanship of the Christs of the Trades is always unskilled.
Plainly it was the poor who commissioned these paintings,
and the poor who found comfort in them.*

There is an example of richer men's fare in the fifteenth
century in a recess in the north wall of the north choir aisle
of Canterbury Cathedral.   I thought it was an old mediaeval tapestry (such were its colours) till on coming closer
I discovered it to be a wall-painting of the legend of St.
Eustace.   St. Eustace, whose real name was Placidus, was
a Roman captain of the guards under Trajan, though no
one would think so to see him here in fifteenth-century
attire in a mediaeval landscape of picturesque ships,
turreted towns and looking for all the world, as he kneels
with hands together in prayer, like the effigies upon late
mediaeval tombs or monumental brasses.   He was converted to Christianity by the vision of a fair stag (there he
is, at the bottom of the picture, many times larger than St.
Eustace, but about as large as the horse upon which the
saint has ridden to the hunt) carrying between his antlers a
'cross of radiant light' upon which hung the image of Christ,

---

* For a full discussion of the subject see Tristram and Borenius,
English Mediaeval Painting, p. 29 *et seq.*

who warned Eustace, 'Thou shalt suffer many tribulations for My sake, and shalt be tried by many temptations; but be strong and of good courage, and I will not forsake thee.' And indeed Eustace met even more tribulations than Job. His possessions were carried off by robbers and pirates stole away his wife; one of his two children was taken by a wolf, the other borne off by a lion as he was crossing a swollen river with them; and when, after fifteen years, the Emperor Hadrian heaped honours upon him, and he met again his wife and children, and cried, 'Surely my tribulation is at an end!' because he refused to offer sacrifice to the pagan gods he and his family were burnt alive in a brazen bull. These scenes are depicted in the wall-painting in a confusing but very engaging medley of queer little trees, a winding river, beasts both wild and fierce and mild and domestic, boats and ships and houses and waves and flowered meads. Perspective does not exist; and as I followed the course of the river from the white stag at the bottom of the picture to the brazen bull lapped in flames at the top I thought the painting more like a tapestry than ever.

It was in the little market-town of Pickering in Yorkshire that I came upon a whole series of murals painted on the inner side of both the north and south nave arcades of the parish church. They looked too good to be true, alas! for by this time I had learnt what to expect when I visited the faded and fragmentary wall-paintings of England. And indeed, as I soon discovered, they were restored in modern times. But I comforted myself by imagining that this was how they had looked in their youthful freshness, when the fifteenth-century eyes of the forefathers of Pickering had been wont to see them.

Here all manner of subjects were gathered together. Here was the story of St. Catherine again, her scourging, her torture on the wheel, and the great, scimitar-like swords of those sent to execute her. Here again, and more distinct than at Trotton, were the Seven Corporal Acts of Mercy – Feeding the Hungry, Giving Drink to the Thirsty,

Entertaining Strangers, Visiting the Prisoners, Visiting the Sick and Clothing the Naked; here at Pickering also appears – it is missing at Trotton – the Seventh Act of Mercy – Burying the Dead. Farther along were the Passion Scenes and Resurrection of our Lord, and below these, in the spandrel of two of the nave arches, Christ calling forth from the vast yawning jaws of Hell, and its fang-like teeth, the souls of Adam and Eve and 'a multitude which no man can number' of others. On the north side of the church St. George, in full panoply of armour, thrust his lance into the mouth of a dragon not unlike a huge shrimp, except that he had a snaky tail which he was twining round the legs of the saint's horse; here was St. Christopher, clinging to a tree-like staff, with the Christ Child holding the orb of the world and a hermit lifting up a lantern at the door of his hut to light the giant over the dark and stormy ford; St. John the Baptist was executed, and Herod feasted at a table covered with plates and displaying two fine salts, before which stood Salome with the Baptist's head on a charger. All were unmistakably in fifteenth-century dress, needless to say.

At Pickering, too, Thomas à Becket, as he knelt at the altar in Canterbury Cathedral suffered martyrdom and St. Edmund stood bound naked to a tree but still wearing his crown (a symbol, of course, of kingship) with his body riddled with arrows; one archer beside him was stringing his bow, two others were drawing theirs, while a fourth stood ready. From the clouds above the foliage of the trees appeared two hands holding a scroll. Upon it field-glasses revealed the words:

> Heven blys to hys mede,
> Hem sall have, for his gud deed.

Again the pageant passes before me of these late mediaeval wall-paintings, too numerous for detailed description unless I were to fill several volumes. One series, however, of outstanding workmanship, must be described in a little detail, and that is the paintings along both the north and south walls of Eton College Chapel. They are similar to murals in the Lady Chapel of Winchester Cathedral, now covered with movable hinged shutters upon which reconstructions of the faded and disappearing originals beneath have been painted. These tell practically the same stories, and are almost certainly by the same artist, whose name, there is good reason to suppose, was William Baker; but the Eton paintings are by far the better preserved. They are mostly in silvery-grey monochrome – grisaille is the technical term – and again, from the distance, they might be mistaken at first for faded tapestries. Touches of red – on a book here, the edge of a robe there – and flesh-tints for faces and hands give accents of enlivenment to the general subdued impression of the paintings, which are somewhat unmediaeval-looking, not only because of this unwonted lack of colour, but also because they were painted on the eve of the Renaissance, and depict figures in the round, with backgrounds in perspective, and a suggestion of space.

On the north wall are preserved representations of various miracles of the Virgin; on the south side there are depicted (with one large gap) the adventures of an empress, falsely accused by her frustrated brother-in-law of infidelity to her husband, and wearing her crown through all her subsequent vicissitudes – banishment to the forest, rescue by a knight (from whom she hides her identity – apparently he does not notice the crown), her healing of the knight's brother of leprosy with a herb which had been given her by the Virgin (a scene pictured, no doubt, where the gap now exists), and her return to her husband, where she performs the same office for his now leprous brother. After which she leaves her crown lying on the ground and the last we see of her she is entering a convent. All the figures in these paintings are beautifully drawn, with a plasticity and truth to nature which loudly cries, 'The Middle Ages are waning, and the Renaissance is at hand.'

So the painted pageant passed before my eyes, of saints

and sinners, kings and knights, Apostles and philosophers, angels, patriarchs, personified vices and virtues, Christ suffering and triumphant in many guises, even that of a poor labourer; scenes from the Old Testament and episodes from the New; the legends of the saints and the miracles of the Virgin (strangely, with the exception of the Wedding Feast at Cana, Christ's miracles are not often represented in wall-paintings); Moralities; some subjects predominating in one century, some in others, certain ones appearing in all. But each century breathes its own peculiar atmosphere, of stark austerity, or gentle, spiritual grace, or mannered aristocratic and rather melancholy affectation, or bourgeois solidity and down-to-earth humanity. The later the century, the greater the awareness of the human foibles of mankind, the nearer to the prosaic realities of everyday life, the nearer to realism and so the easier for all the world to understand. In this last century which I visited in my search for murals, this fifteenth century, I realized many touches which brought the Middle Ages into the present day. I found human beings doing, *mutatis mutandis*, the sort of things we do; I was oppressed by none of the monkish nightmares which had haunted the work of ages long gone by. But with the coming of this warmer humanity and the mundaneness of naturalness the sombre majesty of earlier centuries had fled, taking with it that austere, impersonal greatness which had lifted my thoughts on to a sphere remote from the ordinary world's trivialities and nearer the eternity of heaven.

9

BACKWATERS

〜〜〜〜〜〜〜〜〜〜〜〜〜

B Y now I had necessarily become acquainted with the interiors and exteriors of churches, where nearly all these frescoes and murals were to be seen. It may be that even before I had journeyed in search of murals I had been drawn to study the architecture of ancient churches. By now my pursuit of the art of this mediaeval world had led me into several backwaters, up side valleys and along meandering tracks which sometimes came to abrupt stops and sometimes opened out upon farther views lit by a shining sun; and the journey was becoming all embracing, keeping not to one path, only finding, wherever it led me, fresh fields, new vistas, unexpected landscapes.

One such side-track brought me to Russian icons – that was a track from the highway of Byzantinism. For a while I lived with those dull-gold and red paintings of the Virgin and Child, saints, kings and patriarchs upon wooden panels enclosed in silver frames – devotional products of the Orthodox Church of the East through several centuries, which I had to imagine flickering in the fitful light of votive candles in the gloom of Byzantine churches.

There was the wonderful eleventh-century 'Our Lady of Vladimir', tender and gently melancholy, brown and dim red and old gold; the Holy Child's face in the icon was uplifted for a kiss, His fingers caressed His mother's neck.

In a twelfth-century icon St. Demetrios of Salonika, dark-green and red and gold, sat with his sword across his knees. Then there was the fourteenth-century Descent into Hell, with the vivid splashes of scarlet tunics, set off by dark green cloaks, bringing pulsing vitality to a sombre scene; the fifteenth-century St. George, with his crimson cloak billowing against the brassy background as his silvery coloured horse reared above the green and crimson dragon. There were Nativities in plenty, all Byzantine in type, with Mary lying, as she did in Byzantine mosaics and frescoes, in the mouth of a cave, while Joseph sat below with the Tempter, disguised as a shepherd, feeding his doubts of Mary's virginity; in a corner of the rocky scene the maids prepared to wash the Child – here I was once more far back in the Byzantine world.

There were, too, the brilliant reds and greens of the robes of the scribes in the fifteenth-century scene of Christ among the doctors, with the light brown architecture of the tower in the rear setting off the brownish yellow, relieved by gold stripes, of the classical robes of the twelve-year-old Jesus, who sat upon a semi-circular stepped seat immediately reminiscent of the seat for the bishop and clergy around the apses in early Christian basilical churches. This icon is one which more clearly than any other shows its Byzantine parentage. But loveliest of all was the early fifteenth-century 'Old Testament Trinity' of Andrej Rubljev of Moscow, showing Abraham entertaining the three angels in the Plains of Mamre, a symbolic representation of the Holy Trinity: a beautiful symphony of harmonious colour, luminous blue, dark, glowing crimson, translucent green and radiant gold, while the faces of the angels are pensive, sad and ethereally beautiful.

Another such backwater brought me to the paintings on wood in the stave churches of Norway, where there are forests upon forests and timber enough for everything – for articles of daily use, for ornamental carvings, for the very churches themselves, whose wooden ceilings were in former times brightly decorated from end to end. It was, comparatively, a long time before Scandinavia was Christianized, and in these churches there was a good deal of English influence – very little Byzantine, unless it were filtered through England.

Here, in the vaulting of Torpo church a thirteenth-century Christ sat enthroned, with hectic spots in His cheeks like those of the persons on the Wheel of Fortune at Rochester; there was a book upheld upon His left knee, and His right hand was raised in blessing. A scarlet cloak draped from His left shoulder fell over His knees, but His round-necked, faded green tunic beneath was mediaeval, not classical. Upon the painted boards behind Him, blue above, pale buff powdered with green stars below, were the four evangelical symbols. Another part of the roof depicted on a blue ground the story of St. Margaret of Antioch, the figures, dressed, as usual, mediaevally and completely anachronistically, were short, with over-large heads and again the bright spots on the cheeks. The Apostles, tonsured like monks, had big, spreading bare feet and pointed with enormous forefingers; their innocent, naïve charm atoned for their faulty proportions and unanatomical drawing.

Then there was an Adoration of the Magi, now in a museum in Oslo, but once in Al Stavkirke, with the same naïve and innocent charm, the same rosy spots on every cheek, the same deep blues and scarlets, the same heavy outlines, and with the crazy architecture around drawn as if by those peasant hands which to this day, as they have done for generations, in the snowy winter nights of Scandinavia, paint and decorate in intricate fashion the chimney-breasts of Norwegian houses. Adam and Eve used to sit in a medallion close by in the same church, but now they too are in Oslo. The anatomy of their naked bodies is best not analysed, the drawing of the Tree of Knowledge is primitive, but the naïve charm is unaffected by these considerations.

Under primitive architecture as before, roughly executed, a very lovable, rosy-cheeked Mary embraces an Elizabeth who affectionately fondles those rosy cheeks; the strong blue of Mary's cloak makes a violent foil to the orange-red of Elizabeth's and to Mary's own long gown; the creamy-green background is powdered with large, almost childishly drawn stars. The museum at Bergen has paintings from Ardal Church in Sogn, which are different in colouring but not dissimilar in atmosphere; dark red and brown were preferred here, and though the figures are less fresh and less youthful than those at Oslo they still have a single-minded naïveté which makes one indifferent to their faults. All these paintings are forcefully drawn, with heavy, unmistakable outlines, and their colours are so strong as to be almost, in some cases, crude; inevitably one is reminded of folk art. There is no subtlety in them, and no other-worldliness, no austere majesty. Only that innocent, irresistible, naïve charm drew me to them again and again and opened my eyes to the simple sincerity of their message.

10

'THEY BUILDED BETTER
THAN THEY KNEW'

$\infty\infty\infty\infty\infty\infty\infty\infty\infty\infty\infty\infty$

BUT the main highway of my journey now swept on through the world of ecclesiastical architecture. Architecture is obvious: it stands in our way, confronts us, thrusts itself upon our sight – or at any rate, the architecture of greater buildings does these things. It does not need searching out. It does not hide in museums or libraries, like illuminated manuscripts, or inside undistinguished looking little country churches, like many murals, nor, like these latter, is it sometimes so faint as to be overlooked by the uninitiated. Therefore, in common, I suppose, with everybody else interested at all in the works of our fathers, I had always noticed mediaeval cathedrals.

Long before my journey ever started I had often walked out of London's roar and toil straight into the ancient peace of the cloisters of Westminster Abbey, had been wafted in imagination to the Ile de France as I stood under the soaring arches of Henry III's frenchified transepts and choir. I had climbed Lincoln's Steep Hill to where, sixteen centuries ago, the Roman Forum of Lindum Colonia had stood, where now the great façade and noble towers of Lincoln Minster rise in silvery loveliness against the sky. I had stood on the banks of the Wear at Durham, that city 'half church of God, half fortress 'gainst the Scot', and looked up at the majesty of the cathedral which is St. Cuthbert's shrine, standing aloft upon the crag top, and I had entered it and shrunk to microscopic proportions, confronted by those mighty Norman piers in the nave.

I had travelled over the dead-flat levels of the Fens, and seen the grey form of distant Ely riding like a ghostly ship upon the horizon; long years ago I had walked over the Barham Downs of the *Ingoldsby Legends* and seen that sight that must have rejoiced the hearts of the 'full nyne and twenty in a company' of Chaucer's day, Canterbury Cathedral in the valley below. I had paused a while on the pavement in the midst of the roar of York's twentieth-century traffic, and had admired the Minster's

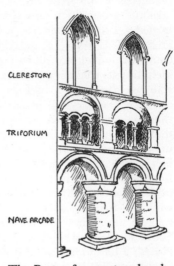

CLERESTORY

TRIFORIUM

NAVE ARCADE

The Parts of a greater church

splendidly ornate west front – as I had paused, but this time in such a gracious peace as English cathedral closes alone hold, entranced by the sheer beauty of architectural composition at Salisbury, built up gable upon gable, roof upon roof, turret upon turret, to the climax of its soaring spire. And how many times had I walked round Wells Cathedral, outside and inside, thinking nothing in architecture so poetic, so perfect, as the stairway to the Chapter House? How many times, for that matter, had I walked round Peterborough Cathedral, the 'beginners' cathedral', as some have called it, because its architectural plan is so easy to understand?

I had rejoiced in the ancient aisles and vaulted roofs of

the crypts at Worcester and Rochester; had watched the sun lighting the fan-vaulting of the cloisters at Gloucester; had thought how good a sight was the burly tower of St. Alban's Abbey, built by the Normans with Roman bricks pillaged from the dead town of Verulamium, seen across the lake and grass which now stretches where Verulamium lies buried.   I had walked, too, through the dark red sandstone arches at Chester, a one-time monastery church, now cathedral, which has all its conventual buildings complete, including its refectory with its exquisite reader's pulpit and staircase thereto.   I had spent hours among the equally exquisite leaf-carvings in the Chapter House at Southwell, that unassuming but so friendly little Nottinghamshire minster.   Just as friendly I had found Lichfield and its unique three steeples, 'the Ladies of the Vale', and the old-French atmosphere of the street leading to its west front.   Chichester in the extreme south, and Carlisle in the extreme north, I knew them both.   Even London's South-wark, in its grimy surroundings, filled with the clatter and roar of the hundreds of suburban trains a day of the Southern Region railway passing its very windows I had visited, I had found admirable things in it.   Just so I had found admirable things beneath the soaring columns of Exeter, rising up to silvery-grey vaulting like a line of palm-branches arching overhead; and never shall I forget how I had once sat in the late-mediaeval, longest nave in England, at Winchester, and heard the choir singing *How lovely are Thy dwellings fair O Lord of Hosts*.   Only one sound have I ever heard more beautiful, and that was the trilling of a chorus of birds in April sunshine echoing among the ruined vaults of the choir of Tintern Abbey.

Of the architectural beauties of the ruined abbeys – Fountains, Rievaulx, Dryburgh, Melrose, Buildwas, Byland – a long, long line of them – I cannot here speak, there are too many of them.   Suffice it to say that even in ruin they are beautiful, though sad, for what remains speaks to us too eloquently of what we have lost.

Yet after all, when it comes to mediaeval cathedrals, England can scarcely hold a candle to France. There is nothing in all the glory of English mediaeval architecture to equal Chartres, or Amiens, or Bourges, Saint-Gilles, Rheims (as it once was), Rouen and, on a smaller-than-cathedral scale, the Sainte Chapelle in Paris, built as a shrine for the Crown of Thorns. But is there any country in the world which has parish churches of such diversity, such charm, such tranquillizing power as England? Do any foreign villages cluster round their churches in quite the moving way that English villages cluster round theirs?

Yet it is a reserved and indrawn charm, that of the architecture of the little ancient English churches, which will not utter a word to the unsympathetic or disclose itself to casual eyes. I did not discover it, or hear it speaking, for some years after I had first started on my journey. The Fenland churches around Wisbech – Leverington, Walsoken, West Walton, Gedney, Elm and March – were my first teachers. After I had learnt from them I ranged everywhere, over the whole land.

Everywhere I went searching for England's parish churches, large and small, in the country and in the town, though best of all I liked them when they were in the country, on some quiet, green hillside, or beside a little stream, or looking out to domes of woodland trees slumbering against a pearly-clouded sky. I went to the red stone town of Bradford-on-Avon, which looks as if it should be in Somerset, but is actually in Wiltshire, and saw the ancient Saxon church which was lost for many years while it existed in disguise as two cottages, inhabited by those completely unaware of the great antiquity of their dwellings. I walked in November rain that hung like a fog over everything from a lonely inn on the Gloucester road to Elkstone, buried deep in the trees of the Cotswold Hills. I left Hadrian's Wall in Cumberland to see the church of the ruined priory at Lanercost, built of Roman bricks from the Wall. I walked out of Canterbury to see St. Martin's on its little

H

hill, the oldest church in England where services are still regularly held.

Among the creeks of the flat lands of Essex I found Maldon, with its triangular tower, looking more peculiar inside than it does out. I climbed up the hilly road to Dover Castle, and beside the Roman lighthouse on the cliff-top, saw St. Mary-in-Castro, which, in the Middle Ages, used that lighthouse as a belfry, and also helped itself, when it was a-building, quite generously to Roman bricks. I found the obscure little church of Hales, in Norfolk, and its round flint-built tower and Norman tympanum carved till it looked like lace in stone over the doorway. I entered the large and dominating church of St. Cuthbert in Somersetshire Wells, so large and dominating that a visitor in there looking about with an uncertain air, came up and said, 'This *is* the cathedral, isn't it?' I took a long and complicated journey to Bradwell-on-Sea above St. Peter's Flats, and meditated in the seventh-century church of St. Chad, standing denuded and desolate up against the skyline where, four centuries before it had been built, a Roman fort had stood. I searched for some while in the humming traffic of Newport on the way to Cardiff before I pulled up a steep hill and lighted upon St. Woolos* with its sturdy Norman nave arcade.

On Anglesey, while the wind roared and wailed around, I found St. Seiriol on Penmon Point, with Saxon carvings and an eleventh-century font. At Long Melford in Suffolk I gazed upon one of the last of the magnificent 'wool churches' of the late Middle Ages. On Romney Marsh I visited Brookland Church with its lead font – one of the few lead fonts in England – depicting the signs of the zodiac and the labours of the months, just as the illuminated manuscripts had done, and saw outside its curious detached timber tower, like some gigantic candle-snuffer.

A small, rackety local bus was the only conveyance I could find to take me from Cirencester to the church of the

* Since 1930, a cathedral.

vanished Abbey of Malmesbury, renowned for its Romanesque Apostles sitting century after century facing each
other in the porch. A walk through a froth of hedge-
parsley on a May day took me down the Adur Valley from
Bramber to Coombes, a church of little note till ancient
wall-paintings were discovered in it, and then on past
Lancing to the churches of Old and New Shoreham. On
another May day I walked through buttercups, apple-
blossom, cuckoo-calls and sun, past thatched roofs and
timber-framed cottages whose gardens were saturated with
the scent of lilac while laburnum dripped over the wayside,
to the church at East Hagbourne, where there was a rarity
– a pulpit of mediaeval date – and queer little stone faces
sticking out of the wall, and a fine timber roof. Subsequently, taking the road under the clear, bold sweep of the
Berkshire Downs, I came into Blewbury, all thatch eyebrows, forget-me-nots, wallflowers, lilacs and larks, and
deep-sunken trees and lanes and interesting-looking grassy
paths leading towards the Downs, and found the church in
one of the tree-filled hollows, and innumerable small points
of interest therein, including a carved mediaeval door.

I threaded the back streets of the city of York till I came
upon All Saints North Street, St. Michael Spurriergate, St.
Martin-cum-Gregory, St. Michael-le-belfry, Holy Trinity
Godramgate, St. Denys and St. Margaret in Walmgate.
I caused amazement to one of the inhabitants of Trotton
when I told her I had come down by train from London
that day on purpose to see Trotton church, the nave of
which, built by the Lord Camoys, cost him only twopence
more, so the story goes, than the beautiful mediaeval
bridge near by. Churches in the Fens and churches
amongst the hills; obscure churches and famous churches;
Saxon, Norman, Early English, Decorated and Perpendicular: I saw examples of them all, and at first hand
realized the differences in the characteristics of all of them,
and learnt church architectural style the easiest and most
enduring way, by seeing it there before my eyes.

Every period had its own attractions.   Anglo-Saxon had
over it the atmosphere of antiquity.   I visited Worth in
Sussex, Bradford-on-Avon, Deerhurst near Tewkesbury,
and in passing looked upon the tower of Holy Trinity in
Colchester, and began to recognize the signs of Saxon
origin – triangular-headed windows, for instance, some-

| Saxon Window (Deer-hurst Church) | Another type of Saxon Window (Worth Church) |

times framed in those thin red bricks I knew to be Roman.
Deerhurst has an internal window of this kind, looking
down into the nave, with twin arches separated by a
reeded column.   It is tempting to think that the reeding
was done by some mason who had seen Roman columns at
some deserted site near by – Glevum itself perhaps – with
their flutings.

Another Saxon feature was baluster shafts, swollen in the
middle, to separate the two lights of a window, as in that
church of many Saxon features, Worth, in Sussex.   Then
there were the tall, narrow doorways with rough pilasters
and primitive capitals thereon, like that at Sompting, on
the Downs behind Worthing.   Often there were traces of
those tall, narrow Saxon doorways walled up in churches
which had obviously been renovated in Norman times.
And at Earl's Barton near Wellingborough in Northamptonshire there was a characteristic Saxon tower, covered with

criss-cross pilaster strips because, probably, the masons could not get out of their heads the timberwork of earlier churches. There were six banded baluster shafts on each face in the belfry stage of this tower, little triangular-headed windows in the third stage, 'long and short' work in the corner quoins, that is, stones placed on end vertically, alternating with stones laid horizontally at right angles, and a typical Saxon west door. What more could one want for an object lesson in Saxon building?*

Saxon Doorway, with 'long-and-short' work

As for timber churches, such as were common in pre-Conquest days, if one walks by the footpath from Chipping Ongar to Greenstead, one may behold a very rare thing: a church nave built of split oak logs, reminiscent of the log huts beside the lakes and forests of Canadian settlers, two or three centuries ago. The existence of this rarity is soon explained. It was in this little church at Greenstead that the body of the sainted Edmund, king of East Anglia, rested for a night in 1016, nearly 150 years after his death, on its journey from London to Bury St. Edmunds, where the Danish king Cnut made recompense for the sins of his ancestors by raising a mighty monastery over the remains of the king they had shot to death. The story goes that when other timber churches were destroyed to make way for nobler buildings in stone, this one was spared because of the sanctity of walls which had stood in close proximity to the venerated body of the saint.

There are, however, later additions to this church; to see a Saxon church uncontaminated I went to Bradford-on-Avon, with its tall, narrow doorways, rough masonry, and

* The battlemented top to the tower is much later.

tiny chancel, and with two carved Saxon angels flying above the chancel arch.   The flat, blind arcading on the exterior gives the church a very different appearance from that other pure Saxon church which I should have visited had I been a northerner, at Escomb, in County Durham. It has been suggested that the chancel arch of this church, because it has the non-Saxon features of proper voussoirs, was a re-erected Roman arch from one of the neighbouring military stations, like the west tower arch of the North-umbrian church at Corbridge.   Bede tells us that Benedict Biscop brought masons from Gaul to build his stone churches, and Escomb certainly has rather a Gallic look.

While on the subject of Roman materials used in Saxon churches I might mention the one at Brixworth in North-amptonshire, where the arches of the original Saxon north and south nave arcades (now filled in, and forming the exterior walls) are built entirely, though crudely, and in a non-Roman manner, of Roman bricks.   This church at Brixworth is not pure Saxon, by the way – it has many later mediaeval additions.

The Normans were great builders.   They had no use for timber churches; theirs must be constructed of stone. Unrestored Norman architecture brought the same sense of antiquity to me as did Saxon.   I felt it very strongly in the crypt at Lastingham Priory in the North Riding of Yorkshire, which is practically untouched since Stephen of Whitby, in 1088, built it over the grave of St. Cedd. Discreet, subdued electric light softly illumined its stout little columns and their heavy Norman capitals, and the vaulted roof with flat, transverse ribs which they supported. In the dark and ancient north-west corner a passage led into obscurity from a high, round-headed, Saxon-style doorway, while in the tiny south aisle were preserved two pieces of ancient timber, one carved with the Viking emblem of the serpent, the other with an equally Scandin-avian winged dragon.

Among these Norman churches several come vividly back to my memory. First, St. Bartholomew the Great, London's only really ancient church (if we except St. John's Chapel in the Tower). Of the minster of the priory founded in the early twelfth century by Henry I's court jester, Rahere, only the choir now survives, with solemn arcades and massy ambulatory pillars. Deep peace and majestic inwardness, belonging to the Norman long ago

Norman Architecture: Nave Arcade, Window
and typical ornaments *a.* Chevron *b.* Cable
c. Billet

and not to the brashness of twentieth-century Smithfield just outside still lie like a benediction upon it.

Next, I remember the 'round' of St. Sepulchre's at Northampton, built, it is said, like all these round churches, in imitation of the Holy Sepulchre at Jerusalem, which

Crusaders saw and copied on their return to their own western lands. Of the more familiar rectangular shape is that other Norman church in Northampton, St. Peter's. It has later Norman, and so more slender, columns with carved capitals which are reminiscent of Byzantine work. Or there is Elkstone, standing deep in the Cotswolds, with its primitive Norman roof vaulting, and Kilpeck in Herefordshire, a tiny red sandstone church with a famous carved south doorway and a corbel table with grotesque carvings of men, intertwined biting beasts, a demoniac figure with outstretched legs, a man playing the rebec, and at the western end projecting dragon-heads with open mouths and coiled tongues. In its apsidal sanctuary the ribs of the vaulting are carved with a heavy chevron pattern meeting in a curious boss with flat, barbaric demon faces; in short, a church, although so far west, impregnated with Viking influence.

Next I remember Walsoken on the edge of Wisbech town; it is just over the county boundary, and so justly claims to have the finest Norman nave in Norfolk; every one of its arches is enriched with chevron decoration, every cushion capital is carved. Then comes to my mind St. John the Baptist at Chester, surrounded by its own picturesque red ruins, the result of a series of bygone architectural disasters, but with a still impressive nave – massive Norman arches below, a beautiful Transitional triforium above. Or there is Barfreston in the south-east corner of Kent; it has, at its eastern end, above blind arcading, a wheel window, a very nearly perfect corbel table round its four sides, a south doorway with four orders of exquisite Romanesque carving, and a carved tympanum above, wherein Christ sits in majesty holding a book on His left knee. This is a mere random list from a very large number of others up and down the land, large and small, rural and urban.

How massive and heavy are the round columns and cushion capitals of these churches, what vistas their barrel

Norman tympanum and nook-shafts

vaults or groined aisles offer, how like a trade-mark do their round-headed windows with a colonette each side become! Norman enrichments soon grow familiar – the chevron and billet mouldings, the reel, the cable, the beak-head, and outside the churches the corbel tables full of grotesque carved faces and figures of monsters and beasts. So do the low, burly central towers, the interlaced blind arcading, and as the Norman century advanced, the order upon order of recessed carvings around the arches of door ways and the characteristic feature of the carved semi-circular tympanum above the door.

Norman architecture is the easiest of all to recognize, to understand and to appreciate. It is a masculine architecture, the architecture of strong but uninhibited, unsubtle piety – for the Normans, for all their wild Viking ancestry, *were* pious – full of strength and power, and without mysticism.

Gradually, as decade followed decade, these things

changed.   A more spiritual vision of the God in whose
honour they were built brought to the churches the same
dreaming grace which appears in the illuminated manuscripts of the time and in the wall-paintings.   The Early
English style of the thirteenth century is not found anywhere outside England.   Those long, 'lancet' windows,
those slender, annulated shafts clustering about a central
pillar, topped with capitals of stiff-leaved foliage, those
steeply pointed arches with sharply cut moulding upon

moulding upon moulding, those
delicate, trefoil-headed arcad-
ings, that dog-tooth ornament,
are as much a hallmark of Early
English as the round arch, massive column and chevron pattern
are of the Norman style.   But
here, in Early English, there is no
burliness, no massive display of
strength; all is light and slender,
soaring aloft like a coil of incense

'Trefoil-headed'

to the Almighty.   If Norman has the overpowering might of
a conquering hero, Early English has the lovely grace of an
uplifted Madonna, saying to the angel Gabriel, 'Behold, the
handmaid of the Lord.'

Salisbury Cathedral is the only ecclesiastical erection
built entirely in the Early English style.   There is, I
believe, no Early English parish church which has not
subsequently had additions or alterations made to it.   But
there are many with some isolated Early English feature,
and several have parts which are pure Early English.
There are for instance, some with Early English chancels.
One of the loveliest is in Cherryhinton Church, just outside
Cambridge.   In the chancel here four pairs of thirteenth-
century lancets with slender annulated shafts to each and to
the blind lancet between each pair, on the north side and
on the south, give a beautiful vision of fourteen shafts and
thirteen arches each side, the effect, especially as all the

lancets have deeply emphasized cinquefoils under their pointed arches, being very rich.

The atmosphere of the chancel of Blakeney Church, which looks across the Norfolk marshes where sea-lavender grows in purple profusion is quite different from that of the later nave – more redolent of the Middle Ages, more remote and spiritual. Moreover, it not only has a stone vaulted roof – a rarity in a parish church – but also a wonderful Early English east window of seven graduated lancets, decreasing in width as well as height towards the sides. The only other instance of such a window which I have met on my journeyings was at Ockham, one of the rural churches of Surrey. This, too, had seven graduated lancets, but was even richer in appearance than that at Blakeney, because the shafts between the lights had foliated capitals, some of them showing, besides the characteristic dog-tooth ornament in the mouldings of the arches, recognizable oak-leaves.

Annulated Column

Another church which is largely Early English is that of Whitchurch Canonicorum, which lies down in a valley against a patchwork of arable fields in western Dorset. Here is a south door of that period, flanked by slender nook shafts with the typical Early English foliated capitals and dog-tooth ornament in one of the mouldings. Here, too, the nave arcade on the north side was early thirteenth century, and one may spend a happy half-hour examining all the carved capitals on the pillars of this side, with their engaged shafts round a central column, for each capital is different, and all are highly original in design, 'stiff-leaf' and 'wind-blown foliage' of course predominating. And when one has done examining the carved capitals in the

Early English Architecture: Nave arcade, Window,
and dog-tooth ornament

nave, one may find more at the chancel arch and in the
north transept, where there is also the shrine of St. Vite.
No one seems to know much for certain about St. Vite, not
even the sex of the saint; but one story says she was a nun
martyred in Saxony in about the eighth century, and
brought back to England and 'interred twelve miles from
Chard'. However that may be, her shrine, here at Whit-

church Canonicorum (which *is* twelve miles from Chard) was very similar to representations I had seen of Thomas à Becket's tomb in the crypt of Canterbury Cathedral, the precursor of the shrine which was once the glory of Canterbury and the Mecca of thousands upon thousands of mediaeval pilgrims. St. Vite's had, like St. Thomas's tomb, lozenge-shaped openings in its side wherein the sick might thrust their diseased limbs and piously hope and wait for a miracle of curing to happen.

Abbey Dore Church in rural Herefordshire, not very far from Kilpeck-reminiscent-of-the-Vikings, is actually, as its name implies, the eastern end of a once large monastic establishment of which the Norman nave has disappeared. The vaulted ambulatory with the remains of five chapels is the only remaining Early English part. Here clustered columns and the simple roll ribs of the vaulting give beautiful vistas, beautiful alternations of light and shade, and the foliated capitals of the columns are particularly attractive.

But all these are Early English only in scattered parts. The parish church which comes nearest to being Early English in its entirety is St. Mary's at West Walton, which looks over the flat lands of the Cambridgeshire Fens for miles, though actually it stands just in Norfolk. I remember walking to it for the first time one rainy February afternoon by a road between sombre-looking orchards which would in due course supply the plums for the Wisbech canneries and jam factories, and seeing far ahead, like a beacon beckoning me on, the mediaeval belfry-tower of the church. As I drew nearer, with only brown fields now stretching away to a fringe of misty trees on the horizon, and saw the village grouped picturesquely around the belfry-tower – even more as I bent round into the main street – a gust as it were out of the long ago caught me up and carried me back seven centuries. I was transported into the world of the Middle Ages.

The huge belfry-tower and its air of venerable antiquity

East Anglian 'Pepper-pot' (W. Walton Church)

dominated the street like a city gate. It served as the entrance to the churchyard, and was completely isolated from the church which stood, towerless, many yards behind it. On it, as on the exterior of the church in its rear, were marks of the thirteenth century: the East Anglian blind arcading with slender, double shafts and pointed arches; the dog-tooth ornament; beyond it the beautiful south porch of the church was an object lesson in Early English, having, in addition to those characteristics the belfry had shown, the conical-topped turrets known throughout East Anglia as 'pepper-pots', which, for some unknown reason, always bestow on that which they adorn an air of remote antiquity.

I found the interior wide and spacious, with the loveliest of nave arcades. There were the central columns again with slender, free-standing shafts grouped around them and banded to them, there atop the columns were capitals of deeply undercut, sometimes parchment-thin, stiff-leaved foliage, there above were the equally deeply cut mouldings typical of Early English pointed arches. While the rain poured down outside I went up into the chancel, and the clustered columns of the noble chancel arch filled me not so much with admiration as with a sense of humbled reverence. Then as I turned at the high altar to walk back I stopped, astonished at the view westwards of all those clustered columns and pointed arches of the nave, with the regular lines of the slender shafts of the clerestory above in perfect perspective and alternating light and shade. 'They builded better than they knew,' I said – for over it all lay the crowning glory of unselfconsciousness.

I walked through the wet grass and the tumbled stones of the graves of the forgotten dead round the outside of the church, and found the fine west door; it had twin arches and a central column or *trumeau* like that of one of the great churches of France – Vézelay, or Amiens, or Rheims, or Bourges – all the dog-tooth ornament of its many mouldings enriching its appearance. Even the ugly later buttresses shoring up the sagging walls here could not detract from its beauty. I saw the north door, a modest version without the porch but with the dog-tooth ornament of that on the south, and then, with one final backward glance at that huge, impressive belfry-tower standing at the end of the village street I came away, heedless of the rain, with the atmosphere of the thirteenth century enveloping me for hours after.

There are other Early English churches more stately than this one; others more compact and neat, but to me St.

Mary's at West Walton will always be the quintessence of the spirit of thirteenth-century mediaevalism.

So I passed on into the fourteenth century, the century of the S-bend, the affected mannerism, the courtly and extravagant graces and posturings of the age when men wore dagged edges to long, flaunting sleeves, hose of one colour on the left leg and of another on the right, and shoes so long in the toes that they had to be chained to the knee to keep them out of the way: the fourteenth century, when, in architecture, what is called the Decorated style came in. Elaboration and great display of the intricacies of technical skill are now the hallmarks. There is complicated tracery in the heads of the windows, and a multiplication of their lights; a sort of double S-bend to stone arches, called the *ogee*, sometimes, if it protrudes out of its own plane, the *bowing ogee*. There are intricately carved and canopied niches with miniature vaults, meant for saints to stand or sit in, but now usually uninhabited, or occupied by a maimed and mutilated remnant of a saint. Elaborations there are of canopied tombs and sedilia, of piscinas, which now no longer have trefoil, but cinquefoil heads; there are chantry chapels with amazingly complex carved retables behind their altars, and tiers of canopied niches; and though few parish churches boast stone-vaulted roofs, yet their timber ones are often fretted and carved — and *coloured*, we must remember — all over. Outside, ornate buttresses have crocketed finials and spirelets upon spirelets, also with crockets, standing up against the sky.

Ogee Arch

I

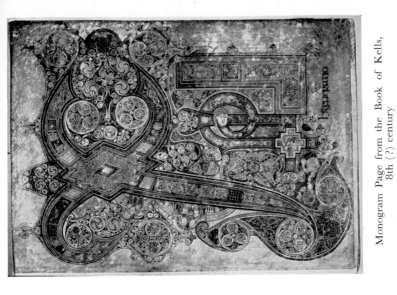

Monogram Page from the Book of Kells,
8th (?) century

Cruciform Page from the Lindisfarne Gospels,
7th–8th century

King Edgar offering to Christ the Charter of New Minster, 10th century

St. Mark, from the Codex Aureus, 9th century

Virgin and Child from Augustine's Commentary on the Psaslm (12th century)

St. John the Baptist, 14th century

Beatus Page from a mid-14th century Psalter

Boating Party, from a late 15th century calendar

12th CENTURY MOSAICS

Above. The Entry into Jerusalem. *Below*. Christ Pantocrator
Cappella Palatina, Palermo

6th CENTURY MOSAICS

Above. Christ calling Peter and Andrew, Sant' Apollinare Nuovo, Ravenna
Below. Abraham entertaining the Three Angels and the Sacrifice of Isaac
San Vitale, Ravenna

Above. Vault-painting in the Chapel of the Guardian Angels; 13th century, Winchester Cathedral. *Below.* The Purgatorial Ladder; 12th century. Wall painting in Chaldon Church, Surrey

Above. Holy Infancy Scenes; 13th century. West Chiltington Church, Sussex.
Below. 'Wheel of the Five Senses', 14th century. Wall painting in Longthorpe Tower, Northants

Above. Early English Architecture: Ambulatory and Eastern Chapels,
Abbey Dore, Herefordshire
Below. Scandinavian influence: South doorway, Kilpeck Church, Herefordshire.
Detail of jamb of doorway

IX

The 'Inhabited Scroll', Easby Cross. Victoria and Albert Museum

Anglian Cross-shaft, Lindisfarne Priory Museum

Left. Pre-Conquest Crosses, Middleton Church, Pickering, Yorks

X

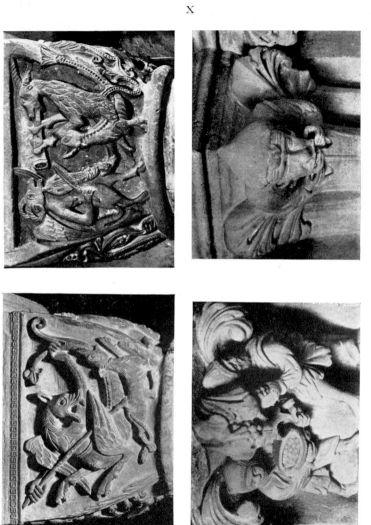

Above. Capitals, Canterbury Cathedral Crypt: Dragon Spearing Dog, and Animals playing Musical Instruments
Below. Capitals, Wells Cathedral: Thieves in the Orchard and the Man with the Toothache

The Death of Cain CAPITALS, VÉZELAY The Wicked Rich Man
tortured by Demons

Above. The Apostles of Malmesbury Abbey
Below. (*Left*) The Royal Ancestors of Christ. (*Right*) Statues in the S. Portal, Chartres

14th century Gothic. Statues on West Front, Exeter Cathedral

Early English. Statues on North Tower, Wells Cathedral

Archway above the Cloister Door, Norwich Cathedral

William the Conqueror;
Choir Screen, York Minster

St. Matthew; Henry VII
Chapel, Westminster Abbey

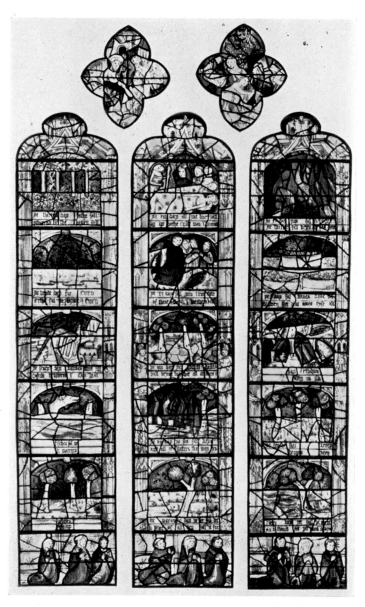

The 'Prykke of Conscience' window, late 15th century, All Saints,
North Street, York

'Figure under Canopy' stained glass, 14th century.

'The Magi behold the Star in the East'. Early stained glass at

An ornament called the *ball-flower* comes
into fashion in some parts of England,
in the exterior mouldings of windows.
Everything is richly decorated, more
lavish, more vainglorious, even if often
handsome. These churches are generally more satisfying in their minor details than in their general effect.

'Cinquefoil headed'

Again, as in the case of Early English churches, I discovered that pure Decorated churches did not exist. Often
the Decorated features had been added to a Norman or
Early English church when some (usually local) influential
individual, lay or clerical, had provided funds to enlarge
an existing church, or when alterations had been made to
increase amenities — small, narrow, deeply-splayed and
round-headed windows, or long, narrow Early English
lancets being replaced, for example, by wide Decorated
ones of three or four lights to bring better illumination to
the church. Or again, after the Decorated features had
been grafted on to a church of earlier style the following
century might add its own features. Most churches in the
Middle Ages were living organisms, always growing, adapting
themselves to changing needs as age followed age and men's
ideas of what was most fitting for the service of God altered.

Still, I found several churches which, though not pure
Decorated, gave a very clear idea of the style. Cley in
Norfolk, for example, which stands just off the main road
running between Sheringham and Blakeney, has a south
door which is an excellent example of fourteenth-century
work, for it has an ogee arch with a cusped trefoil door-
opening under it, and the nave arcade inside is also fourteenth-century. The pillars are octagonal on plan, as
they often are in this century, and there are over them
typically ornamental appendages (so like the fourteenth
century, which loved ornament, necessary or unnecessary)
in the shape of canopied niches. The canopies soar up to
a point, crockets ornament the lines of every angle,

Decorated Architecture: Nave arcade, window,
ball-flower ornament and typical niche

and there are ornate pedestals below them upon which
figures, now gone, used to stand. On the south side
of the church these pedestals, or brackets, are supported by
carved figures. A strolling player performs upon his pipe
and tabor under one of them; a woman plays a viol under
another, and St. George deals with the dragon under a

third. This sort of treatment is typical of the fourteenth century. Everything must be adorned with brackets and finials and crockets and grotesques and tabernacle-work and carved corbels and tier upon intricate tier of canopies supporting canopies which hold up other canopies; and if everything else failed there was always exuberant naturalistic foliage to fall back upon. Richness of detail rather than purity of line, exuberance before restraint, show of technical skill preferred to simple piety; these are the characteristics of the Decorated style.

Finialled and Crocketed Gable

Not that fourteenth-century profusion of ornament is unattractive, even if it is sometimes overdone; it always pays to study details in the work of this century. At Southwell Minster, that lovely old building in Nottinghamshire, there is a fourteenth-century rood screen or *pulpitum* which one could spend a whole morning examining. Carved upon it there are no less than eighty tiny heads, of men and women, demons, beasts and monsters, grinning and grimacing, laughing at jokes, scowling, lugubriously frowning, each a miniature study of character and a work of exquisite art.

But to return to Cley. Here too, there is an example of the homely humour which enlivens this century. At the eastern end of the nave arcade is a carved imp who has an eye made of glass, so that he seems to wink continually and wickedly at those sitting in the pews below.

Then there is Dorchester Abbey in Oxfordshire. The south aisle piers here are of this same Decorated period, one of them having round it, like a collar, a bracket-band carved with a party of sleeping monks, roused by the horn of the devil, who is about to catch them, body and soul, as he catches all the unwary who do not keep everlasting vigil against his wiles. In the choir there is abundance of ornamentation of a most unusual type. The huge east window has elaborately flowing tracery, and on the lower part of this are carved in stone various groups representing the Crowning with Thorns, Christ Scourged at the Pillar, the Resurrection of Christ and His appearance to Mary Magdalene, and a Harrowing of Hell. The sedilia, moreover, are no ordinary ones. There are three seats – an arrangement which, of course, is very common – and a piscina as part of the same architectural group, again not unusual, but these sedilia have in the back of all four divisions a bell-shaped opening filled with ancient glass, and above, more sculptured figures standing on the stone transom of a large window. Opposite, on the northern side, the tracery of the window behaves as I believe it does nowhere else in England, if not in Europe. It takes the form of a Jesse Tree. There is the recumbent figure of Jesse lying on the sill at the bottom, and the carved stone figures of his descendants, that is to say of the ancestors of Christ, stand on the stone branches reaching up into the windows. Low down in one corner is David playing his harp. I have frequently met Jesse Trees in one form or another in churches, as I have met them in illuminated manuscripts, but I have never seen before, nor have I since seen, one taking the form of this example at Dorchester. Incidentally, I found the not very common ball-flower ornament in the mouldings of all these windows, enriching them – or possibly gilding lilies. The Decorated style is rather inclined to gild lilies.

But perhaps one of the finest Decorated churches is the one at Winchelsea, on the edge of Romney Marsh, though we now have only the choir left of it. Accounts vary as to what happened to the nave. Some say it was never more than just begun; others that it was almost complete when the Black Death stopped further building; a third version of its non-existence at the present day, which is, perhaps the right one, is that it was burnt to the ground in one of the French raids upon this coast during the Hundred Years' War. The tower may have fallen soon after. Winchelsea is so fine an example of the period because it was built just

as Early English was expanding into Decorated, in the
latter part of the reign of Edward I, who more or less
'town-planned' the new Winchelsea after the old had been
submerged by the sea some time round about 1288, and
therefore it does not show that lavish over-decoration which
became the bane of later fourteenth-century building.

The church is vast and spacious even in its present
truncated state, and if it really was ever finished, must
have been of noble proportions and considerable beauty –
a king's church in very truth.   The columns supporting
the wide, pointed arches (Decorated arches are never so
steeply pointed as Early English ones) were clustered rather
in the Early English manner, and had among the other shafts
slender ones of black Sussex marble.   They were banded,
too, halfway down, as if they had been Early English, but the
whole atmosphere which lay over them was different.   This
inexplicable, subtle 'atmosphere' of the different periods of
mediaeval architecture is an even surer guide to date than
column styles, window shapes and ornament type.

Beneath the aisle windows were canopied tombs.   Those
on the south were the Alard tombs, those on the north
housed anonymous effigies of an earlier age, as the style
of their carving indicated.   It is said that they came from
the ancient church of Winchelsea which has been lying for
centuries beneath the waters of the English Channel, the
subject of many a romantic legend.

The Alard tombs have scarcely a square inch without
ornament.   Along the base of the tomb on which the
mailed effigies lie are crocketed canopies and pedestals for
vanished statues, with miniature finialled shafts on each
side of narrow crocketed gablets; above, the arched canopy
of the tomb springs from slender, clustered shafts with foliated
capitals; the arch is cinquefoil, and there is carved foliage in
the spandrels.   And as if this were not enough, the back of
the tomb recess is filled with diaper-work.   The ogee arch appears on the tombs in the north aisle, with crockets right up
the side of the gable, and feathered tracery in the spandrels.

A glance through the half-open door of the former abbey church of Tewkesbury, now the parish church, is enough to show that the great nave and its thick, plain cylindrical columns are Norman, but that the vaulted roof and windows above are much later. The elaboration of the lierne vaulting, as well as the window tracery, says distinctly, 'Decorated – fourteenth-century'. In the choir there is more Decorated work, of a more satisfying kind. Lierne vaulting is here also, above the earlier Norman columns, as in the nave; and in its bays there are seven great Decorated windows, with beautiful flowing tracery in their heads. These windows are made more exquisite by the fact that they retain their original fourteenth-century stained glass. Behind the choir is a corona of five (once six, but the Lady Chapel at the crown has vanished) radiating chapels, one of which is now used as a sacristy: St. Catherine, St. Faith, St. Edmund-and-St. Dunstan and St. Margaret, all of the Decorated period. In the chapel of St. Edmund-and-St. Dunstan there is a carved boss showing the legendary wolf who guarded between his paws the martyr king's head when the sorrowing royal servants came seeking it.

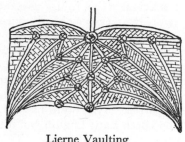

Lierne Vaulting

A fashion for chantry chapels came in during the fourteenth century. These were erected in churches, by those rich enough to build and endow them, so that priests specially appointed for that office might in them, on behalf of the souls of those buried therein, sing masses *ad aeternitatem* (little did they foresee how all that would end, two centuries later); and at Tewkesbury, around the choir, there are more of these chapels than there are in many a cathedral. Some of them belong to the fifteenth century, but when I was studying the Decorated style I went into the Trinity Chapel, which is the chantry of Edward le Despenser, built towards the end of the fourteenth century, and there I saw one of the earliest examples (the very earliest is in the cloister at Gloucester) of that miracle of carving known as fan-vaulting, which was to develop so marvellously in the century following. The lord Edward, for whose soul's repose this chantry was built, is painted with his wife on the east wall, where a contemporary mural of the Holy Trinity is just discernible; but there is no effigy of him lying beneath the fan-vaulted roof. In his helmet and mail, his gauntleted hands joined in everlasting prayer, he kneels under an ornate canopy (floodlit nowadays) on the roof of his chantry, turned towards and gazing at, as long as the Abbey shall last, the high altar of the God into whose hands he had commended his spirit.

How different is this memorial from the cenotaph of John Wakeman, near the chapel of St. Edmund-and-St. Dunstan! On the tomb here lies carved a half decomposed body which is being devoured by a snake, a frog, a mouse and a snail. This gruesome effigy should by rights be lying underneath, and on the tomb should be the figure of Wakeman, last abbot of Tewkesbury before the Dissolution, clad in his pontifical robes in all the glory of his earthly state.* This example of a mediaeval *cadaver* is, of course, much later than the fourteenth century, but I mention it here because it is typical of the waning Mediaeval Age, and has the same moral as the murals and illuminations in manuscripts depicting the Three Quick and the Three Dead: *Vanity of vanities, saith the preacher, all is vanity.* Or, as James Shirley was to say, 300 years after the choir of Tewkesbury was built,

> The glories of our blood and state
> Are shadows, not substantial things.

* He surrendered the abbey to Henry VIII in 1540, and became Bishop of Gloucester.

On this note the fourteenth century passed into the fifteenth, which was to sound it ever more frequently.

The worldly, bourgeois fifteenth century – the age of the rise of the towns and prosperous merchants, of the Wool Staple, the glorious zenith of the wool trade in the Cotswolds and East Anglia. The time when men – often to save their souls, less often from purely spiritual motives – built those glorious churches which clothed the land from one end to the other of the limestone belt, and over the counties where men had knapped flints from the dim past of prehistory, with another 'white robe of churches' as lovely as the first had been, over 300 years before, in the land of France; churches not comparable with, because utterly different from, the sombre, gloomy piety of the Norman church, the uplifted, rarified spirituality of the Early English, the exuberant love of decoration of the fourteenth century.

In noble, shimmering array they stand again before my mind's eye. Long Melford and Lavenham, close to each other, each in its picturesque Suffolk village; Gedney in the flat lands of Lincolnshire, St. Nicholas in all its splendour in the ancient Norfolk port of King's Lynn; Chipping Camden and Northleach, two of the glories of the Cotswolds, and Cirencester, which has a three-staged south porch (rebuilt) which once served as a meeting hall for guilds; St. Peter Mancroft overlooking the market-place at Norwich, city of churches. Those wonders, too, of the Suffolk coast, Blythborough and Southwold, and the two beautiful shrines which 'have everything', not far from the Norfolk Broads, Cawston and Salle; these are a few which rise most readily to my memory out of many. Mighty churches, all of them, stone frameworks for mighty expanses of glass, with openwork parapets and panelled buttresses, and richly carved stone porches (in East Anglia, of flint flushwork, like the body of the churches), beautifully proportioned, majestic and serene, the wonder of their own age and the glory of ours; and, in Somerset especially, where the church itself is often poor by comparison, uplifting tall, pinnacled towers worshipfully into the sky.

I see in my mind's eye, too, their interiors, their lofty aisles, one grand sweep from the high tower-arch at the west to the High Altar far at the eastern end, their slender, often octagonal columns, their wide-windowed clerestories, the mullions of the four-, five- or six-light aisle windows running in long perpendicular lines to the symmetrical tracery in their heads, the whole church flooded with light, even to the timber hammer-beam roof and its carved angels up above. Of course, they lack the appealing other-worldliness of the earlier churches. They were not built in an other-worldly age. They were built in the fifteenth century by prosperous wool merchants with an eye to the perpetuation of their names, and certainly to spiritual main-chance. One would not in these circumstances expect them to be other-worldly. But they are a glorious feast for the eye and a wonderfully uplifting aesthetic experience, which can easily become a spiritual tonic; and to see one standing alone – as for instance Gedney does – or on an eminence, like Long Melford, in all its almost cathedral-like proportions, is to feel an overmastering desire to worship Him to whom such miracles of beauty were raised.

In my journeys I saw many of them wondering, as I approached them, at the breath-taking harmony of their perpendicular lines, their fretted and carved battlements and crocketed finials and pinnacles standing against the sky; the cinquefoil-headed panellings on every one of their numerous buttresses (much needed, when the walls were, except for those buttresses, composed almost entirely of glass windows); their canopied niches and their wealth of carved ornament so different from that of the fourteenth century. For whereas fourteenth-century ornament sprawled in curves and circles Perpendicular was dis-ciplined between upright parallel lines; and when I entered Perpendicular churches, there I saw those upright parallel lines moving away in regular perspective to a point where

Perpendicular Architecture: Nave arcade, window
and typical ornament

four-centred arch and high-soaring, slender columns
merged in one grand play of light and shade.

Very often nowadays these churches serve a village of
most insignificant proportions. Gedney Church, for
instance, stands conspicuously like some crystal cathedral,
isolated in the dull, flat fields around Holbeach, a great
stone skeleton of ribs with a glittering expanse of glass
between, but Gedney village might be overlooked by one
driving through it in a fast car. At best, they soar over
small country towns, as does the magnificent flint and stone
Lavenham church, which has a south porch which would not
shame a cathedral, and ranges of aisle and clerestory windows

considerably more impressive than those in some cathedrals.

One of the most famous among Perpendicular churches is that at Long Melford in Suffolk. It is an impressive pile, with its lengthy range of clerestory windows on the south glittering in the unclouded light of the sun. Its lofty proportions, and the various architectural devices employed to give it an appearance of even greater height and length, are magnificent, and it has a Lady Chapel such as I have seen nowhere else – a small, entirely self-contained building, which adds still greater length to an already abnormally long church. The tower at the west end, though built in the Perpendicular style, is modern, but all the rest dates between about 1484 and 1496.

The interior is enormous. The lofty clerestory is made to look even loftier by cinquefoiled panels extending down to the arches of the nave arcade, and by the vertical stone shafts, on which rest the timbers of the roof, between each window. You may stand by the tower-arch and look eastwards upon a vista of great beauty right down the long nave to the chancel and sanctuary, and see the roof and clerestory running in one unbroken line throughout the building; then, moving down the church, at the end of the north aisle you come upon the Clopton chapel. The effigy of Sir William Clopton clad in fifteenth-century plate armour with his hands making a triangle in prayer lies upon his canopied tomb, and the floor gleams with Clopton memorial brasses. Through a small vestibule, under a fan-vaulted ceiling, is the Clopton chantry. Here is another Clopton tomb, with shields in sunk panels and twelve beautifully carved canopies above them. The whole chantry shines with mediaeval painting: a figure of Christ in red and green, showing His Wounds, on the vault of the tomb; carved scrolls interlaced with foliage and flowers in red and green and gold along the cornice; a Virgin and Child in black and white and grey on the splay of the hagioscope which looks through into the Clopton aisle of the church; and upon the red and green painted roof-beams are white scrolls on which appear IHU MERCY and GRAMERCY alternately in blackletter.

To get to the Lady Chapel one must go out into the churchyard again and enter it through its own door. This arrangement of a Lady Chapel is, I think, unique. The aisles, the 'cloister ther abowte', as its founder, John Clopton, described it, form an ambulatory round the chapel proper. Canopied niches over empty pedestals stand at the two outer westward angles; canopied niches, crying out for their vanished statues, stand also at the internal angles; delicate shafts on each side of the ambulatory arches support the timber roof. And here, as elsewhere in the church, is fifteenth-century stained glass of great interest and beauty; a mediaeval alabaster; and a fifteenth-century carved oak seat from Granada Cathedral.

The last buildings I would mention are not parish churches; but as I went on my architectural journey through the fifteenth century I could not pass them by, for they possessed superb examples of that most characteristic Perpendicular architectural feature of all – fan-vaulting. Fan-vaulting, though by modern canons of functional design it fails lamentably, is one of the most beautiful types of *stone* roofing in existence. Much of it is purely ornamental, and serves no useful, that is to say, no functional purpose whatever, but to me that does not matter in the least. Man cannot live by bread alone. The sight of those inverted cones of delicately panelled stone, stretching out to touch one another across the roof, their ribs like an avenue of palm branches, their parallel segmental lines making a flowing pattern down long aisles as if pebble after pebble had been thrown into pool after pool of water, sending ever widening ripples to a distant bank, is as soothing to the eye as the serene beauty of arching lines of symmetrical curvature is satisfying to the senses.

And what of the cloisters at Gloucester, especially the roof of the Lavatorium where the monks of the convent used in days gone by to wash their hands before entering the refectory? What of the nave vaulting of Sherborne Abbey? or of St. George's Chapel at Windsor Castle? What, above all, of that exquisite *tour-de-force*, fraud and deception though it be, the roof of Henry VII's Chapel at the east end of Westminster Abbey?

No spider's web encased in frost was ever more delicate, no object of stone was ever more reminiscent of spiders' webs; nor did stone ever hang before, nor has it done since, as if it were veils of misty lace drooping in a void above the earth. Blatantly, in unrepentant prodigality, ornament is piled on ornament, lilies are gilded as shamelessly as the fourteenth century ever gilded them. The result ought to be a masterpiece of meretricious vulgarity, instead it is a miracle of lightness and grace and beauty. Much depends, perhaps, on the fact that here the cones are pendent, and also on the fact that at regular intervals highly ornamented semi-circular beams span the chapel, tying the roof together into a disciplined whole, and giving a point of stability on which the eye can rest amongst the mazes of filigree pattern. By these means it avoids, too, that fault to which Perpendicular style was prone: monotony; for too frequent a repetition of parallel lines did tend after a while to become as great a bane of the Perpendicular as over-loading with ornament had been of the Decorated style.

As I look up now at the roof of Henry VII's Chapel I suddenly realize that I have travelled a long way from those unselfconscious, clustered columns of West Walton, the purity of those lancet windows at Cherryhinton, the simple spirituality of Early English. I realize that this roof above me now is the last manifestation of the Gothic genius which started with such buildings as West Walton's church of St. Mary. As I stand under those ethereal pendants I can see the torch of the Renaissance, which has been leaping in brilliant flame for the past 150 years in some countries on the Continent, steadily approaching English shores, and I know that in Henry VII's Chapel at Westminster I am standing on the threshold of the modern world.

11

THE CROSSES OF
THE TWILIGHT OF THE DAWN

～～～～～～～～～～～～～～～～～～～

O N the threshold of the modern world – but I am not
yet ready to return to it. Almost as soon as I had
begun my pilgrimage to cathedrals and churches
I had realized that their interest did not lie in their architecture alone. All too often the architecture is a book from
which the text has been ruthlessly torn. Almost invariably
– at any rate in parish churches, but sometimes in cathedrals as well – there are niches destitute of the saints they
were made to hold, screens which are meaningless tiers of
canopies sheltering nothing. Sculpture in the Middle
Ages was not an ornamental addition, standing isolated like
Cromwell on his pedestal outside Westminster Hall, or
Peter Pan by the waterside in Kensington Gardens. It was
part and parcel of the architectural design. It belonged to
the building trade, not to what we nowadays call the 'fine
arts', a term which would have been incomprehensible to
the mediaeval mind. Masons, not artists in our sense
executed it. It was inseparable from buildings, and
naturally, as I studied buildings I met the remnants of
mediaeval sculpture in or on them. And so my path now
led me through one of the most fascinating of all the lands
of mediaeval art – the land of sculpture.

At the outset of my journey through this land I received a somewhat unnecessary warning; unnecessary because I saw all around me statues without heads, arms or legs, cruelly mutilated and incomplete; crosses without their tops, carved reliefs obliterated by the axe, defaced effigies lying upon tombs whence all the little 'weepers' mourning in their canopied niches had vanished; canopies themselves knocked to pieces. What mediaeval carvings I was likely to see, I was rightly reminded, were only a fraction of all the treasure of sculpture which the Middle Ages knew. Time has worn away a few of them. The smoke-laden atmosphere of industry, and the vagaries of our climate, most unkind to delicate finials and exposed crockets, has defaced more, especially external ones. But the great destroyers of our heritage were neither Time nor Climate, but first the commissioners of that royal and greedy vandal, Henry VIII, and second, the fanatical reforming zeal of the Puritans, self-appointed judges of what it was good for posterity to see, who attacked everything which to them smacked of 'Popery and superstitious practices'.

I therefore found that France was richer than our land in existing mediaeval sculpture of the eleventh to the fifteenth centuries – with the exception of tomb effigies. If France had no Puritan Revolution against 'Popery', England had no political one crying, '*Liberté, Egalité, Fraternité*', and in England the tombs of the aristocracy and landed lords were left, as the Revolutionaries did not leave such in France, for the most part unmolested. If they are mutilated in England it is usually through indifference or neglect, or because someone wanted to erect something else inconveniently near them.

So much for the sculpture of the later Middle Ages – 'High Gothic sculpture'; but what of that which came before the eleventh century? Here the path led me far back – farther back than I had ever dreamt of going, into the dim mists of antiquity in wild barbaric lands that knew art when the Roman Empire was an embryo in the womb of

Time, before the sixth century B.C. It led me back to
Scythia and Sarmatia, the steppe lands stretching from the
Carpathians to the Don, the legendary realm of the Cim-
merians who lived in perpetual twilight, where Perseus
found the Three Grey Sisters in the 'Unshapen Land,
where the air was full of feathers and the soil was hard with
ice, by the shore of the freezing sea, nodding upon a white
log of driftwood, beneath the cold white winter moon'.*
The Scythians spent the spring and autumn on the open
steppe, and in the winter and summer came to the rivers
Don, Dnieper and Volga; and they ornamented their
armour and weapons – their breastplates, swords, scabbards,
belts, ear-rings, clasps and buckles, the bits of their horses
and all their horses' gear with bizarre patterns: animals
twisted into decorative lines, geometric designs, rosettes,
wheels and screws, motifs freely borrowed from other
cultures with which, in the course of time, their migrations
brought them into contact.   These people, when they
reached the shores of the Black Sea – the Euxine of Greek
legend and ancient history – mingled with the Greeks
already there, and took from them the classical *rinceau* and
the acanthus-leaf pattern.   For years they dwelt on the
confines of Persia, and from Persia borrowed what Persia
had long before borrowed from Assyria and Babylon: confronted animals, twisted serpents and dragons, grotesque
monsters and the double-headed eagle.   With this rich
artistic inheritance these nomads went wandering still over
the plains of southern Russia; they met Germanic tribes,
Herulians, Visigoths, Ostrogoths, Vandals, the barbarians
who, bringing what they had learnt of Scythian and
Sarmatian art with them, in the fifth century after the birth
of Christ overran the Roman Empire of the west and
destroyed it – including Gaul and Britain.

This barbarian art, abstract, dynamic, whirling, tending
always towards pattern, although it had taken certain
motifs from classical sources, waged for centuries a ceaseless

* Charles Kingsley: *The Heroes.*

battle with the reasoned, symmetrical and realistic art of the Graeco-Roman world which made Man the centre of the universe and the measure of all things. In the art of the so-called 'Dark Ages' the struggle is in being; but the end was inevitable when Christianity conquered the northern lands. Barbaric art had no future. Its death was hastened by the inescapable fact that it could tell no story. And Christianity demanded that very thing, which classical, representational art alone could give it. Therefore, in the end, the art of the Mediterranean world won the fight and abstract art vanished from the scene till centuries after the Middle Ages had waned and died.

I would meditate upon all this as I gazed upon the great stone Celtic crosses at Bewcastle and Ruthwell, Hexham and Easby,* Rothbury, Aycliffe and Irton, and the fragments at Jedburgh, Aldborough and Lindisfarne Priory. What purpose they all served is not certain, though a good many would appear to be tombstones to the once distinguished but now forgotten dead. Since, however, it is said that the early Christian missionaries to these lands used to erect wooden crosses where they preached – on the same principle, presumably, as surgeon-barbers in the Middle Ages stuck a bandaged pole outside their premises – and since Bede tells us that in the year A.D. 634 Oswald, king of Northumbria, erected 'the standard of the Holy Cross . . . in the place which is called in English Hefenfelth of the Heavenly Field † and on his knees prayed to God that He would assist His worshippers in their dire need' before he advanced to defeat the British king Cadwallon on that spot, we may assume that afterwards such wooden standards were perpetuated in stone, and that such crosses as are not tombstones are memorials of some special event now long forgotten.

The best are in the north of England, and they are also

* Now in the Victoria and Albert Museum, South Kensington.
† Now Heavenfield, in Northumbria, near Hadrian's Wall, just south-east of Chollerford. A modern wooden cross still marks the spot.

the earliest. Scholars still wrangle about their dates, but they seem to belong to the time of Northumbria's prosperity, of which Bede writes in his *Ecclesiastical History*, that is, the hundred years between A.D. 650 and A.D. 750. The best of all are the majestic structures at Bewcastle, about seventeen miles north-east of Carlisle, and in Ruthwell Church, Dumfries. The Puritans wreaked their fury upon the latter, overthrowing it as a superstitious and idolatrous monument, but the idolatrous pieces have been re-erected for us to wonder what idolatry anyone can ever have seen in them.

Both crosses show Christ treading upon the beasts, in illustration of the words of the psalm, 'Thou shalt tread upon the lion and the adder, the young lion and the dragon shalt thou trample under feet';* they both show St. John the Baptist, 'him that crieth in the wilderness, "Prepare ye the way of the Lord"', with the lamb in his arms: 'Behold the Lamb of God, which taketh away the sins of the world'; they both show St. John the Evangelist, accompanied by his evangelical symbol, the eagle, carved with a careful perception of the nature of the bird which is a characteristic of Celtic art, which, with no influence to guide it other than that long heritage setting out ultimately from the Scythian steppes, always delineated animals with masterly sureness when it fumbled naïvely – whenever it introduced it at all – with the human form.

Both crosses have Runic inscriptions. Those at Bewcastle, incised between the panel showing Christ trampling on the beasts and that with St. John the Evangelist turning to regard his bird, have not been translated with certainty, but those which make a decorative border for the strikingly carved scene on the Ruthwell Cross of Mary Magdalene wiping Christ's feet with her long hair have been interpreted as referring to an ancient Anglo-Saxon poem, written, perhaps, by the poet Cynewulf, *The Dream of the Rood*. In this poem the Cross is made to say,

* Psalm xci. 13.

Then the young man, who was God Almighty, stripped himself, strong and steadfast. Bold in the sight of many He mounted the High Cross, when He would redeem mankind. I trembled when He clasped me, yet I durst not bow to the ground or fall to the lap of earth.

The great monument of red sandstone at Ruthwell, with its long, narrowing shaft ending in an equal-armed Maltese cross, rears up over seventeen feet. The grey sandstone one at Bewcastle, standing still where it has always stood, in the burial ground of St. Cuthbert, is a mere fourteen feet high, and it has lost its cross-head. It carries no narrative scenes, and has figures on only one face, the other three faces being filled with scroll-like coils of the True Vine and little birds and beasts perched on the tendrils thereof pecking at conventionalized bunches of grapes, or with interlaced strapwork and plait design like those in the illuminated manuscripts of the period. The Ruthwell Cross has narrative scenes on the back and the front: Christ healing the blind man, the Annunciation, the Flight into Egypt, St. Paul and St. Anthony breaking the bread which was sent them from heaven by a raven, an illustration of a legend of the hermits of the Egyptian desert in the earliest days of monasticism; above all, the scene of Mary Magdalene and Christ. In the three large panels representing Christ which appear on these two crosses there is a gracious and tender dignity in the figure of the Saviour which is far removed from the Celtic barbarism of the pecking creatures in the coiling scrolls; and on the Ruthwell Cross, although the Magdalene's hair is clumsily carved and her right hand is a huge, ill-proportioned monstrosity, the reverent, adoring turn of her head is as moving as the humane nobility of the Christ whom she is worshipping, standing above her.

Whence came these great, majestic figures, so far in advance of all other carvings of their age, so monumental and so moving, so Byzantine in all but their gracious tenderness? Explanations are many, proofs that any

explanation is the true one there are none.   One theory is
that the Northumbrian bishops, Wilfrid and Benedict
Biscop, visiting Italy in search of craftsmen, found and
brought back with them refugees from the seventh-century
Mahommedan conquests of Syria, Egypt, Africa and Spain,
and that these artists, bred in the classical tradition, carved
the figures, or taught the Anglo-Saxons to carve them, while
the English dictated the form of the monuments (such
crosses are not found on the continent of Europe) and
insisted on the barbarian scrolls and pecking birds and
beasts.*

There are many of these crosses, and hundreds of fragments of cross shafts in England and Scotland and Ireland.
There is the cross of St. Patrick and Columba at Kells;
there is a cross at Donaghmore in Tyrone, a splendid
example at Monasterboice, and two crosses at Castledermot,
Kildare.   They are to be found at Collingham and Nun-
burnholm in Yorkshire, at Sandbach in Cheshire, Irton in
Cumberland, Kirby Stephen (which bears an interesting
chained Norse devil) in Westmorland, Rothbury in
Northumberland, Bakewell in Derbyshire, in Durham
Cathedral Library, and even in the south of England, at
Codford, Britford and Ramsbury in Wiltshire.   Obviously
I could not visit all the specimens of this type of pre-
Conquest art which still exist, still less, in a limited space,
describe them all.   It must be enough to mention a few
(not necessarily the best) which I did see on my travels in
the dim twilight of these pre-Norman centuries.

One of the first was the Acca Cross, in the south transept
of Hexham Abbey in Northumberland, which looks across
to the tombstone of a pagan cavalryman of the Roman army
at the foot of the famous night stair to the bygone dormitory
of the bygone monastery.   It dates from about A.D. 740
and is decorated with thin, rather wiry and wandering vine
scrolls, highly conventionalized, like the triangular bunches
of grapes appearing at regular intervals among them.   No

* A. Gardner: *English Mediaeval Sculpture*.

birds or beasts peck the fruit on this cross, and its patterns are now much worn and weathered.

In the museum attached to the ruins of Jedburgh Abbey in the Lowlands of Scotland there is a fragment of a cross-shaft carved with what are known as 'inhabited scrolls', that is, coiling tendrils and foliage with birds and beasts perched in the windings thereof. On this shaft at Jedburgh, which was carved possibly about the same time as the Acca Cross, or perhaps a few decades earlier, the birds confront each other across the dividing line of the main stem of the Vine, and while a fox is eating the grapes in one scroll at the bottom, in the opposite one a small mouse with forward poking head and big ears is peering round one of the stems.

On the high-tide island off the Northumbrian coast, now called Holy Island, where in the seventh century St. Aidan, apostle of Christianity to Northumbria, founded a priory in which St. Cuthbert later lived and held office, and where he was originally buried, fragments of cross-shafts and tombstone slabs are preserved in the museum beside the ruined mediaeval priory church which succeeded St. Aidan's. To the sound of the North Sea waves seething among the rocks St. Cuthbert knew long ago, amid the screeching of the sea-birds winging their way from Inner and Outer Farne as they did when St. Cuthbert lived his hermit's life on an island hut in their midst, I examined the ancient stones: their heavy strapwork and interlacings and plaited strands, the incised designs on three of them, which called to mind instantly the cruciform pages of the Lindisfarne Gospels which had been written possibly at the same time as the stones were carved in the priory near by. On one broken, semi-circular headed slab primitive little men on one side represented the wild heathen of Northumbria waving their battle-axes in what was certainly intended to be pagan ferocity, though the carver's skill did not match his intention, and they appeared to be marching as sedately as any disciplined Roman legion; on the other side were those same wild heathen after St. Aidan had converted them to Christianity. They were now no longer brandishing battle-axes, they were bending in adoration before a Cross with the sun and moon above (just as I had seen it in the Byzantine Crucifixion at Santa Maria Antiqua in Rome, and in countless early representations of the scene). These human figures, like others which appeared on several heavily interlaced strapwork shafts at Jedburgh, were extremely crude, and reminiscent of the efforts of young children; but their naïveté and obvious sincerity have their appeal in a world growing weary of its own sophistication. Some of these shafts and slabs might have been as late as the eighth or early ninth century – the comparatively late date may account for the frequent appearance at Jedburgh of the human figure among the more customary Anglo-Saxon coils and plaitings and interlaces.

I also saw, on the edge of the famous Moor, three crosses in the churchyard at Ilkley, carved in the first half of the ninth century. Only one has a cross-head, and that does not rightly belong to it; but what is most noticeable is the coiled pattern on the sides: simpler than others, and the spirals were tighter, as if they were a well wound spring, and they had a rather unusual beaded edge. Inhabited scrolls also appeared, with confronted birds and creatures that looked more like long-eared rabbits than anything, rubbing noses. There were also beasts liberated from the confining scrolls, rearing and snarling, their tails elongated into a wispy pattern of interlacing – this fantastic tail often occurs later – it is a Danish feature.

Even in London I was able to see a cross, although, of course, it was in the alien atmosphere of a museum – the Victoria and Albert at South Kensington. This was the Easby Cross, which once stood by the abbey of that name in Yorkshire. Its four surviving fragments were collected together in modern times, and mounted as a shaft. Birds of the eagle family and beasts of a species unknown here tramped and perched upon the tendrils of the vine. The birds and beasts were still biting and pecking in determined Anglo-Saxon style, but the tendrils of the vine twined more loosely, in a more natural way, as if they had been carved by a hand accustomed to the art of the ancient classical world. Consequently it was not surprising to see, on another face of the shaft, the haloed busts of the Apostles looking for all the world like Roman portrait heads, in compartments with beaded edges, and a seated Christ, doubtless a Majesty, without the great monumental qualities of the Christs on the Bewcastle and Ruthwell crosses, but classically humane. These carvings were so unlike the uncouth figures at Lindisfarne Priory that they must have been carved either by foreign craftsmen or by Englishmen strongly influenced by that resurgence of Classical art which is associated with the Carolingian Renaissance. This supposition would imply that they were carved in the late eighth or early ninth century. Some, however, would place them earlier,* in which case Wilfrid's or Benedict Biscop's refugees from Islam might have executed them.

Other crosses showed signs of unfamiliar influences – Danish-Norse-Viking (they are all in essence the same). Why these Scandinavian flat, linear style patterns? These beasts with tails intertwining interminably and illogically? These creatures broken into geometrical designs? These weird animal heads with uncanny expressions? This sudden plague of dragons and serpents and fearful misshapen monsters?

I look around as I stand in this twilight of the dawn, this pre-Conquest land. Long since the prosperity and supremacy of Northumbria, which had produced the great carvings of Ruthwell and Bewcastle, has waned and died. By now, too, the power of Offa's Mercia, which succeeded it, has passed into the days that are over and done. As the years have gone by, and the eighth century has merged into the ninth, it is the southern kingdom of Wessex which has

* Gardner places them *c.* A.D. 680.

risen to power, and it is the kings of Wessex, and first and foremost the great Alfred, who are fighting a new invader as, four centuries earlier, the Romanized Britons under Arthur had fought the invading Anglo-Saxons, Alfred's forebears. All along the eastern coasts the Danes are raiding, 'spreading terror and devastation wherever they went, plundering and burning and desolating the country . . . they made lamentable havoc in the church of God in Holy-island, by rapine and slaughter'.*   It is Alfred who is checking the advance of the Danes, but he saves only the south and west; north of a line from London to Chester the Danes are settling down in the land and spreading their influences everywhere. As I move nearer to the tenth century I find that Alfred's successors have driven the invaders back and recaptured York, so that for the rest of this century there is comparative prosperity and room for the great monastic revival associated with the name of Dunstan, Archbishop of Canterbury but also a craftsman and worker in metals, who, when the devil, as the story goes, tempted him in the guise of a fair woman, seized him by the nose with his hot tongs, so that the Evil One began to roar and bellow, and leaped twelve miles at one bound away to Tunbridge Wells. But the 'Northmen' return to the attack as the eleventh century opens. By 1017 the old Wessex kings have been supplanted by the Norseman Cnut, and Viking influences are everywhere.

It was in these 'times of the troubles' no doubt that the fragments of wheel-head crosses in the church of St. Andrew in the one-street village of Middleton, a short walk from Pickering in the North Riding of Yorkshire, were carved. In the background, standing up against the east window of the north aisle, was the upper half of a cross mounted on a modern base to give it something of its original height: a queer old Anglo-Danish cross, with a lopsided hammer-head top and a protruding rounded boss in its centre; its vague and rather mazy decoration continued from the

* *The Anglo-Saxon Chronicle.*

wheel-head without a break down the shaft – a sign of its late date. The wheel-heads of all earlier crosses are self-contained units in their decoration. To the left was another cross, one half of its wheel damaged; in a long panel below the rather tight coils of strapwork in that wheel stood a warrior, primitive and naïve, in a pointed helmet, with little, dangling arms and with his legs, although he faced front, turned awkwardly sideways. Around him, regardless of perspective, hung in a vacuum as it were his weapons: sheathed scramasax, a sword with a semi-cylindrical pommel, a disproportionate, tiny round shield with a boss, and a long-handled axe. At the back of the cross, there was all Scandinavian legend in a melancholy-eyed, bilious looking dragon drooping in the midst of interlacing bonds. He was outlined with the double contours which Norse craftsmen loved, the flatness of the pattern he made in his panel caused him to look like a beast chased on some metal belt or torque.

A third specimen, short and dumpy, possessed a perfect wheel-head, and below it, in the same sort of oblong panel, was a hunter with a spear in his right hand and a scramasax in his left, apparently crouching, but looking more as if he were kneeling. His hounds stood below, and a portly beast cavorted at the bottom, all being very clumsily carved. At the back of this cross also, there was another bound dragon, also in double contour lines and making a metalwork kind of pattern, but this one struggled against his bonds, coiling and writhing, and his eye was alight with wrath. He might have been Fenrir's Ulfr, the howling wolf of the deep, Loki's fierce son, whom Thor bound in vain with the strong chain Laeding, and the still harder bondage of Dromi. All these crosses had interlaced coils down their sides, all of them plainly showed Scandinavian influence not only in their dragons, symbols of evil, but in their shallow surface-carving and broad strap and knot-work, utterly different from the rounded scrolls and flowing coils on the Easby Cross, and the human figures were poles apart from the humane graciousness of those at Bewcastle

and Ruthwell. They explained in five minutes the difference
between early and late 'Celtic' crosses, classical-Byzantine
inspired and Viking-influenced; and their crude little
figures with their pointed helmets, round eyes and dangling
arms (there was another such small warrior with his
scramasax on his lap on the window-sill) brought an
atmosphere of heathen Asgard into that little Christian
Yorkshire church.

Having seen something of the so-called Anglian crosses –
a form of sculpture destined to die as these pre-Conquest
centuries died – I turned to other forms of Anglo-Saxon
sculpture. And going back a little – and for the last time
– into the twilight I had been on the point of leaving, in
the newest part of Peterborough Cathedral I came upon the
oldest stone – the Hedda Stone; an eighth-century shrine-
shaped block with a gabled lid decorated with the now
familiar pattern of interlacing strapwork and the Scythian
confronted animals. But below, under an arcade on the
two long sides of the stone, stood the twelve apostles, six at
the front and six at the back, not so much worn away that
their classical ancestry could not be seen. The stone
indeed, lid-interlacings and animal apart, was very much
like one of those Roman sarcophagi one may see in the
aisles of Sant' Apollinare in Classe, or in the museums and
churches of the old Rhône towns and villages of Provence –
Arles and Avignon, Orange and Montmajour.

A hundred and fifty miles or more from Peterborough,
among the South Downs, one meets the Norse beasts of the
interminably twining tails. Opposite the south door of
the village church at Jevington, let into the north wall, is
a slab with a figure in very high relief on it, as stiffly carved
as if it had been a child's wooden Dutch doll; by the
cruciferous nimbus, however, and the long-shafted cross it
holds, it proclaims itself as Christ, triumphing once more
over the beasts. The one at Christ's right foot is an
ordinary beast except for his hind leg, which mingles with
his tail to wind and twist and interlace in a fashion known

as the 'Urnes' style; at our Lord's left side is a more dragon-like creature rearing up, bewildered and lost, in the flat convolutions, coils and inter-twistings of the tail into which its narrow body has dissolved.*

The Jevington Slab

There is another Viking style, the 'Ringerike'. The Guildhall Museum (now housed in the Royal Exchange Building) has an example. Here is the tomb-stone, broken into four pieces, of some long forgotten Viking warrior who perhaps came to England with Cnut, and it represents the Scandinavian theme of the contest of the Lion and the Serpent. The carving is flat and linear, with incised lines, twisted round into coils to represent joints, and the serpent, rearing angrily before the chest of the great lion, is a tight interlace below of lines that bind and entangle his foe's driving legs. The beast's tail is confused with a mass of fiercely curled tendrils which wave behind him in the air; his tongue shoots out from his backward twisted head; his eye is full of fire. This is a powerful, heathen, barbaric work, and when in its original state, that is to say, painted, it must have been more powerful still. Its Danish ancestry is beyond all doubt when one looks upon the Runestone at Jellinge, Jutland.

A reminiscence of this 'Ringerike' style exists in the minster at Southwell. Here, in the north transept, is a blocked door; and its lintel, evidently re-used, for it is far older than the transept, or indeed any part of the existing

---

* T. D. Kendrick places this carving at the beginning of the twelfth century (*Late Saxon and Viking Art*, p. 120), but this late date is not universally accepted.

church, is carved with a crude representation of St. Michael and the dragon.   The archangel, with drilled eyes, a fierce expression, surprised looking wings and garments flaring outwards at the hems, wields his stumpy sword against a

dragon all flat, geometrical pattern, with an incised decoration on his body and his tail twisting and turning in a maze of convolutions till it ends illogically in what look like leafy tendrils. To St. Michael's right more normal looking beasts appear, one with snarling jaws and his tail coiled between his legs and circling over his back; further to the right is David, rending the creature's jaws.

Animal head label-stop (Elkstone church)

The uncanny Viking animal heads appear in many places, but one of the best acts as a label-stop in the tower arch of the partly Saxon church at Deerhurst, a riverside walk from Tewkesbury Abbey.   There it is, looking out upon the church with melancholy, eerie eyes; its jaws snarl, its ears are stylized, although it is in the round it is still scored with lightly incised lines.   Why it looks so pagan and so barbaric it is hard to say, unless it is that it shows so plainly that it was carved by one who still felt in the wolf (for it surely is the head of that animal) the macabre power of the dreadful werewolf itself.

But there are angels as well as beasts in these pre-Conquest days, although the beasts predominate.   There is no Viking influence in the angels – they are Byzantinesque rather, stern and unsmiling.   There is the upper part of a damaged one in a niche of the external wall at Deerhurst, and two more lying with up-kicked heels high up over the narrow but lofty chancel arch of the pure Saxon church at Bradford-on-Avon.   Indeed, it was the discovery of these angels in the seventies of last century which roused suspicions as to the true nature of a building which had long been used as a school-room and a cottage. There is yet another, with an overlarge head, looking back awkwardly at similarly up-kicked heels at Winterborne Steepleton in Dorset; he perhaps is the sternest of them all.

Seeking pre-Conquest sculpture in this dim Anglo-Saxon world I wandered far removed and apart, along the abandoned trackways of antiquity. I could say much of all I saw, but one more carving must suffice, and that is the majestic crucified Christ in the wall of what was once the cloister at Romsey Abbey in Hampshire. I had already seen, inside the abbey, pre-Conquest carvings on capitals and panels, and the sun was moving over to the west when I came out to where the cloisters used to be, a rockery now, with seats among ancient grave-slabs, and saw the Crucifix from afar, with the golden light of the evening sun full upon it. The figure of Christ upon a Cross now flush with the wall was nearly lifesize, and carved in high relief; the arms were extended stiff and straight, the head was not drooping, but triumphantly upraised, and as it was flat on top it originally had probably worn some sort of victor's diadem or crown. There was no sign of suffering in the erect, uncontorted figure, but rather a grandeur and majesty which the unclouded sunlight seemed to accentuate. It was a body, too, plastically modelled with classical feeling; and the sight of the great, carved *Manus Dei* – the hand of God – emerging from the cloud above the halo of the Crucified took my mind back over lands and seas and centuries till I was in front of Byzantine mosaics again. The carving was obviously executed by an Englishman – the type of triangular folds upon the loin-cloth clinging as it were damply to the thighs proved that – but as obviously it was executed under strong Byzantine influence, as if Byzantinism from the eastern parts of the ancient Roman Empire was already filtering through to these far islands even as early as the tenth century. The frontal pose, the lack of human weakness and human reaction to torture, the impassiveness, the elemental majesty of a Being uplifted above all mortal frailty and bearing within Him the remoteness and aloofness of the Eternal – all these Byzantine characteristics were there.   I stood in body among the quiet Hampshire gravestones in the light of the sunset of an English summer evening, but in spirit I was back again in Ravenna where Time stood still in the presence of the Infinite.

12

ALL HEAVEN AND HELL
IN STONE

〰〰〰〰〰〰〰〰〰〰〰〰〰

I step forward fairly now into the twelfth century, and
on the other side of the Norman Conquest find myself
in a changing world. Of course, some pre-Conquest
features linger for a while, for the Normans are 'Northmen'
themselves, of barbaric Viking ancestry, and right into the
twelfth century many Viking features appear on the
churches which they built. What could be more Viking
than the open-mouthed dragon-heads with coiled tongues
standing out against the sky on the western gables of
Kilpeck Church? Or the grotesque, ugly heads with
ringed eyes and gaping, animal jaws of its corbel tables?
Or the enrichments of the jambs of its south door, with
curious, so-called human figures in extraordinary garb
entangled in a maze of twisting stems and writhing dragons?
All these are in red sandstone, but even so the figures seem
made of wire, and the entanglements of the stems and
dragonesque bodies winding around them are reminiscent
of nothing so much as the intricate wood-carvings to be seen
to this day on Norwegian stave churches. Round the arch
of this same south door there are, too, medallions containing
the signs of the zodiac linked by the strangest nightmarish
faces, so that the whole looks like a metalwork chain; and
in the order of the arch below this outer one there is an

example of beakhead ornament – Viking in origin, though it becomes, as the century wears on, a hall-mark of Norman decoration. In this beakhead at Kilpeck – a very rich example – are fearful and hideous monsters, neither all bird nor all beast, nor wholly anything ever created in the natural world, but a composite of frightfulness conceived in the barbarian imagination, with their beaks closed upon the arch's roll-moulding. (When on another occasion I visited Iffley Church near Oxford, I saw the beaks in more ordered array, surely more than half a hundred of them, cruel, eagle beaks biting the roll-mouldings of the arch of the west door.)

Beakhead Ornament

Inside Kilpeck Church there are strange little figures of apostles with big heads and staring eyes and tiny arms, standing on each other's heads to act as shafts of the chancel arch, three on each side. The idea of human figures acting as arch shafts may have been brought to England by pilgrims to Spain who had seen them at the shrine of St. James at Compostela, but the wire-drawn technique of the figures themselves is as Viking-inspired – though now at two or three removes – as the rest of the ornament at Kilpeck.

Whence, too, came the theme of that tympanum over the south door at the peaceful Buckinghamshire village church at Dinton, a bus ride out of Aylesbury? Below, in a horizontal panel immediately above the door, an archaic St. Michael with little, starting wings fought a large-headed dragon which was baring its enormous teeth, but in the lunette above two beasts representing the souls of the righteous were devouring the fruit of the Tree of Life – and what was that Tree of Life but the old heathen 'ash Yggdrasill, the first of trees, the symbol of ever-enduring time, with one foot in the formless elemental abyss, one in the giant land, its branches spreading over the whole world, one reaching up to the unseen'?*   And at Bradbourne church, Derby, there were, round the arch of the door, actually Norse beasts creeping, with those interminably, illogically intertwisted tails, their interlacing spreading behind them to form that 'Urnes' style exemplified at Jevington in Sussex.

Norse influences, however, were now meeting others; this process might be seen on the carved capitals of columns. It was often entertaining, sometimes amusing, always instructive to keep a watchful eye upon column capitals. Some early ones – they were carved within the decade following the Norman Conquest – met my gaze in the hoary chapel of Durham Castle, so redolent of the Norman past.   The Norse influence here was mingled with classical ideas filtered through Norman funnels.   There was for instance, a capital with volutes quite in the classical manner, but between them appeared a cat-mask above a curled leaf, distinctly unclassical, but very Norman.   Another had two confronted animals with their heads acting as the angle volutes – a northern, not a Mediterranean motif, like their flat, unmodelled bodies, decorated (if that is the word) with a pattern of diagonal incised lines; they stood upon a background diapered with giant stars.   There was also a snake coiling on a similar diapered background, and upon this capital definite curling 'Ionic' volutes.   On another capital the subject spread over two faces.   On one was a stag and a nimbed figure who may have been St. Eustace, and on the other the horse which the saint was leading by the bridle.   Figures of both man and beast were carved in a clumsy, primitive style.   Equally primitive was the human mask of what one might call the 'pancake type' on the diapered background of yet another capital; the 'Ionic' volutes of classical inspiration still appeared, but at the neck of this capital was a decoration here first seen, later to become very popular in Norman work – the cable pattern, looking like a twisted rope.   And finally, in this

* Mallet: *Northern Antiquities.*

L

chapel at Durham, four figures of supporters were placed at the angles of a capital, their arms upraised as if they were straining to uphold the weight of the chapel vaulting. What were these but reminiscences of the classical giant Atlas, on the mountain peak beyond the Garden of the Hesperides, kneeling as he held the heavens and the earth apart? Such Caryatids are found in France; now that England, through the Norman Conquest, had become a part of the continent, French influences, starting as a rivulet, were destined to become a flood and eventually almost a deluge.

In France also, at Tournus, there are strange, square capitals, one of them carved with a primitive human mask; and in the eleventh-century crypt of Gloucester Cathedral there is just such a squarish capital with rough volutes and between these a human mask even more primitive than the French one. It has arched eyebrows and staring eyes, and – a most unusual feature – a wide, military moustache with twisted ends. This capital is a godsend to jocular guides driving their flocks round the crypt chapels.

But the most accomplished series of capitals of these early years is in the twelfth-century crypt of Canterbury Cathedral. Here a demon figure with hideous ears sits astride two confronted monsters, his hands in their ravening jaws, their legs entangled in meshes of what look like tautly coiled and beaded metal-work (Viking influence again); here a winged creature in a maze of metallic stems plays a triangular harp while another beast, perhaps a dog, standing on its hind legs, 'governs the ventages' of a recorder-like instrument with his claws; here a lion with a somewhat human face and benign expression belying the cruelty of his tusks raises one of his front paws in an heraldic gesture while his tail coils round his hind leg and circles over his back to end in a leaf and berries. Storm and stress rage on another capital, where on one face a two-headed creature with a female body rides a monster which is part bird, part fish, part quadruped spreading a many branched tail, and on another a winged dragon with terrific force spears a running hound – a masterpiece of power and dynamic movement, perhaps the best capital of all. There is, too, a bird trampling forcefully upon a twining serpent which he holds by the throat in his eagle beak, as if ready to devour it – this subject so pleased the carver, apparently, that he repeated it. And the two *jongleurs* must not be forgotten – the conjurors, contortionists and gleemen of the Middle Ages – doing their music-hall turn upon yet another capital, one stretching up his arms to hold another above his head, while the upper circus artist does a juggling act with a bowl and a large, fat fish; nor the animal musicians performing in their turn – a goat playing a large flute as he straddles a mild little dragon-tailed creature who appears to be begging him to desist, while a hoofed quadruped with the curling horns of a ram and wings folded behind him plays a pear-shaped rebec in a very slovenly manner with a badly held, bent bow.

But now, on a capital in the north aisle of Romsey Abbey (where I had seen the pre-Conquest Crucifix), there appeared a different type of capital carving altogether. Here sat a bilious and unhappy looking owl unfolding his wings as if he were about to take to flight – as he easily could have done, for, significantly, no coils or meshes of foliage tendrils imprisoned him. He stood free at last, a decoration in his own right, almost in the round. Then, in the British Museum, I came upon another capital similarly three-dimensional. This one was from the sad ruins of Lewes Priory. Gone were the linear designs, the flat, abstract patterns of light and shade, the last of the Viking influences; for this carving, representing two apostles pulling in their net with the miraculous draught of fishes, was deeply undercut, in such high relief it was again almost in the round. The hair of the fishermen was stylized and striated and wig-like, their net resembled a heavy handled basket; the carving had the effect of massiveness because a large mass was concentrated into a small architectural space, everything being subordinated to the outline of the architectural unit. In short, I had now reached mid-twelfth century, and that great period of sculptural art of the Middle Ages – the Romanesque.

I had met Romanesque before, in the solemn, hieratic, Byzantine-inspired illuminated manuscripts, in the austere, staring, other-worldly wall-paintings. But in sculpture I found Romanesque art at its greatest, its most architectural, its most monumental. To feel the full power of its greatness, however, I had to go to France, where the vast tympana over the processional west doors of cathedrals, and the statuary of their portals, surpassed even the best that I could find in England.

To Vézelay, then, to St. Trôphime at Arles, to St. Gilles du Gard, Toulouse by the Pyrenees, Moissac, Souillac, Conques, built in, or shortly before, the days of the Wandering Scholars, those *Scholastici*, 'schoolmen', who tried to give rational form to their Christian beliefs, and taught in the universities of Paris and Chartres a theosophical philosophy. The days when Abelard lived, poet, philosopher, theologian and scholar, the 'heretic hounded by the councils',* author of the controversial *Sic et Non*, and tragic lover of Heloïse. He came to the Abbey of Cluny 'and by so coming enriched us with a wealth beyond all gold', as Peter the Venerable said after Abelard had died there, and Philippe of Hervengt announced that Lucifer, the star that brings the morning, had set. The days, too, of Abelard's great opponent, St. Bernard, and of Peter the Lombard, Bishop of Paris; the age when the Church could excommunicate kings. That age had begun fifty years before, when, giving an exhibition to the world of the relative importance of the spiritual and temporal powers, the Church had kept Henry IV of Germany waiting in penitence for three successive days, barefoot in the snow in the outer courtyard of the castle at Canossa among the Apennines, and it was still continuing 100 years later, when the

* Helen Waddell: *The Wandering Scholars.*

Emperor Frederick Barbarossa had to admit defeat at the hands of the Pope's Lombard League and kneel for forgiveness in the porch of St. Mark's at Venice before Alexander III.   Here, in these days, among the Romanesque sculptures of mediaeval France, I am still deep in the times when, although there were intellects like Abelard's which pierced as a sword, most men walked hand in hand with blind faith and superstition, could believe miracles and see visions both of heaven and hell, and when the fiends who 1,000 years before had been the pagan gods were still realities to them.   This was the age when Guibert de Nogent, Abbot of Nogent-sous-Coucy, could tell how in his youth the devil brought the shapes of dead men before his sleeping eyes, and how once in the dead of night there rose a cry of many voices, and looking behind him he saw in the vast and shadowy darkness a devil in bodily form standing by him.   He tells us too of a novice who had to hold with his teeth the monastic habit he had put on, to prevent a company of demons from tearing it from his body. The monk Gauchelin tells of an army of fiendish ghosts he once saw fleeing through the night; one in the form of a knight carrying a black banner touched him on the cheek and left a burn from his finger tips, hot with hellfire.   Others were scourged in their sleep by the minions of Satan, and when they awoke, found that their bodies bore in reality the wounds of these scourgings.   All the world, but especially the monastery, was an embattled camp against the onslaughts of the legions of the Evil One.   The powers of darkness and the passions of the human soul became incarnate in monsters and fiends; and terrified monks dreaming their frightful nightmares in the twelfth century represented him who had once been that Satan of whom it was said, 'How art thou fallen from heaven, O, Lucifer, Son of the Morning!' in a foul and terrifying guise in which he had never appeared before and in later centuries was not to appear again.

Such are the ghastly visions of Evil which appear on some

of the twelfth-century capitals of the church of the Madeleine at Vézelay. These carved forms are not comic – it was not till the fourteenth century (largely through the influence of the Mystery Plays) that the devil became a figure of fun. They are as horrifying to the rational eyes of the twentieth century as the visions which provoked them were to dreaming twelfth-century saints and sinners. As I look upon them my blood runs cold. I feel an uncanny sensation of being in the presence of gross, unmitigated Evil. Such power has Romanesque art to rouse the spirit of man even across eight centuries.

Here is the death of the wicked rich man, lying upon his bed, a compressed, Romanesque figure with a disproportionately large head to suit the shape of the capital; his quailing soul is being torn from his mouth with pincers by a demon with frightful jaws and glaring eyes. Another, trampling upon the dying man, with gaping mouth and talon teeth, his hair, like his companion's, erect and bristling as in the heat from an oven, lays a vice-like grip upon the victim's arm. On another capital is a man tortured by demoniac winged creatures, scrawny and vile-jawed, more foul than ever the eyes of nightmare saw; his hair is being dragged from his head, his arms pulled from their sockets, his body is caught in a vice from which all his writhing will not free him. Two men on the lateral faces of the capital look on in justifiable affright. On another capital a similar devil with bristling hair leaps out of the mouth of the Golden Calf, elsewhere a fiend seizes the voluptuous, naked body of Luxury.

But evil does not always triumph. On one capital an angel has caught a demon, with the same kind of scrawny thighs, bristling hair and huge mouth, and is twisting his arms behind his back. On another, St. Benoit, his pastoral staff in his huge hand, the folds of his garments mere incisions in the stone, his disproportionate head crowned with striated hair like a wig, blesses a tree which the heathen are pulling and hacking so that it may fall on him, and all their efforts are unavailing against his goodness. On yet another St. Peter and St. Paul, small, stumpy figures covered with those incised lines like the pen-strokes of an illuminator of manuscripts, stand on either side of a bound figure and pray with uplifted hands for the conversion of the world.

The capital was an essential part of a Romanesque column, and there are hundreds of them, all carved, in these French churches. All manner of subjects appear. Noah constructs his ark, apparently out of wickerwork; Eve among twining foliage tempts Adam with an enormous apple. There are legends of the saints and signs of the zodiac. Dives feasts at a crowded table while on one of the lateral faces of the same capital the dogs lick Lazarus' sores; Samson, his cloak flying out stiffly behind him, seated astride the lion, rends its jaws with his bare hands. Even classical tales appear, Ganymede, for example, carried off upside down in the beak of Jupiter's eagle. And there are combats upon combats; for all these represent Mankind's everlasting struggle against the powers of evil, and are symbolic:

> Gird your heavenly armour on,
> Wear it ever night and day,
> Ambushed lies the Evil One,

they cry; and so mailed knights fight mailed knights, men fight ravening beasts, they also fight personifications of the Seven Deadly Sins and all the Vices. Here among the capitals is an everlasting Psychomachia, a Battle of the Soul against all that would lead it to hell.

In Romanesque art there was a passion for symbolism. According to Romanesque ideas, everything that exists in the world is an image of the divine power, and is a symbol of the presence of God. Every deed that is done in the Old Testament prefigures some event of the New. The sacrifice of Isaac is a symbol of Christ's sacrifice upon the Cross; Elijah's flight from his own country and his sheltering with a Gentile of Zarephath symbolizes Jesus, rejected by the Jews and accepted by the Gentiles; Joseph sold for twenty pieces of silver to the Ishmaelites prefigures the selling of Christ for thirty pieces by Judas. And so the statues of the prophets and apostles are placed by the pillars of the portico which leads into the church, sometimes even acting as atlantids, supporting the lintels, because they through the ages have supported the Church, and it is through them that we are enabled to enter the sanctuary. Therefore on one side of the great inner portal at Vézelay, St. Peter and St. Paul stand – great, monumental, architectural figures, with massive proportions, garments clinging to their thighs then leaping out as in a wind-blown swirl at the edges, feet almost dancing in a manner typical of French Romanesque. Other apostles are on the other side, while the lintel of the tympanum above rests on a great mullion with the figure of John the Baptist bearing the Lamb – because by Baptism alone can the Church be entered. All the figures are a harmony of incised lines flowing with dynamic perpetual motion which vitalizes their essential massive inertness and lightens the dead weight of the manifest stone – for in Romanesque carving there is no soft flesh. All is hard stone, with skin stretched tightly, or garments as tight as skin, over elongated, austerely gaunt frames. Here is no realism. These are not men who once walked the earth and lived as we do; they are compelling, overwhelming personifications of spiritual force, impersonal, demonstrating above all else the power of God, giving visible human shape to the Divine, once more symbolizing in the finite the measureless Eternal.

But what can one say now of the mighty carved tympana of those French churches – the 'pilgrimage churches', as they are sometimes called, because they stood on one of the four routes to the far-famed shrine of Santiago da Compostella in north-western Spain – Vézelay, Conques and Moissac, Saint-Gilles du Gard and Saint Sernin at Toulouse? As they were placed above the processional entry to the church they obviously called for some exalted, triumphal theme.   So at Vézelay I saw in the midst of the tympanum a huge Christ seated in glory in a mandorla, a cross-nimbus behind His head, the swirling lines of His garments twisted into whirling circles upon His knees and on His thighs.   He stretches His arms out wide as if to enfold the whole world, and from His fingers come streams of Grace (or perhaps blood) upon the heads of His disciples seated below.   He is sending them forth to evangelize the savage world not yet touched by Grace; and around this central scene, framed by a semi-circle of medallions where the signs of the zodiac mingle with the labours of the months, this grace-less world appears, carved in panels. Here the people of pagan lands are discussing the truths which have been preached to them by the disciples: some are displaying palsied limbs which have received new power, bodies which have been cleansed of leprosy, the effects of miracles which have converted them.   On the lintel are strange races of the earth: the panotii, who can fold their ears about their heads; the dog-headed Cynocephalae, inhabitants of the Cimmerian land, beings who await in darkness the coming of the light; the pigmies who are so small they have to climb ladders to get on to their horses' backs (here they may be seen doing it); and pagans carrying bows and arrows and driving cattle to sacrifice to their pagan gods.   On all of them the divine light of revelation is about to fall as they make their way towards two tall figures in the centre: St. Peter and St. Paul, no doubt, symbols of the Church and of Rome.

At Vézelay Christ is the Redeemer of the World; at St. Foy at Conques He is seated in the tympanum as Judge and Saviour, in a cloudy mandorla with angels disposed around Him; a great Cross rises behind His aureole, symbol of the sacrifice He made that erring men might live.   The rest of the tympanum shows that scene which is often repeated later: the Elect and the Damned.   On Christ's right the blessed approach, led by the Virgin Mary and Apostles;

angels with scrolls fly above them. On the left of Christ
the angels hold a book, a censer, a sword and a lance;
beyond them are the Damned amid tortures indescribable.
Two gable-shaped lintels appear below. Under one of
these is Abraham, holding in his bosom the souls of the
righteous; under the other is Hell. It is significant (everything is significant in a Romanesque carving) that Christ's
right arm, on which side are the Elect, is raised to heaven,
whereas His left, the side of the Damned, points down to the
frightful fanged monster-mouth which opens upon the
maw of hell.

In the tympanum at Moissac is a representation in stone
of the Apocalyptic scene pictured in the 'Beatus' manuscript of the monk of that name, which he wrote in the
eighth century in the monastery of Liebana, in northern
Spain. In the centre appears an exceedingly elongated,
Byzantinesque Christ, surrounded by angels and the
symbols of the four Evangelists. In three registers on either
side of Him and below, the twenty-four elders of the Book
of Revelation, with cups and vials in their hands, turn their
heads up to gaze upon Him where He sits, a crowned and
kingly figure, upon the throne of His glory. Twelve of these
occupy the long lintel that separates the tympanum above
from the portal below. Underneath them there is a purely
classical style lintel, with rosette ornament – a reminder
that this part of France, which in the twelfth century must
even yet have been full of the ruined works of the Romans,
still copied, if it did not actually incorporate, Roman
motifs, designs and architectural units.

And indeed, Saint Gilles du Gard has a façade which
seems to have been deliberately designed on the pattern of
a Roman triumphal arch, with three portals – a central
large one and two smaller – free-standing half-columns in
front of the portal (without architectural function) and full
columns on each side, adorned with classical Corinthian
capitals, and even with classical fluting on one or two of
them. A frieze runs right along the façade, carved from

end to end with small figures crowded together, strongly reminiscent of Roman sarcophagi, or Roman carvings on Trajan's column or on the triumphal arches.   There are many scenes; the striated lines on garments, however, and the linear flatness of all the figures, proclaiming that they belong to the twelfth century, not to the second, even if their subject matter did not do so; for here are the Entry into Jerusalem, the Kiss of Judas and the Flagellation.

At Saint Gilles Christ in Glory with the evangelical symbols occupies the central portal, the Virgin and Child with the Magi and Shepherds one of the smaller ones, and a Crucifixion the other.   But even more interesting are the entirely non-classical, Romanesque statues of apostles and saints between the portals.   Grave and dignified they were, monumental and mighty, but as I looked upon them I seemed to see the grand, impersonal, transcendental Romanesque withdrawn just one step into enclosing shadows.   There was a roundness not of the Romanesque about these figures; a slight droop of relaxation, away from the austere Romanesque tautness.   The folds of their garments were rounder, their faces more human, their eyes gentler; and I was not surprised to hear that Saint Gilles is late Romanesque, already in some details foreshadowing the Gothic of the thirteenth century.

At St. Trophîme at Arles, the old Roman Arelate on the banks of the mistral-lashed Rhône, everything is on a very small scale.   One of the three portals of Saint Gilles, in fact, serves as an exemplar for the whole front of Arles. Here the tympanum is relatively unimportant: Christ sits enthroned there amid the evangelical beasts, with serried ranks of winged angels in the archivolt over Him, and immediately above His head two angels are sounding the Last Trump.   The Apostles sit in the lintel at His feet, the Blessed walk in procession to Abraham's bosom in the frieze below on His right, the Damned on His left into the flames of hell, both cortèges being depicted in somewhat monotonously repetitive lines.   In the niches between the rather classical-style columns (Saint Gilles again) stand rigid, stolid saints. The best Romanesque carvings at Arles, to my mind, are the lively pillar carvings of the cloister, and the equally vivid carving of the capitals of the double columns there, depicting such scenes as the Entry into Jerusalem, the Nativity, the Resurrection and the Annunciation.

So on to where, between Rhône and Pyrenees, in old Languedoc, stands Saint Sernin in Toulouse, where there is a tympanum above a side door carved aboout 1100, so harking back to earliest Romanesque. This, too, is a small affair, and plainer, as befits its earlier date, than the others I have seen. Plain mouldings in the arch surround it – there is none of the elaboration of Vézelay here – and a small, plain lintel bearing stumpy figures spaced out in linear distinctness in one plane, stands over the door below; the only other carvings are in the capitals of the nook-shafts and two figures of apostles in the spandrels. This tympanum represents Christ's Ascension. All the figures again stand in one plane, but there is a roundness about them as if memories of antique art still lingered on in this Pyrenean part of France where Roman influence had once been so strong.

But my time in France is growing short: I can see only one more Romanesque tympanum out of the many there are still to be seen at Beaulieu-sur-Dordogne, Saint Nicholas de Civray, La Charité-sur-Loire, Bellegarde-du-Loiret, Charlieu, Saint Bénigne de Dijon; this last one is at the cathedral of Saint Lazare at Autun. Here is a flat, elongated, and altogether remote Christ (His head is missing, only the cross-nimbus remaining) sitting in Judgement in a mandorla upheld on the shoulders of straining angels. All the rest of the available space is crowded with the serried ranks of the figures of the Blest and the Damned, with St. Michael weighing souls while a foul fiend tries to falsify the balances, and hell-mouth swallows its victims behind. Below in the lintel a procession of figures is no doubt that of souls risen from their graves and awaiting judgement. All the figures in the tympanum itself are exaggeratedly elongated and emaciated; all show the Romanesque pattern of incised lines across the drapery of the legs, and in some instances the swirl into a whizzing coil at the hip-joint. The devils have the scrawny thighs and huge mouths and nightmarish aspect that makes the blood run cold among the capitals of Vézelay.

I cannot, however, leave France without looking again at those strange Romanesque figures of Souillac, Moissac and Beaulieu-sur-Dordogne: the twisted figure at Souillac of the prophet Isaiah, from the portal of the former abbey church, but now set in the rear wall of the baroque façade of the present one is a mighty work, as forceful as if it had been galvanized, as unrealistic as an ideal conception, as grandly arresting as only Romanesque can be. His clothes are stretched tightly on his contorted form, his left leg is extended over his right, his whole body is swung round at the waist in the manner of some of the figures of English pre-Conquest manuscript drawings; his beard is parted into what Chaucer would have called 'colpoons' of stringy hair, his left hand clutches the remnants of the original wall. St. Peter in the angle of the portal at Moissac has a similar contorted stance as he tramples on a vanquished monster; his head is thrust forward in a forceful gesture, his large hands are back-spread, palms outward; there are almost horizontal incisions in the stone about his left leg representing creases in the drapery, and sharp, straight lines upon his stony cloak. One is never allowed to forget the stone, the massy stone, out of which Romanesque figures are carved. At Beaulieu-sur-Dordogne an elongated figure of a prophet holds up the lintel like an atlantid; and imprisoned on one of the lateral faces of this figure-mullion is an extremely attenuated and compressed man with his head bent forward, and his hand gripping one thigh as if he were straining to push himself out of the compression of the stonework encasing him. Here is Romanesque architectural style carried to an uncomfortable and haunting extreme, for the man, if it were not for the sense of straining effort which he gives, would look like a corpse squeezed into a coffin too narrow for him. I find this statue more than a little macabre.

Regretfully, then, I leave France and return to England, and with France fresh in my memory go first to Kent, to the west door of Rochester Cathedral, and see reproduced there a carved tympanum which brings back a rush of French impressions. Here is Christ again seated in a mandorla supported by elongated angels and surrounded by the evangelical beasts just as He appears in France, and below Him there is a lintel with little stumpy figures of apostles. Here, too, are the Romanesque incised horizontal lines across the drapery of the legs, but the fact that both Christ and the beasts are almost in the round proves this to be later Romanesque. Moreover, the elongated, straight contours of the frenchified column figures on either side of the door – representing, one supposes, Solomon and the Queen of Sheba – bring to mind the figures at Chartres (which I consider step over the borderline into Gothic) – except for the shallow incised lines which do duty for folds in the draperies and draw those royalties back into the twelfth century.

About the 'Prior's Door' – the entrance into the destroyed west walk of the cloister at Ely Cathedral – there can, however, be no doubt. It is pure Romanesque to the last line. The immense and exaggerated Christ in Glory with His book upheld on His lap, seated with His knees wide apart, His feet brought close together, with V-shaped incised lines down His long legs, His mandorla upheld by the twisted, extended forms of angels starting away from what they are supporting, one arm of each grotesquely enlarged and bent back over their heads to touch the mandorla, all filling the tympanum with a linear pattern of flowing line and sharp light and shade – these are all

Romanesque characteristics. Romanesque, too, are the richly decorated doorway and tympanum of the village church at Barfreston, not very far from Dover; although the Christ in Glory here is of moderate size and less austere aspect the regular pattern of lines covers his garments in the approved Romanesque manner as He holds up His right hand in blessing and with His left supports the indispensable book on His knee. Twining foliage around Him makes medallions for grotesque beasts and the heads of two royal persons and angels; more foliage tendrils in the arch, making more medallions, hold secular subjects: animals playing musical instruments and little men brandishing swords or engaged in other secular pursuits; and on the capitals are knights on obvious shire-horses gallantly tilting. The dead weight of Romanesque monasticism sat but lightly upon the hand of the carver of the Barfreston doorway.

But in pursuing Romanesque one cannot for long be out of the stern company of the eternal verities. One cannot stir more than a step out of this grey, purposeful, grim and earnest world, obsessed by thoughts and visions of sin and temptation, death and judgement, the eternal combat of the soul of man with the embattled powers of Evil. The stone frieze on the west front of Lincoln Cathedral brings me back to the consideration of God's works and purposes, as told in the Hebrew scriptures, and of this life as being nothing but a preparation for the next, whether that be heaven or hell. To the right of the main west doors there are scenes from Genesis. Here are Adam and Eve – stiff, primitive figures, with short arms and large heads – expelled from the Garden of Eden by a stern-faced angel who pushes Adam by the arm to make plain his commands; the father of us all looks round as who would say, 'Who do you think you are, pushing me?' (It is usually Eve who wears the expression of truculent disdain.) Cain and Abel till the fields; God speaks to Noah, and Noah, hammer over shoulder, builds his boat-like ark – its clinker-built prow may be seen behind him and the young helper to whom he is giving his orders.   Then suddenly Daniel appears (in what is plainly a misplaced panel) his garments being carefully patterned with parallel incised lines, sitting with a self-satisfied expression in the midst of a pride of apparently mild-mannered lions.   Then we are carried back to the Flood, and the prayer in the Ark from five big-headed, naïve figures crowded into a most unseaworthy-looking vessel; after that, in a well-designed pattern of symmetrical heads and parallel folds of garments eight people leave the Ark and God meets Noah again: 'And God said, "I do set my bow in the cloud, and it shall be for a token of a covenant between me and the earth." '*

On the left of the door are Last Judgement scenes.   In a maze of coiling, writhing forms which strongly cradle and contrast light and shade there are devils again, as in France, torturing the Damned: foul creatures tearing at the adulterers, snakes biting the wrists and coiling round the legs of a miser borne down by the weight of the money-bag round his neck, and two fiends with animal heads laying frightful hands upon him.   Near by, Christ stands before the gaping jaws of Limbo; and to offset the lurid scenes in hell is a tranquil, ordered procession of the Blessed, in relief as slight as that of the Panathenaic frieze of the Parthenon, of part of which it reminded me in the fine lines of the idealized draperies, in its calmness, its atmosphere of shadowy silence.   In contrast again there was Dives crowded between two others feasting at a table in life, while in death his soul tumbled headlong into hell-mouth; a grinning devil prodded the souls there as if he were stirring in a cauldron some macabre and hellish brew.   But angels with beautifully conceived wings took the soul of the prostrate Lazarus and bore it to Abraham's bosom – there sits Abraham up aloft, a tall figure holding the souls of the righteous in the folds of his enveloping robe.

Different parts of this frieze are in quite different styles,

* Genesis ix. 13.

and it is plain that several carvers worked on it in those years
of the second half of the twelfth century; but all have the
massive strength, the geometric, angular, linear pattern,
the grim forcefulness and the elevated didactic purpose of
a monastic world which saw nothing in this life save an
unremitting struggle against the snares of hell.

Two ancient but well preserved slabs are now incorpor-
ated in the wall of the south choir aisle at Chichester
Cathedral.* Here, carved in relief, is Christ visiting the
sisters of the dead Lazarus, and raising their brother from
the dead.   In agonized supplication the sisters of Lazarus
appear under the arcaded turrets of the gateway of Bethany,
which has been flung wide behind them as they have rushed
forward and raised their hands while Mary cried, 'Lord, if
Thou hadst been here, my brother had not died';† now,
with her sister behind her, she kneels before the approaching
Christ, His divinity manifest in His towering stature,
greater than that of any round about.   He looks out beyond
them as One contemplating the sorrows of the whole
world, and His heart is filled with divine pity; and as He
says, 'Where have ye laid him?' His disciples behind Him
gaze with solemn, grief-stricken intensity at the scene
before them.   In the second panel Christ has cried 'with
a loud voice, Lazarus, come forth', and the four-days dead
man is rising from the tomb.   The stature of Christ is
greater than ever, and the carver, no doubt to give vitality
to the facial expressions of the participators in the scene,
has adopted a curious but effective mannerism: the eyebrows rise steeply to a furrow above the nose, the eyes
complete what is almost a triangle beneath the brows, and
the corners of the mouth droop down, with a marked ridge
from nostril to lips.   This gives to each face, with the
hollows of the deeply drilled eyes, an impression of mingled
grief, astonishment and awful consternation as the dead

* Some authorities deny that these are Romanesque.   Gardner places
them in the pre-Conquest period.   Their date is still disputed.
   † John xi. 32.

M

man glides up from the grave and the grave-clothes fall from him, and Martha and Mary clutch their cheeks in frenzied horror. Not even in Byzantine mosaics had the raising of Lazarus ever been so dramatically conceived. Only the little, coarse-featured gravediggers, levering up the tombstone, are of ordinary clay; everyone else is caught up and sublimated by the near presence of that awful and eternal majesty which can cross even the river of death and say, 'I am the Resurrection and the Life; he that believeth in me, though he were dead, yet shall he live.'

Romanesque head with 'striated' hair (from the Chichester Reliefs)

Such great themes did Romanesque art set itself to picture – in stone, as it had done upon painted walls and in illuminated manuscripts.

There are many other Romanesque carvings, large and small; but I will sum up Romanesque scuplture by describing two lunettes which I consider the most typically and impressively Romanesque of all. These are inside the porch of Malmesbury Abbey. Six apostles sit under a semi-circular arch on each side and an angel flies horizontally above each group; they look towards Christ, who appears in a comparatively unimpressive tympanum over the south door. Everything that is Romanesque is in these two lunettes: the massive monumentality of the large limbs, the stiff, mannered gestures of the great, back-flung hands, the angular postures of the heads, the widely spaced knees, the harmonious pattern of parallel incised lines on the garments, resolving into circles at the knees and shoulders and elbows, the double contour lines, the large and massive bare feet; although the great figures are virtually in the round, and although in their roundness they make a contrasting pattern of light and shade, they still give the impression of something linear, something drawn, as an illuminator might have drawn it.   Both groups are equally powerful, equally impressive; sitting above the arcades of the porch they are like ageless shapes formed in the morning of Time out of the primeval mountain-tops,

> Like Druids of old, with voices sad and prophetic,
> Like harpers hoar with beards that rest on their bosoms.*

Is it not their great glory — was it not, indeed, the purpose of their carver — that they could not be portraits of any men who ever trod this earth, but in their unrealistic greater-than-manness should symbolize the universality and timelessness of the Apostles of Christ?

So, after Malmesbury, I step forward out of this great, brooding, Romanesque world, where strict realism plays little part, where the rhythmic flow of sinuous lines across and around forms larger than life suggests the slow, deep harmonies of a sea ceaselessly surging on granite rocks; where the super-worldly majesty of carved figures is like high mountain ranges lifting their eternal snows into the clouds of heaven. Once more, then, the impersonal greatness of the Romanesque falls behind me; out of the grey twelfth century I go onward into the golden world of the thirteenth — the first century of Gothic.

* Longfellow: *Evangeline*.

13

FRETTED CANOPIES AND
SYMPHONIES IN STONE

~~~~~~~~~~~~~~~~~~~~~~~~~~~~

T HERE are some who would place the sculptures of
Chartres Cathedral amongst Romanesque art. But
even the earliest of them – those on the west front,
which date from the middle of the twelfth century, and are
therefore strictly, in point of date, Romanesque – seem to
me to have made that one step forward which brings them
out of the Romanesque age and into Early Gothic. They
are still architectural, still elongated, the earliest still show
the linear pattern of parallel incised lines swirling into
circles at knee and elbow joints; still angels tend to lunge
forward with a far extended back leg, or hold cloudy
mandorlas, or portions thereof, with contorted forms and
heads turned away from what they are doing; still Christ
sits enthroned among the four beasts, and the apostles in
the lintel below awkwardly crane their necks to look up at
Him; still in the arch-mouldings around Him are the signs
of the zodiac and the labours of the months, as at Vézelay;
still the dead rise pell-mell from their graves, devils haul
away the souls of sinners and the souls of the righteous sit
in Abraham's bosom. But there is a difference. The
weight has gone out of the stone. Even the earliest statues,
those of Old Testament characters acting as columns for
the Portail Royal, though they bear all these marks of the

Romanesque, are softer and lighter.   Their garments cling
to them as if they were made of fine wool, not stone; some
of them wear a half-smile; they are beginning to descend
to sunlit human earth from the cold grey craggy mountain-
tops, whereon, austere and remote, the
giants of the Romanesque age lived.
Christ, who sits aloft in the mandorla,
wears a robe scored with the narrowest
of parallel or near parallel lines, holds
the Romanesque book on His knee,
raises a Romanesque hand in a Romanesque blessing; but His hair waves softly,
His expression, though unsmiling, is far
from forbidding – it is the face of One
who judges, but who judges with compassion for the frailties of the judged.
Nevertheless, realism is still far off.   The
line of figures representing the ancestors
of Christ on the columns of the Portait
Royal arc as columnar as figures can be,

Christ in a
Mandorla

exaggeratedly elongated, and straight and narrow as pillars.
Yet there is something most attractive about their straight
unnaturalness; or is it the rhythmic harmony of those finely
scored parallel lines which is so satisfying?

But when one comes to the later portals on the north and
south, then one stands in the radiance of the full glory of the
thirteenth century.   Could anything in the sculpture of
any age be lovelier than that line of Apostles in the portal;
and has not humanity returned to stone in the statues of
St. Martin, St. Jerome and St. Gregory the Great (with
the dove on his shoulder) in the portal of the Confessors?
Gone now are the sharp, incised lines.   Robes fall in soft,
natural, clinging folds.   Gone are the exaggerated gestures,
the massive limbs, the Byzantinesque elongated forms; gone,
above all, are the lofty, aloof, noble but awesome expressions.   These apostles and martyrs and confessors are
kindly saints, for whose aid one might well supplicate.

They look upon the world with sad pity rather than juridicial condemnation. They gently hold the emblems of their several martyrdoms – they too have suffered, and can feel for our suffering, and though they tread their persecutors underfoot it is without ferocity or exultation; they represent only righteousness predominant over evil. Their heads have a slight inclination which suggests meditative tenderness; the best in this respect is John the Baptist, who carries the Lamb of God in his left hand; though Simeon on his right, with the tiny, doll-like form of the Child Jesus in his arms is an appealing figure too. And what of the beautiful head of the compassionate Christ on the *trumeau* of the south portal?

There is nothing like the Chartres statues in the whole world of mediaeval art. Their graciousness, their moving tenderness, their tranquil loveliness, their perfect harmoniousness, do more than please the senses. They stir the spirit with a passionate desire to worship – and so, no doubt, fulfil the purpose of their creation.

We have in England nothing so wonderful as Chartres; but we are not without our smaller thirteenth-century glories. I had started my English Romanesque journey among column-capitals: I did the same as I went wayfaring amongst Early Gothic in England. At once I found that even these were lighter, more delicate, less oppressive. Instead of the inert, dead weight of the Romanesque patterns there was now the airy beauty of stiff-leaved foliage. At Deerhurst, at West Walton, at Lincoln Cathedral, at Whitchurch Canonicorum, at scores of places it appears, but best of all at Wells Cathedral, where there is some of the earliest work. Demoniac nightmares no longer haunted the craftsmen of Wells. Sometimes comparatively well-mannered beasts trampled the foliage; more often it enshrined little figures, or heads, or small genre scenes, as of the countrywoman (or is it a man?) pulling a thorn out of her foot, a little cobbler at the 'trivial round, the common task', the poor little fellow with the toothache who has, perhaps, come to seek relief from William Bitton, whose shrine is near by, and the intriguing series (on four capitals) of the robbers in the orchard. 'Take care – someone is watching!' the round-faced malefactors seem to be hissing in the first. 'Up torch and sticks – thieves in the orchard!' cries the yeoman-owner in the second. 'Take that – and hand me back my fruit!' is the theme of the third, as the owner brings down his cudgel upon the head of the wry-faced robber, while the series is concluded with a 'Caught this time – the Foul Fiend take thee!' as the farmer catches the thief by the ear and prods him with a pitchfork on the fourth. Very different this from the monsters and horrors of hell at Vézelay!

At Lincoln Cathedral there are not only rich foliage capitals but long, hanging tendrils of leafage forming cone-like corbels; at the foot of one of them is the famous 'Lincoln Imp'. The story goes that when the cathedral was being built the Devil and the Wind came together to prevent the building; the Devil went inside to see what he could do and was turned to stone as he climbed the walls. There he still sits, a gruff, hairy little dwarf, with one leg crossed over the other, while the Wind wails and howls outside as he waits for his companion. Did *this* devil make my blood run cold? Did *he* fill me with a sense of the brooding presence of monstrous evil? Would he be called the 'Lincoln *Imp*' if he did? No. The oppression of nightmare has folded its pennons and winged its way from the earth; the frightful demons of Vézelay have become merely spiteful and malicious sprites about whom picturesque legends may be told, not fiends of hell from whom we avert our eyes in horror, whose names we dare not breathe lest we conjure up the real presence of Evil by so doing.

In the Chapter House of Southwell Minster there is an unsurpassed array of very late thirteenth-century foliage capitals. They are extraordinary because they are crisply carved, extremely deeply undercut, and so naturalistic that the species of every one may be identified, and this is very rare in the thirteenth century, which carved foliage stiffly and conventionally. There, in the Chapter House, is a facet of the English countryside in stone: buttercup leaves, maple leaves, oak, hawthorn, mulberry and vine leaves; the leaves of the ivy, the rose and bryony; and perhaps the most attractive of all, hop leaves and with the leaves the hop's highly decorative flower. On a few of these capitals figures appear: the hounds chase a hare amongst the ivy, small and harmless-looking dragons sport amongst the vines, two pigs grub up the acorns under the oak leaves – one cup, empty of its acorn, stands up among the leaves exactly as the carver must often have seen it in the Nottinghamshire fields round about.

But to come to larger things, and first of all to the great west front of Wells Cathedral, like a vast, sculptured screen, or an altar reredos on an enormous scale. It was intended to be a kind of Bible in stone, telling the whole story of the Fall of Man and the coming of sin into the world, the birth, life, death and resurrection of Him who by His sacrifice brought about the Redemption of Man and the resurrection of the dead. Christ in majesty sits in the central niche far above all the other carvings of the façade; below Him are the Nine Orders of Angels and the twelve Apostles; below them again, in niches with trefoil headed arches, the resurrection of the dead is carved – naked figures leaping and climbing out of their graves, pushing their tomb-slabs aside so that in many cases they stand up on end. Even lower still come three tiers of niches in which appear evangelists and the doctors of the Church; saints, male and female; and kings. Also, in quatrefoils, (such storied quatrefoils appear in France) are scenes from the Old Testament, from Creation to the Flood – amongst them Noah building his ark again – and episodes from the New, two very noteworthy ones being Christ's Transfiguration and a group of disciples listening to the preaching of John the Baptist.

Bishops, hermits, confessors, kings and nobles, mailed knights, saints and evangelists, the holy women and royal ladies: there they all stand or sit in their simple, canopied niches, tall and dignified, the fine, soft folds of their clinging draperies falling in V-shapes in front or sweeping down in long, fine curves from shoulder to knee; the grave-faced kings are crowned with mediaeval circlets, the ladies toy delicately with the band that fastens their flowing mantles, the mitred bishops raise a hand in blessing, the knights still bear the kite-shaped shield and wear the flat-topped helmet of the twelfth century. Some of the faces have a sad and meditative beauty, like the figures at Chartres, and there is about them the same atmosphere of serenity and quiet, noble graciousness.

Quatrefoil

Serenity – the thirteenth century dreamed less of demons, and more of angels. I went to Westminster Abbey to see what Early English carvers could do with angels. Unfortunately, the angels at Westminster are so high up in Henry III's lofty triforium – in the spandrels of the two transeptual triforia – that even with field glasses it is difficult to see their full beauty. The angelic forms censing on the south are the more pleasing. Their glorious wings fill the background of the spandrel, their draperies flow over the knees that rest against the outer-most moulding of the pointed Gothic arch. Gone completely now are the stony incised lines that did duty for the folds of garments in the twelfth century; the rippling lines of the angels' sleeves, the sweep of the robe below the waist is softly appealing. The more easterly angel swings his (unfortunately now destroyed) censer with a noble, almost imperious action that matches the nobility of his expression; the more westerly is a somewhat feminine figure, with the round contours of youth and the face of a maiden unaware of her own fresh loveliness. Two similar angels in a similar position fling out their censers in the north transept also, but they are a trifle stiffer and harder, and their expressions are considerably more stern.

From the transepts I went to the Abbey's Chapter House, where there are two Annunciation figures over the doorway, the Virgin and the angel Gabriel. These are courtly, aristocratic figures, with sharp and angular draperies. Mary has the gentle restraint of a high-bred lady as she raises a deprecating hand and slightly bows her head as who would say, 'Be it unto me even as Thou wilt'; but Gabriel (partly, no doubt, because his wings have now vanished), looks more like a courtier than an archangel, and his back-bent attitude has just a suspicion of mannerism.

They dreamt of angels in the thirteenth century at Lincoln as well as at Westminster. There are twenty-six of them there (not counting the unaccountably winged harpist, David) sitting high up in the spandrels of the beautiful Early English choir dedicated to St. Hugh, and named after its heavenly messengers, The Angel Choir. (Field glasses are again called for.) Their far outspread wings fill the empty spaces of the spandrels, some showing two wings, some one, according to their position,* and they are engaged in various pursuits. One pushes an indignant Adam and a disdainful Eve out of the Garden of Eden with a very determined hand and elbow, wearing a grimly pugnacious expression the while; others smilingly hold wreaths or spears (symbols of Christ's Passion), one tenderly lifts up an *eidolon*, a little soul, perhaps that of St. Hugh; others point to prophecies in books or unroll scrolls; there are some who swing censers, and many who play musical instruments — pipe and tabor, trumpets, lutes, harps and an enormous viol. They hold up the sun and moon, the martyrs' palm or crowns of victory, or, rather surprisingly, hawk, lure and gauntlet; and St. Michael the Archangel is amongst them, engaged, as he usually is when he is not

* Some are misfits, proving that the wings were carved on the wall before the angels were put into position.

spearing dragons, in weighing souls. Some of them look earnest, a few of them intent, a very few stern; the majority have the most charmingly roguish expressions, especially one on the south side with a ribbon-like scroll held up in both hands, and another on the north, twanging a harp. The one with puffed cheeks blowing a large trumpet – surely the Last Trump, intended to waken the dead – resembles nothing so much as a small boy making as much noise as he can with an ill-advised toy. The most charming face of all is that of the angel with the hawk, lure and gauntlet. He might well be one of the outstandingly mischievous mediaeval choir-boys metamorphosed into stone and fated to sit aloft as long as the Minster shall last, looking down on the scene of his pranks of centuries gone by.

The fact that one can talk like this about the angels of Lincoln is proof that all the Romanesque awesomeness has left them. No Romanesque angel could ever be a metamorphosed mischievous choir-boy. Romanesque angels do not look roguish or smile sweetly as they finger musical instruments. The atmosphere of the age, like the angels' stone draperies, has lightened, expressions have softened, garments now flow gracefully in sinuous folds with rippling hems; there is a refined naturalism about the forms of all sculptured figures. The Madonna who sits holding the Child at the south-west end of this same Angel Choir is a high-born lady, graciously inclining her head; Christ, on the north, attended by a small, hurrying angel now, alas, headless, presenting to Him a soul also now headless, is benign even in the act of showing the Wound in His side. There is nothing of the awfulness of the Supreme Judge about Him.

In the museum of the Philosophical Society at York there are some life-size statues discovered in 1829 in the grounds of the ruined St. Mary's Abbey near by. These must belong to the earliest years of the thirteenth, or even to the late twelfth century, for they have all the marks of transition

from the style of one age to that of the next.   Some of them
in their sternness and monumentality – notably one which
probably presents Moses – are almost Romanesque, and
reminiscent of the earliest figures of Chartres.   (It is impossible to forget that in these days England possessed vast
territories in France, and that intercourse between the two
countries must have been incessant.)   The beard and hair
of this figure are striated in the earliest Chartres manner;
its stolid dignity, however, and its solidity, is more reminiscent of St. Trophîme at Arles – there is nothing in the York
figures of the elongated asceticism of Chartres, and the folds
of the garments are thicker and heavier.   On the other
hand, the more youthful figure (might it be St. John?) has
the curled hair of early Gothic, and early Gothic's humane,
idealized features; the fluent folds of his garments, too, are
finer, though he displays a curious little loop of drapery
over his right arm, a mannerism which may be seen at St.
Trophîme.   But the St. Mary's Abbey figures are not to be
classed as Romanesque.   One has only to look at the
classically modelled feet and hands, so different from the
heavy, block-like massiveness of the twelfth century, to
realize that; the right word to describe them is Transitional.
Some of them are so weathered and decayed that their
original quality cannot be estimated.   It is not even always
possible to decide who they were meant to be, except in the
case of one with bare legs who holds up a vestigial small
animal on his left arm, and who is surely John the Baptist
with the Lamb of God.

Detailed descriptions of all the other carvings in trefoil-
headed niches and in spandrels, on roof-bosses and in arch-
mouldings are not possible; individual mention cannot be
made of the hundreds of little carved heads, exquisite and
grotesque, real portraits and caricatures, human and
animal, gracious and monstrous, that peep and peer from
hood moulds and vaulting shafts, that lurk as corbels at the
bases of columns or smile or scowl as label stops inside and
outside every mediaeval cathedral, abbey and parish

church.   This is not the place to go into details about the
rather dry, stiff, stringy carvings in the spandrels of the
south transept arcade at Worcester Cathedral (beware of
Victorian restoration here); nor about the interesting scenes
from the Old Testament round the Chapter House at
Salisbury, nor the Judgement Porch at Lincoln (beware
again of restoration) so like the great French Judgement
Porches; nor the beautiful statue of Queen Margaret (so-
called) not far from this Judgement Porch, and scores of
lesser but no less lovely figures – or more often, alas,
fragments of figures – which are to be found in little, humble
parish churches.

Neither is there time as I hurry on to do more than merely
mention French early Gothic, other than that at Chartres;
the 'Beau Dieu' of Amiens, with its noble head, at Amiens
also the grave and gentle angel of the Annunciation; the
laughing angel – '*l'ange au sourire*' – of Rheims, and the
gracious Virgin of the Visitation there, with the poise and
idealism of an Hellenic statue.   Over all, French and
English alike, that same golden light of a dreaming tenderness shone that I had noted in the illuminated manuscripts,
the same serenity, the same beautiful simplicity and
humanity that I had seen before irradiating the age of the
Poverello, the little Poor Man of God.

But I must now leave this age behind as I pass onward
into the fourteenth century.   How very clever and skilful
with the chisel was the fourteenth century!   How it could
prink and tittivate and garnish, pile ornamented gable upon
ornamented gable, and floriated ogee arch upon arches
bearing figures of knights holding heraldic shields – as in
the Percy tomb at Beverley in Yorkshire!   How it could
build up finial upon finial, pinnacle above pinnacle, all
soaring up to a conical canopy of tabernacle work bewildering in its complexity, a forest of spires, a maze of inter-
linking cusped gablets!   How it could trick out the long
pendent corbels of the choir at Exeter Cathedral with
masses of foliage surrounding the figures of saints or Virgins

almost lost in the leafage, with censing angels above in a flutter of wings! Never was there such an age for the *horror vacui* as the fourteenth century.

And how the draperies of its statues billowed and swirled, how it loved outstanding bunches of frizzed curls protruding at the sides of its sculptured male heads! Drolleries and grotesques it loved also, though it was wood, not stone, which gave carvers their greatest opportunities, and it is when one tips up miserere-seats in cathedrals and abbeys, or studies the pew-ends in Norfolk churches that one sees genre and grotesque – as well as moral – carvings at their best. But woodwork belongs more properly to the fifteenth century, and is a separate art.

Once again I beheld the cascading draperies, now in stone, which I had seen drawn in fourteenth-century illuminated manuscripts; as, for instance, on the figure of Edward I's Queen Eleanor, standing in her highly ornate niche in the crosses at Waltham and Geddington and Hardingstone, on the fringes of Northampton, who wears garments that both cascade and at Headington billow extravagantly. More and more naturalistic grow the draperies as the century wears on, rounder and more exuberant the folds, of more and more human proportions do saints and bishops, priors and apostles, kings, ladies, Madonnas and angels become. Increasingly individualistic are expressions, so that we are bound now to presume that most of the heads that adorn corbels and label stops in this age are portraits of someone. There are, for example, wrinkles on the brow of the old man in the moulding of the Chapter doorway at Rochester. He is probably an Evangelist, for he is seated at a writing-desk, but surely some aged monk of the convent acted as model for the sculptor? The head of a youth from Clarendon House is certainly a portrait, so, most likely, are the heads of Edward II and Isabella, Abbot Hugh and the master mason, Geoffrey, at St. Alban's. And for realism, what of St. Christopher at the church of Terrington St. Clement near King's Lynn in

Norfolk, who has the appearance of any large-boned, brawny peasant?

Virgins are now inclined to simper; or, as in the gateway at Winchester College, or at Amiens Cathedral in France, to stand with draperies falling in generous sweeps in proud attitudes of queens who know their worth, the Child being a plump, laughing and very human baby – how far removed from the deep-eyed, solemn Eternal Logos of Byzantine mosaics, seeing all futurity spread before his eyes!

It was not enough for the fourteenth century to place plain figures in a plain row as the Romanesque carver did at Malmesbury; they must have decoration of some kind behind or over them. So on the archway above the east cloister door at Norwich Cathedral there are, radiating across the mouldings of the arch, seven figures under ornate crocketed canopies: Christ in Judgement sitting in the centre, displaying the Wound in His side, with an angel standing, each under his own canopy, to right and left of Him; St. Peter sitting further on the right, wearing ecclesiastical vestments and a papal tiara, and with the keys of heaven in his hand; and beyond him again St. John the Baptist, in a short, skin shirt. Beyond the angel on Christ's left is the crowned St. Edmund (a saint naturally very popular in East Anglia) in kingly tunic and mantle, and beyond him stands Moses with the Tables of the Mosaic Law; they all show a slight S-bend. The general effect is interesting, rich, striking, especially now that its original colour has been renewed;* but where is the grand monumentality of the Malmesbury apostles, the stern greatness of those who were more than ordinary men – the dedicated ones chosen by Christ Himself to carry His Word to all the nations and establish His Church on earth? If you like your Bible in the language of everyday, and your saints and apostles brought down to the level of the man in the street, then you will not complain of fourteenth-century statuary;

* By Professor E. W. Tristram, 1935-36.

but if you prefer sometimes to tread upon the mountain-tops and breathe more rarefied air, if there are times when you long to escape from the commonplace and gaze upon the heroic, then sometimes, you will look back in longing towards those mightier men of old who saw all heaven and hell in blocks of stone and carved the timeless giants of twelfth-century Romanesque.

However, no one would wish to live forever upon the mountain-tops, and there are times when one is glad to come down to earth among the human foibles of the fourteenth-century, and to forgive it its passion for elaboration. None of its sculpture has the majestic solemnity and grandeur of former ages, none exudes a rarefied atmosphere of mystic spiritualism, but it can be picturesque, attractive, even beautiful in an entirely physical way. It is instructive to compare the west front – the 'Image Screen' – of Exeter Cathedral, which belongs to the fourteenth century, with the west front of Wells. At Exeter there is an array of kings, knights, apostles, prophets and angels, eighty-eight statues in all, in two tiers of niches and on brackets under the lower tier; a few of these being modern substitutes or having restored heads, while others are decaying fast. The very earliest of these figures is 100 years younger than the images of the stone screen at Wells, and they are in a different style altogether. The canopies of their niches are much more ornate, running up delicately to crocketed finials; the figures under them are picturesque where those at Wells are statuesque; they are restless where the Wells figures are tranquil; all angles and joints while those at Wells form 'closed contours', their robes falling straight in long, unruffled folds to the ground; Exeter's figures are complex, where those at Wells are simple. Several statues at Exeter sit with one leg crossed over the other, an attitude which seems in the fourteenth century to indicate kingly, or at least noble rank; most appear to be about to start up to do something, or they are stroking their beards as if contemplating animated movement. At Wells the vast

majority is still and quiet.   The general effect at Exeter is
thicker, 'crustier', if one may use such an adjective; richer,
but less serenely dignified.

Not so decayed and mutilated, and therefore showing
fourteenth-century style better, are the kings over the west
door at Lincoln Cathedral.   The richness of the tabernacle
work over their heads is almost unbelievable, and they
themselves are quaint figures, all crowned, with short legs
and long bodies, and all are dressed alike in tight-fitting
fourteenth-century jupons and long, flowing cloaks.   They
have been called, unkindly but not altogether unjustifiably,
'playing-card kings'.*

After the kings, angel musicians.   On the north side of
the nave of Exeter Cathedral there is an unusual and
picturesque feature – how often does that adjective rise to
the mind in the fourteenth century – the so-called 'Minstrels'
Gallery'.   In the Middle Ages this was used during Palm
Sunday ceremonies, but nowadays the cathedral choir goes
up into it to sing carols on the afternoon of Christmas Day.
It is a projection into the nave from the clerestory wall, and
in front it is decorated with highly ornate niches under arches
curving up to extravagant cusped points; there are finialled
buttresses between, and in each niche stands an angel playing a musical instrument.   The whole mediaeval symphony sings in their names: cithole, bagpipes, recorder,
viol, harp, Jews-harp, trumpet, organ, gittern, shawm,
timbrel and cymbals.   Some of the musicians sway in the
S-bend; they all exhibit the rather wilting, aristocratic fourteenth-century slimness, and they wear garments tight-
fitting to the waist, whence they flow down smoothly to lie
in ripples about the feet.   Several years ago the grime of
centuries was cleaned from this gallery, and all its figures in
their mediaeval colours were revealed.

This is a thing of which we ought constantly to remind
ourselves as we look at mediaeval sculpture: that once it was
all brightly painted.   I tried to visualize the west front of

* Gardner: *English Mediaeval Sculpture.*

N

Wells – of Exeter – painted; those Malmesbury Apostles; the demons at Vézelay. We have nowadays grown so unused to painted sculpture that we imagine it would look garish. I wonder if it would – painted mediaevally. Anyhow, I would give much to see Wells and Exeter and many a statue shining in the red and green and white, the blue and gold of the Middle Ages. There is, besides, a very practical consideration; in our unkind and capricious climate painting preserves the stone.

There is a typical example of fourteenth-century elaboration – which, however, gives superficial pleasure to the eye – in Gloucester Cathedral. The murdered Edward II was buried at Gloucester, and the monks there speedily made capital out of their possession of his body by hailing him as a martyr, and inviting pilgrimages (and funds) to the tomb which they had built for him. So there, under the cuspings and crocketings, the pinnacles and finials, the gables and ogee arches and lavish ornamentation of the fully developed Decorated style, under a canopy which looks at a distance like a tropical forest of luxuriant, drooping vegetation, lies the marble effigy of the poor, weak king, unidealized, and unhandsome enough to be something of a portrait, if portraits of kings were indeed introduced as early in the fourteenth century as this.

Many other fourteenth-century carvings could be mentioned, both in England and in France: the shrine base of St. Alban at the Abbey dedicated to him, deliberately destroyed at the Reformation and in modern times pieced together from 2,000 fragments; the little knightly figures on chargers in the lobed trefoils of the gables of the steeply pointed canopies over the last resting-places of the great in Westminster Abbey, and the charming little weepers standing in trefoil – or later, cinquefoil – headed niches round the tombs of nobles, here and elsewhere; in France, in the Louvre, little cowled monks whose home was once the church at Citeaux, act as bearers of the effigy of Philippe Pot, seneschal of Bourgogne. Or there is the blindfold figure of the Synagogue with her broken staff at Rochester, or the crowds of little grotesque heads which poke, grin, leer, snarl and stare from the stone choir-screen at Lincoln, but which are all too tiny to be at all disconcerting; and scores of other stone carvings of all kinds.   But I must again hasten on, passing all these by.

I come into the fifteenth century, when work is growing stereotyped, and the curse of mass-production which began in the fourteenth century has now settled upon the land. It is the same tale as with manuscript illumination.   The days of the guilds, urban prosperity, wealthy and in-fluential merchants, are now here.   Craftsmen are exclu-sively laymen in these times, and the spirit of religious devotion is passing away.   The hitherto unassailed power of the Church has now been attacked.   In England John Wyclif, 'the Morning Star of the Reformation', has already, towards the end of the fourteenth century, sent out his 'Poor Preachers', the Lollards, to undermine some of the fundamental tenets of the Roman Catholic Church.   In Bohemia, Hus, a martyr for liberty of conscience, and strongly influenced by Wyclif, has been burnt as a heretic (1415).   In Germany, Luther and his protests against Indulgences are not far off, and in Picardy, just after the turn of the century, in 1509, Calvin was to be born, Calvin with his blasting views on Predestination.   It would not be long now before the Puritans, the arch iconoclasts of Eng-land, would be on the scene, destroying what the Commis-sioners of the greedy Tudor monarch, Henry VIII, had left of mediaeval treasures.

A few last glimpses then of late mediaeval sculpture before the hammers of the iconoclasts descend, and the broken stone clatters in shattered pieces upon church and abbey and cathedral floor!   I remembered the fourteenth-century 'playing-card' kings of Lincoln as I saw the stone choir screens, first at Canterbury Cathedral, then at York. At Canterbury the Saxon Ethelbert, and Edward the Confessor, the Plantagenet Richard II, and Henry IV and

VI of the House of Lancaster, carrying sceptres, and in some cases orbs, stand in niches with lacily carved, fretted and finialled canopies, vaulted underneath with miniature lierne ribs. They may or may not be the rulers they purport to be, but though hardly portraits, they are fine, kingly figures. In their robes they show the characteristic fifteenth-century voluminous folds, sweeping, deeply under-cut, and somewhat baggily, to the ground.

In York Minster also, as at Canterbury, standing in niches on the west side of the choir screen, are more so-called English kings from William the Conqueror to Henry VI.* These figures bear no resemblance whatever to the kings whose names are on the pedestals. I was, for instance, surprised to find William the Conqueror, whom I had always imagined as bull-necked, bullet-headed, clean shaven and with close-cropped hair, as he appears in the Bayeux Tapestry, flaunting a long, curly beard here at York, and wearing great bunches of curls sticking out above each ear. Needless to say, like all the figures, he was dressed in a long tunic with thick, heavy folds, of fifteenth-century fashion. The others are equally unrecognizable, with their bunched and curled wigs, haughty attitudes, and general resemblance to each other.

In Hexham Abbey one may see a fifteenth-century curiosity: the carvings on that side of the base of the Leschman Chantry which looks into the north choir aisle. Here are some very queer Northumbrian figures of gro-tesque and primitive aspect, clumsy, unrealistic, awkward, strongly resembling the more rural aspects of the Roman-esque art of 300 years before. (Their actual date is *c.* 1480). In ugly squareness a block-like figure with a huge mouth and the features of an ogre clasps his head as he kneels, elbows on the ground before him, on the west angle of the chantry base; a neckless, humpty man with wide-spread, thick legs plays some expiring bagpipes with shape-

* The original statue of Henry VI was removed long ago, and the present figure is modern.

less hands; a fox in monk's habit preaches (as one may often find him doing on pew-ends and misereres) to a group of stiff geese; a monkey-headed creature sits on a pile of flat cakes or loaves devouring buns – an obvious picture of Gluttony; a disproportionate border-raider with the famous Greek 'archaic smile' upon his pancake face, and his head twisted painfully at right angles to his body, carries a stolen lamb across his neck – among other equally archaic, bulky figures. This, of course, is a fifteenth-century oddity, not typical of an age of increasing realism and prosaic matter-of-factness. The primitive workmanship is no doubt due to the Abbey's remote position, near the Border country.

Once upon a time, in many cathedrals and abbey-churches, there were, behind the high altar, mighty reredoses, with tier upon tier of richly canopied niches and saints and ecclesiastics standing in them upon ornate pedestals. Sometimes the niches remain, but the original statues have all vanished, victims of the iconoclastic destroyer. Such a reredos exists at Winchester Cathedral, being filled now with modern figures; but many fragments of mediaeval statues, especially heads, have from time to time been discovered in the ground round about which may, five centuries ago, have stood complete in that splendidly ornate array of fretted canopies and finialled shafts. The greatest of these heads, in my opinion, is that now called 'The Almighty'. It is a noble conception of the Ancient of Days, quite different from that in Byzantine mosaics, but just as moving. The Almighty is crowned, and His hair flows over His shoulders; His sweeping beard no doubt formerly reached to his breast, His eyes are cast downward, His expression is of one who, while carrying the whole cosmos upon His shoulders, the Creator who set in motion the revolution of the spheres, can yet look down in pitying sadness upon the world He made, a Father grieved at the foolishness of His children, but merciful in His judgement of them. This is the God the Father of whom Christ spoke in the parable of the Prodigal Son: 'when he was yet a great way off his father saw him, and had compassion, and ran, and fell on his neck, and kissed him.'*

The fifteenth century does not often rise to such heights – at least, as far as we know.   This is the kind of thing that makes us despair, in realizing what we must have lost of mediaeval art, and sharply reminds us that we may be gravely miscalculating when we criticize each century's work.   How can we be sure we are judging fairly when we have left to us, especially in sculpture, only a tithe of what must have been produced?   And how can we be sure that what still remains is the best that there was?   In fact, if we had no illuminated manuscripts, we should have no right to judge at all; but they are the one branch of mediaeval art that escaped both the iconoclast and the restorer, and even largely the devastation of Time, and there is no reason to suppose that the characteristics they show deviated from those of other forms of art, except in so far as the technique required by the different material forced them to do so.

The fifteenth century, then, with exceptions, no doubt, as 'The Almighty' reminds us, was matter-of-fact, down to earth, prosaic.   The soaring pinnacles of fourteenth-century canopies tend to flatten out; the slim, aristocratic, swaying figures of the preceding century grow more squat and stout, more bourgeois, as the years of the fifteenth century pass.   To see a gallery of statuary of the mid-fifteenth century I went to Westminster Abbey, to the chantry chapel of Henry V, which forms a sort of bridge over the ambulatory, behind the Royal Chapel.   From the ambulatory one may look up at carved scenes representing two episodes, one on each side, of Henry's coronation – the Acclamation and the Homage.   There is, too, a representation of the king on horseback, perhaps as he rode at Agincourt, on a richly caparisoned beast, though here his mount's legs are widely outspread as we see them on ancient seals.   The canopies all show the fifteenth-century flattening and loss of delicate intricacy.   The statues have

* Luke xv. 20.

no courtly affectation, and stand naturally – in some cases with considerable dignity. Edward the Confessor, dressed in mantle and robes very like those in which Richard II is dressed in his gilt-bronze effigy lying beside that of Ann of Bohemia on a tomb in the Chapel of the Kings not far away, is an erect, impressive, bearded figure, with the heavy folds of his garments falling realistically to his feet; he stands, with other figures, on one of the staircase towers. St. Edmund, one of those other figures, is clad in the baggy-folded exuberant robes more characteristic of the fifteenth century.

Shortly after the Second World War there was an exhibition in London, at the Victoria and Albert Museum, of the little statues which normally stand in niches around Henry VII's Chapel at Westminster Abbey; they had been taken down and kept out of harm's way while the bombs were nightly falling on London, and when hostilities were over and they were brought out of hiding, they were put on show at close quarters before being replaced, each standing by itself, clearly visible, in the Museum galleries. They charmed all London – which had never noticed them when they were up on their pedestals at Westminster. And there is the adjective which best describes them – charming. They are not other-worldly, monumental, inspiring; they are homely, appealing, domestic, with many happy touches. Did not everybody enjoy St. Anthony's pig, and the little bell hanging from the fingers of the saint's right hand? Were not St. Matthew's spectacles the talk of the town, and the subject of letters to *The Times*? They are not great as the Malmesbury apostles are great, but they are full of character – ordinary character, such as we see all about us every day.

St. Matthew the Evangelist peers over those heavy spectacles like some shortsighted old don, as he supports the book on which he is writing upon a little angel's head (how are the great visionary evangelical symbols fallen from the heights of mystical symbolism!); St. Dunstan with his tongs is tweaking a little devil by the nose as if he were a careful householder picking up one lump of coal to put on the fire; a comfortable, matronly housewife – actually St. Anne – looking like the Nurse in *Romeo and Juliet*, teaches a little girl, her daughter, the Virgin Mary, to read.   Prophets in enormous hats and baggily folded clothes unroll scrolls as if they were merchants of the Staple, checking over their bills of lading; one of these prophets looks over his spectacles like an aged grocer surveying a small customer behind the counter, another has the thin lips, long nose and quizzical expression of the keen man of business, though his taste in hats is extraordinary.   An executioner near St. Sebastian must have been a portrait of someone, his face is so un-exaggerated, unidealized, lifelike.   St. Roche, too, in his picturesque hat, realistically pulls down his hose to exhibit the plague sore on his thigh; and the burly St. Christopher, an old, bearded giant, cheerfully carries his divine burden. St. Paul, with his long forelock curling over his bald fore-head, studies his book like an absorbed scholar muttering into his beard; St. Mark has a toy lion on the book he holds in his left hand, and points downward with a long fore-finger; the folds of his robe are extravagantly voluminous, almost blanket-like.

When these little statues had all been replaced I went to Westminster and saw them standing in their late-Gothic niches.   They looked like old friends, familiar, chatty, delightfully approachable.   Late Gothic – very late indeed, standing there on those almost Tudor pedestals under the filigree wonder of the extremely late-mediaeval fan-vaulted roof; not even fifteenth century, indeed, but early sixteenth. They are the last in that long line of sculpture of the Middle Ages which stretches back into misty perspective, far off across the centuries on to the Northumbrian moorlands, where the great stone crosses were set up.   Turning from them, I faced about, and was confronted with Henry VII's tomb.   A Renaissance tomb, in the newest fashion of the opening years of the sixteenth century.   The waning

Middle Ages are sinking into the shadows of that which is past; now the Renaissance is at hand in England too, and the classicism which departed with the Roman legions is returning, with some differences, after 1,100 years. Here, where I stood before my journey back to Ruthwell and Bewcastle, and saw, under those ethereal pendants of the last phase of the Perpendicular style, the torch of the Renaissance steadily approaching English shores, I stand again, knowing once more that I am on the threshold of the modern world.

14

SOLEMN HARMONIES OF COLOUR

AGAIN I look onward, and then turn back. There is one more thing that, as I have journeyed, has caught me up in the enchantment of its beauty, and which I must return to the Middle Ages to study, before I come out again into the glare of the present. Is it the loveliest of all the products of the Middle Ages? It is difficult to say. Illuminated manuscripts, mosaics, wall-paintings, architecture, sculpture, all have their own peculiar qualities, and they are none of them comparable. But whatever the uninitiated may say of any of those things, not even the uninitiated will deny the exquisite beauty of this final glory: mediaeval stained glass.

When I first began my journey, as I said at the beginning, it was in times of war. My pursuit of stained glass was delayed because my journey started in the war years. I used to read descriptions of it: 'a mosaic of jewels', 'solemn harmonies of colour'. I longed to see for myself; but in those days there was not a scrap of mediaeval glass anywhere visible. Up and down the country, in village and town, from tiny hamlet-church to vast cathedral, the tragically fragile thing had been taken down and buried where neither cannonade nor bomb-blast nor fire could destroy it, and the windows which it had once turned into a glory were now dead and colourless – their plain glass only a protection against the weather. Providentially.

During one of the air-raids on Canterbury the plain glass in every window of the Cathedral which had held the priceless mediaeval treasure was smashed to smithereens.

Pitifully fragile thing – at the mercy of the destroyer! Care prevented the twentieth-century destroyer from harming it; but the destroyer of the seventeenth century, when he 'rattled down proud Becket's glassy bones' on to the floor of Canterbury Cathedral swept into oblivion half the glorious mediaeval heritage which should have been ours. And so we execrate the name of Richard Culmer and all his Puritan iconoclasts, and can never forgive them, self-appointed judges of what it was right for us to see, for the loss of all that beauty of which they have irrevocably robbed us.

During the last of the war years I longed in vain to see a piece of mediaeval glass. I shall always remember the first piece I did see – not an outstandingly beautiful or famous or even noteworthy piece, but the *first* piece – it was in the church of St. Leonard at Leverington, near Wisbech, in Cambridgeshire.

I came upon it unexpectedly in the north chapel of the church, just two months after the war in Europe had ended. It represented a Jesse Tree. It had been restored in 1900, but practically the whole of the glass in the tracery lights was complete, and from that I was able to get some idea of what mediaeval glass looked like. It was the blues that were most enchanting. They were liquid loveliness, and I could not imagine why the restorers had had to deaden the effect of other fragments of old blue in the windows below by their strips and patches and oblongs of murky brown. I certainly gained my impression of what mediaeval glass looked like in spite of, rather than because of, the restoration.

As the months passed on into years, gradually the glass came back to village church and cathedral, to tiny isolated windows and the great ranges of cathedral nave and clerestory. Nothing in all mediaeval art has such power to move as mediaeval stained glass. In the contemplation of a beauty of colour that has never been surpassed one may come nearer communion with God than one does in verbal prayer. For God is Light, and stained glass holds the light in its inmost heart of hearts, and without the light it falls into nothingness and dies; the light is its life, and takes the vibrant colour in its arms and cradles it as the shell cradles the iridescence of mother-of-pearl. When one looks upon mediaeval stained glass – particularly thirteenth-century stained glass – one seems to be looking upon the Infinite, where Past, Present and Future no longer exist.

During this journey I did not have to travel so far back into the mists of time as I had done before. Nothing still existed of those 'coloured' windows which St. Gregory is said to have placed in the church of St. Martin at Tours in the sixth century, nor of those with which, a century later, Benedict Biscop (who seems to have had a finger in every artistic pie) adorned his churches of Jarrow and Wearmouth. Nobody seemed to know for certain when *stained* glass was actually introduced. The Romans glazed their windows – even without the evidence from many a museum in Britain that is clear, for did not Seneca write that glazed windows were one of the luxuries of life which did not add to a philosopher's happiness? but there are no references to *coloured* glass, at any rate in western Europe, before the sixth century. None of that glass remains, and there are not even descriptions of it. By the eleventh century the Chapter House at St. Benedict's famous monastery of Monte Cassino was filled with 'coloured glass glazed with lead and fixed with iron', a description which fits well with our ideas of stained glass, but it had all vanished centuries before Monte Cassino was reduced to rubble in the Second World War.

There is, however, a little piece of coloured glass in the church at Brabourne, in Kent, which is certainly the oldest in this country, and it may have been made in the eleventh

century.   It is only a simple pattern of leaded white glass
with pieces of coloured glass formed into a rosette design,
and not really what we understand by 'stained glass'; and
in Dorchester Abbey there is glass in the bell-shaped
openings behind the piscina and sedile in the chancel,
which is said to have been taken from the now vanished
Norman east window.   This is closer to our idea of stained
glass, for the four pieces represent a Pope blessing, St.
Birinus receiving his commission to preach the gospel in
what we now know as Oxfordshire, the Holy Eucharist and
a mitred figure.

France is richer than we are in glass of this date.   In the
south aisle of the cathedral of Le Mans there are some panels
of stained glass which certain authorities consider to be late
eleventh century, which show, on alternate ruby and blue
backgrounds, twelve figures of apostles in Romanesque
attitudes, and up above, in a separate panel in the top row,
the Virgin Mary.   Their nimbed heads are all at awkward
angles as they gaze upwards, and some have their arms
uplifted.   This is obviously an Ascension scene, although
no figure of Christ is now apparent, but it is evident that
the panels are not in their original state or probable
original arrangement – very few mediaeval stained glass
windows are.   But whether this window is late eleventh
century or early twelfth, it shows all the characteristics of
the earliest period of stained glass of which I could find any
examples.   The ruby background is aglow with deep and
luminous colour, of varying shades; the blue is of vibrant
intensity, inclining in places to purple;* the figures on their
plain backgrounds are tall and Byzantinesque, exaggerated
and occasionally grotesque in gesture, and highly conventionalized; their garments are blue, maroon or yellow
with small patches of green and touches of white.

A little later in the twelfth century comes the Crucifixion

* These variations in shade were not intentional.   They were caused
by the craftsmen's inexperience in mixing their materials, but they
actually give life and interest to the plain colour.

window – the main east window – at Poitiers.   The colours are brighter – one might almost say shriller – than those of Le Mans, shriller than anything ever found in England, ruby and blue predominating again.   The figures are still elongated, Byzantine fashion, especially that of Christ on a glowing ruby Cross, and Christ in Glory in a ruby and blue mandorla above the Cross, in the round head of the window.

But the loveliest window of the twelfth century is probably the one in the south choir aisle at Chartres, showing a huge Virgin and Child surrounded by angels censing or holding lights, and known as *La Belle Verrière*. She is an extremely Byzantine figure, crowned, and robed in clear blue with bands of ruby, sitting frontally with knees wide apart, and staring frontally, like the statuesque, formal Child in ruby upon her lap; the Dove of the Holy Spirit hovers with outspread wings above her head. Here, indeed, is that mosaic of glowing jewels of which I had heard, the glory of intense colour sparkling and flickering in points of fire, scintillating with every change of my position, darkening and brightening as the clouds behind it pass across and away from the sun.   It seems sacrilege to investigate the cause of this mosaic effect, and to realize that it was the early craftsmen's very deficiencies of technique which brought it about; but the fact is that at this period all such panels were made up of a huge number of tiny pieces – one writer has computed that there might be over fifty to the square foot* – each chipped into shape with the grosing iron and all leaded together.

In England there is not much indubitably twelfth-century glass to be found.   There is one little panel in the north aisle of York Minster – a little figure in clinging draperies holding in each hand the branches of what must have been a Jesse Tree; but the largest collection is in Canterbury Cathedral.   First there are the large Romanesque figures there representing the ancestors of Christ.

* Le Couteur: *English Mediaeval Painted Glass.*

These were originally all in the windows of the clerestories, but some of them are now in the clerestories of the choir only, some in the eastern transepts, and the Trinity Chapel, and one amongst much later glass in the west window. There they are, under plain or extremely simple trefoil-headed arches, large, elongated, Byzantine figures plainly influenced by France, seated with knees mostly wide apart, often with awkwardly twisted heads and gesturing, mannered hands – except Adam, who, his brown, lean, elongated body naked except for a fleece about his loins, digs with a mattock against a background of intense blue broken only by the horny whiteness of a stylized tree. The intensity of the blue is deepened by the narrow, glowing ruby border round three sides of the panel, and Adam digs wearily on, standing in a rocky furrow between two baulks of vivid green.

Then there is the patriarch Enoch, with twisted uplifted head and outspread arms, in a white robe with a yellow girdle, his legs swivelled round in the manner of Christ's in the tympanum at Vézelay; Zorobabel, tall and dignified in his white robe and murrey mantle, sitting upon his bright green throne as if he were expounding the law; Juda under a turreted arch, Ragan, Phalech, Lamech and Mathusala (I take these names as they are spelt on the glass, where they are written in large, Lombardic letters behind the patriarch's heads). They all sit enthroned against the background of that same intense blue; there were once eighty-four of these majestic figures, now there are only thirty-eight, and some of them are so high they are difficult to see; but they give that same sense of giant, brooding presences that one feels when looking upon Romanesque sculpture: of heroes of old seated, for all their contorted attitudes, in kingly dignity against the blue of the Eternal.

'Figure windows' like these are one type of early mediaeval stained glass glazing; even more common are the 'medallion windows'. The medallion windows in the north choir aisle at Canterbury, patched up and partially

restored as they are, are a moving manifestation of mediaeval art.   It is with a sense of tragic loss that one learns
that in the Middle Ages there were twelve of these windows,
with about 174 jewel-like pictures in them; now only thirty-
three panels are left, and they are mostly not in their right
places.   Is 'Blue Dick'* the arch thief atoning in some
inferno for his crime against posterity, whom he robbed of
so much beauty?   Before one examines the details of these
north choir aisle windows one wonders at their colour: and
here 'solemn harmonies' is the description that comes first
to the mind.

> Storied windows, richly dight,
> Casting a dim religious light

said Milton, who was a Puritan too, but who happened to
be a poet and lover of music as well, and that made all the
difference.   Their deep, muted glow, transforming the
light passing through them into a mystic radiance, is some-
how like the sound of an organ; it is music and poetry
intermingled, irradiated with slow-pulsing, majestic light.
Why are these windows so beautiful?   Is it only their
colour?   Or is it the spirit of the faith that lay in the minds
of those who wrought them long ago, living on still and
breathing its message to any who will pause awhile to
listen to voices across the centuries?   I do not notice who
passes as I stand here.   Gazing upon this solemn beauty I
seem to be alone in communion with God.

   Yet presently one should look at details, for in the details
the Middle Ages are telling the great story of the Fall of
Man and his redemption by the Saviour Christ, with all the
prophecies of His coming and the great consummation of
His Sacrifice: simply and clearly, when one understands
their almost childlike conventions: these 'celery-stick'
trees, these wavy lines of cloud to show we are in the open
air, or a couple of round arches and a column or two to
indicate that we are indoors; these gold coins as big as

* Nickname of Richard Culmer – see above, p. 195.

saucers (to make sure one sees them), these enormously long flexed forefingers (to draw one's attention to the most significant thing in the story); this Christ, showing by His over-large size His greater importance.

The very mind of the people of the Age of Faith is mirrored in the anti-types and types represented in the medallions – that is, a New Testament scene in a medallion with (originally) a medallion scene from the Old Testament on each side of it which was regarded as having prefigured it. In many cases the original arrangements have gone, but one may still see the Three Wise Men on their journey, garbed in the conventional loose Oriental trousers and seated on their horses; one is pointing to the large star shining in the wavy band which does duty for the clouds above their heads, while another seems to shade his eyes as he looks back at it from the city gateway which he is just entering. This is the New Testament anti-type, and on the left of it is one Old Testament type, Baalam riding on his ass with his cloak streaming out behind him and his hands outstretched before him to the star in the central medallion as he cries, 'There shall come a Star out of Jacob and a Sceptre shall rise out of Israel'; and on the right is the other Old Testament type, Isaiah the prophet, a toga'd figure before the turreted gateway of a city at which he looks back as he too points to the Wise Men's star, prophesying, 'The Gentiles shall come to the light and kings to the brightness of thy rising.'

Lower down the window, too, the Magi are adoring the Christ Child on His Mother's knee, with the shepherds on the other side. The Virgin stares straight ahead just as in *La Belle Verrière* at Chartres or in Byzantine mosaics, two Wise Men bring caskets and the third kneels as he offers a handful of coins. All of them are under arches or a pediment, showing that the scene is indoors, and the mauve and yellow and green of their garments stands out against the blue – always in these medallions the blue – of the backgrounds. This roundel is between Old Testament

o

scenes of offering: The Queen of Sheba followed by her retinue with some queer equine creatures who are probably meant for camels brings the treasures of Punt to Solomon seated upon his throne on one side, and on the other Joseph's brethren bring their gifts to their brother who is raised aloft on a high throne while Egyptians offer theirs also.

Then there is the anti-type of Christ presented in the Temple, with Simeon at the altar and Joseph and Anna carrying long candles and the basket out of which peep the heads of the two turtle-doves; prefigured by, on the one side, Eli receiving the child Samuel, on the other the type has gone; there is only a medallion telling the parable of the Sower, a figure in a short, clinging green tunic holding the seed in a fold of his cloak and with a vigorous movement of his backswung right arm broadcasting the seed that fell by the wayside and upon stony ground. The yellow furrows curve behind him like the hull of a boat, birds of various colours fly around, and a highly conventionalized grey tree waves rather ghostly arms in the background against the deep blue sky. Lower down there is another Sower scene. This Sower walks to the right instead of to the left, like the other. He carries his seed in a two handled basket, and some of it is falling among the curiously shaped thorn-bushes in the foreground. The baulks running diagonally across the scene are evidently the good ground upon which the seed fell which 'brought forth fruit, some an hundredfold, some sixtyfold, some thirty-fold'.*

In the next window the types and anti-types are a good deal muddled, or missing altogether, so it is best to take each medallion as an entity, while remembering that the Middle Ages never intended this. There is the twelve-year-old Jesus in the Temple among the doctors; the Miracle at Cana, with Christ sitting at a crowded table much like those in the illuminated manuscripts. In another part of

* Matthew xiii. 8.

the window appears the Miraculous Draught of Fishes. Noah is in a half-medallion, a green-robed figure with ruby sleeves leaning from a casement in the roof of a tiered and colonnaded Ark, receiving back a white dove with an olive branch in its beak. The waves below are gloriously coloured, purple, blue and green, with white crests. This was originally a type of the Baptism of Christ – 'the first devouring flood submerging everything with its pervading flow purified all things and signified baptism'. These are perhaps the most outstanding medallions and panels, and with this window we reach the end of Canterbury's twelfth-century glass. Some would say that even these north choir aisle windows are early thirteenth century, and not twelfth century at all; but if this is really so they are very early thirteenth century and have all the twelfth-century characteristics, including marks of strong French influence.

There is more early glass in the window in the east wall of what is known as the *Corona* or 'Becket's Crown', in the Trinity Chapel, or Chapel of St. Thomas, behind the high altar, near the spot where that shrine 'with golden plates embossed with golden wires, pearls and precious stones' stood flashing and blazing throughout three centuries, 'whereof (as Erasmus tells us) the meanest part was gold, every part glistened, shone and sparkled with very large jewels'. Here pilgrims old and young, rich and poor, men, women and children laid their offerings; and here, in 1538 came the destroyers, who carried off to Henry VIII's royal treasury twenty-six cartloads, they say, of jewels. This window I look upon now probably dates from about 1200. It shows Our Lord's Passion, Resurrection and Ascension, and the familiar Romanesque theme of Christ in Glory – and the types beside the anti-types again. Some of these medallions are modern, though put together from bits of ancient glass, so that they still glow with the subdued harmonious jewel-like fires of early mediaeval colour. The Crucifixion is one such. It is the anti-type to Moses striking the rock with a rod, reminiscent of Longinus' spear;

whereupon a twisting stream gushes down – as the stream of blood gushed from the Saviour's wounded side. It is also the anti-type to the Sacrifice of Isaac, where Abraham stands with his sword-arm raised to strike the child kneeling at what looks very like an altar, while the ram caught in the thicket stands at the other side. In a lozenge above is the purely ancient scene of the Entombment. The stiff and shrouded body of Christ is being lowered by two bearded men into a sarcophagus across the dim, twilight blue of the background, and as dimly lean over it figures in a green which has been 'kept back' – that is, toned down to the prevailing solemn hues of death – with the fine brown enamelled lines of the garment-folds upon it. The story of Jonah and the Whale is close by, for it is the type of Christ's Death and Resurrection. The prophet, in bright ruby, is being lowered into the gaping jaws of a vividly green fish emerging from waves of green, deep blue and brownish ivory, and the crew stands up in an unseaworthy looking ship against the deep blue background which is the rule in all the medallions.

At the top of the window sits Christ in Majesty on the arc of the rainbow, and angels kneel on each side of Him; the Dove of the Holy Spirit hovers with outspread wings, and from a cloud below His feet eleven crimson streams of fire pour down upon the heads of the apostles seated below, all gathered together into one place on the Day of Pentecost. At the bottom of the window, and easily seen because it is at eye-level, is a half-medallion wherein a spy in a brilliant ruby tunic and another in one of pale pink, carry on a pole slung between them an outsize bunch of grapes. These are the Grapes of Eschol, the type of Christ and Simon of Cyrene and of the vintage of the wine of the Eucharist, giving the foretaste of the Promised Land won by the Passion of Christ. The uneven depths of blueness of the background are here at their most effective, and a touch of green ground at the bottom is a miracle of artistic judgement – like the slight touches of white in all this early glass.

Between all these medallions are coiling scrolls of yellow and green and blue against ruby backgrounds – solemn harmonies in themselves.

I turn back into the Trinity Chapel, called the Chapel of St. Thomas because twelve windows here, in the aisles and the ambulatory, once held glass depicting various miracles believed to have been due to the sanctity of the Saint's near presence or to his intercession after his murder in the Cathedral that dark December afternoon of 1170. Only nine windows now have ancient glass in them; only seven of these some or all of the glass which originally belonged to them. They are not much different in style from the 'Theological' Windows in the north aisle or those of the *Corona*. There are still medallions leaded in various designs, still the same deep, solemn harmonies of colour, the intense blues and the glowing ruby; still the little figures in their short tunics girdled softly at the waist ride, run, gesticulate and point as they go about their business or bring their diseases and their offerings to the Saint's tomb, or stand amazed at the miracles wrought there.

These, then, are the 'Miracle' windows. The saint's tomb in the crypt, where he was buried till his remains were translated in 1220 to the Trinity Chapel, is represented in several windows, and there are two pictures of the later shrine – the one which Erasmus described. St. Thomas, too, appears many times, usually in a vision to some sleeper – mitred and vested, and carrying his pastoral staff or archiepiscopal cross. The scenes are mostly easy to see, the lowest being almost at eye-level: a crippled child at the tomb of St. Thomas; Stephen of Hoyland delivered from nightmares (represented as demons at his head) and tearing at the bedclothes; there are pilgrims, some disabled, on their way to Canterbury. William, the priest of London, is cured of paralysis by drinking a drop of the saint's blood; the whole story of Eilward of Westoning is told in four scenes. Robert of Cricklade, Prior of St. Frideswide's, who suffers from swollen feet, totters towards

the tomb, upheld by two servants, and then is seen barelegged, bowing over it.   Lepers and dropsical women and
maniacs and those sick of a fever are healed.

There is the story of William of Kellett, the carpenter,
whose axe slips as he is working at his bench, and makes
a fearful gash on his shin.   With his leg swathed in bandages, he lies in bed, where St. Thomas appears to him,
and when the bandages are taken off soon after hardly any
trace remains of his horrible wound.   Rodbertulus of
Rochester and his friends are amusing themselves after the
manner of certain detestable small boys by stoning frogs,
when Rodbertulus (that is, Bobby) falls into the Medway.
Two of his friends rush off to Bobby's parents with the
news.   In a panic they arrive at the scene of the disaster,
but find that by the intercession (presumably) of St.
Thomas the tide has gone out, and so the tiresome Bobby
is drawn alive out of the mud, which always seems a better
fate than he deserves.

And so they go on, miracle after miracle; I will mention
only one more out of many, the tale of William of Gloucester, told in several scenes.   He is directing some deep
digging operations when the earth collapses upon him and
buries him.   His mates rush off to spread the news, and
the bailiff rides out to see what can be done.   The hand of
St. Thomas points to the spot where the luckless William
has been overwhelmed, and bending down, the bailiff hears
the buried man's groans.   The parishioners are then seen,
spades over shoulders, marching off to the spot; and by the
grace of the saint they dig poor William out alive.

It is said that craftsmen from France came to England
to make this thirteenth-century glass at Canterbury.
Whether all of it was made by French hands – some
certainly was – is open to question, but no one can deny
that it was made under strong French influence.   I looked
at the prophets and disciples in the windows of the choir of
Bourges Cathedral – Micah and Jonah, Amos and Nahum,
St. Peter, St. Paul, St. John – thirteen feet high, all of them,

standing, not sitting, and with other subtle differences to distinguish them from the great Canterbury ancestors of Christ, but obviously related to them in their stiffness, their mannered gestures, austere countenances and Byzantine attitudes.   I looked, too, at the long line of gigantic saints of noble majesty which fills the clerestory at Chartres, and knew whence came the inspiration for those huge figures which once, at Canterbury too, filled all the clerestory windows.

Then I turned to Chartres to the Scenes from the Life of Christ in the central window over the main doorway.   The shepherds with their 'hockey stick' crooks gazing up at the angelic host above them, and gesturing towards them are similar in type to countless peasant figures in St. Thomas's Miracle windows. The innocent-looking faces of the crowned Magi are depicted in just the same way as those pointing to the Star in the north choir aisle at Canterbury, they would seem to be the selfsame kings who there stand before Herod.   Here are the same solemn harmonies as one played at Canterbury; here is the same glorious colour throbbing with its intensity, as for instance in the Visitation scene, or the medallion showing the death of the Virgin surrounded by the vibrant luminosity of the ruby and blue scroll decorations around it.   Yet there is a subtle difference, especially in the giant figures – they are all over twenty feet high – in the upper windows at Chartres. There is about them a certain restlessness; they flicker and dance in colour, they flash like a suddenly opened casket of jewels; the hues, and consequently the light, is more broken.   They have not the static quality of Canterbury's figures.   Their colours too, especially those of the great archangel with the thurible in the apse, seem sharper, more piercingly and excitedly 'French'.   This may be partly due to the frequent use at Chartres of 'mosaic diaper' to fill the spaces between the medallions.   Scroll-work is not used at Chartres to anything like the extent that it is at Canterbury.

These shriller colours are less evident at Bourges, where there is the story of the Prodigal Son, the pictures of the Last Supper, the Washing of Peter's feet and the Last Judgement window in the ambulatory bearing colours muted more in the Canterbury manner.

I remembered two things about Sens. One was that William the Frenchman, called in to rebuild the choir of Canterbury Cathedral after a disastrous fire had burnt down the old Norman building in 1174, was a native of that town; the other that Becket took refuge there during his exile from England. It is therefore not surprising to find in the Sens windows scenes from Becket's life, and over-whelming reminiscences again of certain Canterbury medallion windows; and it seems that the same craftsmen must have made some of the Sens glass and some of that at Canterbury – especially that in the *Corona*. In the Becket scenes at Sens the same mitred and vested figure of St. Thomas appears as in the Miracle windows; there is the same grouping of crowds of riders, in this case as Becket enters Canterbury; the same blue and green conventional waves through which his ship makes its way to the landing-stage in England where the archbishop disembarks; the same blue and yellow scroll decorations on a ruby ground be-tween the medallions, the same deep blue backgrounds and intense glow of solemn light. There is even a type and anti-type window at Sens.

The frequent recurrence of the parable of the Good Samaritan in stained glass of this period is instructive. The parables, for all their picturesqueness, are not often repre-sented in mediaeval art; when they are it is because the mediaeval mind, overlooking the crystal simplicity of their teaching, read subtle symbolism in them. The 'man who went down from Jerusalem to Jericho' was Adam, leaving the Paradise of the City of God; the thieves who set upon him were the Seven Deadly Sins; the Priest and the Levite who forsook him in his suffering were the Law of Moses, the Old Testament; the Good Samaritan was, of course, Christ

the Saviour.   For this reason only was the story represented in the windows of thirteenth-century churches.

There is another kind of thirteenth-century glass less
expensive, no doubt, and with the practical advantage that
it admitted more light.   This is *grisaille*.*   In such windows
the glass is mostly white, with elaborate patterns of circles
and lozenges all overlapping or intersecting one another in
painted line-work; there is sometimes a coloured border,
and often what one might call 'studs' of colour at intervals
over the glass.   I thought *grisaille* glass must be very dull;
then I went and looked at the mid-thirteenth-century 'Five
Sisters' window in the north transept at York Minster.
They are the finest *grisaille* windows, I believe, in the world:
five exaggeratedly narrow Early English lancets only five
feet wide but fifty high, filled with glass whereof I did not
study the painted pattern in detail; I gazed upon it as a
whole.   It was like opal and mother-of-pearl with rubies
caught in the silvery sheen of them.   It cannot be ade-
quately described; it must be seen to be believed.

They say Westminster Abbey had *grisaille* windows in the
Middle Ages; Lincoln still has some; and still, at mal-
treated, eighteenth-century desecrated Salisbury some is
left.   The pleasures of *grisaille* are utterly different from the
emotional impact of coloured windows.   One is a Mozart
symphony, the other a tumult of Wagnerian chords; one the
still, calm beauty of full moonlight on a sheet of water,
the other the sun going down in triumphant glory among
the bars of crimson and purple of descending twilight.

* French: *gris* . . . grey.

15

THE AGE OF CANOPIES

∞∞∞∞∞∞∞∞∞∞∞∞∞∞∞∞

WE are told that after fire had destroyed nearly all of Chartres Cathedral in 1194 the citizens, rich and poor, old and young, nobles, merchants, craftsmen, peasants, were consumed with a burning passion. One thought only lay in the minds of all: to sacrifice everything they had to rebuild the House of God. Some gave money for this end, some stone and timber and lead and everything else necessary; some provided the workmen with food; and some who were too poor to give any of these things, gave, regardless of their personal affairs, their labour, even harnessing themselves to carts to drag stone to the building. They thought of nothing else till the work was done; and great princes, nay, kings, were fired by their enthusiasm, and made their offerings too. St. Louis of France gave the rose window of the north transept and the lancets beneath it, and other royal donors followed his example; and in a white flame of zeal and faith the guilds of the City of Chartres gave forty-seven windows – with little panels at the bottom of them showing the bakers and butchers, the money-changers and furriers and all the rest of the ordinary workpeople at their everyday, bread-and-butter tasks. So did whole communities, social rank forgotten, feuds forgotten, sluggishness and dissatisfaction put by, work together when occasion arose, all animated by a single emotion – in the thirteenth century, the Age of Faith.

But the years passed by and the white flame of inspired devotion sank and died. The fourteenth century came, the age of disillusion, broken ideals, doubts of the spiritualism of a Church swollen with riches and comfortable living, the age of heretical questionings from a Wyclif and satiric criticisms of a Langland in his *Piers Plowman*. It was the same story that may be read in all mediaeval art, from illuminated manuscripts through wall-paintings and architecture to sculpture, and now it recurs in stained glass: decline of spiritualism, disappearance of mystical symbolism, increase in technical skill at the expense of profundity – but withal (one must of course admit it) an aesthetic attractiveness, a grace and charm, sometimes an innocent quaintness very pleasing to the senses even if it gives no inner serenity to the soul.

The fourteenth century in stained glass is the age of canopies. It is also the age of single figures upon plain or *grisaille* glass. It is the age of yellow and gold; for it is the century of the invention of silver stain. The fourteenth-century craftsmen discovered that if they painted white glass with silver oxide or chloride such painted parts, when heated in the kiln, would turn all shades of yellow from pale lemon to the colour of brass, according to the amount of silver used. This meant a great saving of labour and expense, because now hair, or crowns, or haloes or canopies or any gold or yellow detail could be painted on one piece of glass, and did not need a separate piece leaded in. Yellow of varying shades consequently begins to pervade fourteenth-century glass; so much so that it seems the predominant colour of the century as far as stained glass is concerned.

There are no more medallion windows, no more deep blue and ruby plain backgrounds. When such appear at all they bear painted diaper patterns which deprive them of their glowing luminosity. There are no more solemn harmonies, no more types and anti-types, no more giant figures of austere majesty, gazing down from lofty clerestories. Austerity gives place to graciousness, majesty to charm, Byzantine stiffness to the lithe and willowy S-bend. Above all, the canopy grows and grows. It puts on arch upon arch, gable over gable, crocket upon crocket, finial upon finial; it piles Pelion on Ossa, it is a Tower of Babel rising even unto heaven. Sometimes it fills two-thirds of a light, dwarfing the saint or holy one who stands beneath its monstrous superstructure.

The first fourteenth-century type glass I ever saw was in the chapel of Merton College at Oxford – it actually belongs to 1283. These panels of coloured glass, ruby on blue or green and gold on red, or sometimes murrey on blue ran across the middle of all fourteen windows, and represented little monkish or bishops' figures kneeling, one on each side of St. Peter with his keys, St. Paul with his sword, St. Andrew with his cross, and so on. They were charming looked at as a whole, but like the much later figures in the chapel of All Souls had, when looked at in detail, a certain monotony and repetition which became the bane of the fourteenth century, as it endeavoured to hide by skilful technique the fact that it was losing inventiveness.

After that I saw fourteenth-century glass again in the seven great windows at the east end of Tewkesbury Abbey. It was now obvious to me that the old thirteenth-century style had to pass away, for here were large windows with three, four or five lights, and with tracery in their pointed tops; a totally different type of window from the round-headed Norman ones of Canterbury. A single figure in each light therefore appeared in all but the east window. Here was the last sunset ray of that old theme, the Prophets and Ancestors of Christ. They stood in two windows on each side of the main east one; they were attractive, graceful figures, very rich in colouring – red and green and gold – under the inevitable but effective canopies; but the gigantic forms, the brooding majesty had gone from them. And as if to emphasize the worldliness of the age, the next window westwards on each side contained

knights in armour with heraldic jupons representing the
chief Lords of the Manor of Tewkesbury.   In the main east
window Christ was seated in Judgement, however, with the
apostles and the Virgin Mary, and below them the just
souls, risen from their graves and being welcomed by an
angel, and the resurrection of the damned, bound with a
chain by a small green figure, obviously the devil.   Typical
of the fourteenth century is the appearance of a donor – in
this case Eleanor de Clare – kneeling in one of the lower
panels, and lowest of all is a row of coats of arms.   The
glory and honour of this world, in all its glittering colour,
has now entered into what had hitherto been exclusively a
paean of praise to the Saviour and the Creator.

But as I had had to go to Canterbury Cathedral to know
twelfth- and thirteenth-century glass, to know that of the
fourteenth I had to go to York Minster.   The Minster has
ancient glass in 109 windows,* from the earliest period to
the latest, but it is very rich in glass of the fourteenth
century.   Most of this is in the clerestories (difficult to see
without field-glasses) and in the nave.   Memories of the
glass at Canterbury and that at York cannot possibly
become entangled, for the styles are as different as the spirit
of the thirteenth century was different from that of the
fourteenth.   Instead of the deep blue and glowing ruby of
earlier times, green and gold predominate at York; but an
even greater difference is that no longer was the whole
window, as at Canterbury, filled with deep and luminous
colour.   In the fourteenth century the rule was to have
coloured panels alternating with the silvery sheen of
grisaille.   Moreover, as at Tewkesbury, the windows
themselves had changed in their shape.

At York there is the same general arrangement in all the
nave windows: two horizontal bands of coloured panels
across all three lights in each window, separated by panels
of *grisaille*, and surmounted, of course, by canopies; and at
the bottom a whole panel devoted to a kneeling donor, for

* F. Harrison: *The Painted Glass of York*.

the age had now arrived when men no longer dreamt of keeping their pious benefactions anonymous. The green of the fourteenth century, too, is duller, a more olive green than the brilliant, sharp colour of the thirteenth century; the glass seems thinner and flatter, without the intensity of the earlier age, and without those accidental but beautiful variations of shade. No doubt, also, because the reds and blues were so much flatter, it had been found necessary to give them the vitality that their depth had hitherto provided by scratching diaper patterns like fern-fronds or filigree windings over their surface. And the canopies, the 'passion of pinnacle and fret', as Ruskin called it! Amongst the flying buttresses and windowed finials, the crocketed niches and traceried spandrels, among a forest of spires like the view from the top of the Sheldonian in Oxford compressed into a thousandth of the space, there are even tiny figures of kings and ecclesiastics, standing one above the other under their own little canopies in the niches of the border shafts of the great canopy. All of which is intriguing, but it diverts attention from the main figures in the windows.

There is no longer any theological or any other kind of scheme in the windows. They no longer tell a coherent story of the Fall and Redemption of Man, nor do they prefigure the events of the New Testament by those of the Old. There is no symbolism worth mentioning. To understand them, all one needs is a working knowledge of certain stereotyped events in the lives of the more popular saints. There are not even now any particular conventions to understand. Spiritual depth has vanished, devotional mysticism is no more. This, for all its elegance, is a mundane world, and we worship God and honour the saints rather from habit than conviction. The craftsmen represented the subject which the donor of a window wanted represented in a window – which subject would very likely have nothing to do with that chosen by the donor of the window next to it.

In the south aisle are windows representing under gold (silver stain) canopies the miracles of St. Nicholas, the story of Edward the Confessor and the ring, St. William crossing Ouse Bridge, a somewhat mutilated Jesse Tree; the exploits of St. John the Evangelist, a Crucifixion, and figures of saints and ecclesiastics. The north aisle shows an equally heterogeneous array of subjects: the martyrdoms of various apostles and saints, Passion scenes and Christ in Glory; the tortures of St. Catherine in the midst of a good deal of heraldic display, and one unusual window, the famous 'Bellfounders'' Window, given by Richard Tunnoc, a bellfounder of York. He is shown kneeling in the lower panel of the centre light, presenting a model of the window to an archbishop; but the most interesting part of the window is that containing the panels showing the casting and tuning of a very long, conical-shaped bell. Everyone comes to look at this window, but the multiplicity of little bells in the borders and hanging in rows from all the canopies – hundreds of little bells – is inclined to make the window fretful and fussy.

It is not for their details that I found these fourteenth-century windows so pleasurable an experience, but for their clear, liquid colour. They reminded me before anything else of the gold and green and red pages of illuminated manuscripts – cream parchment leaves lit up with ancient colour. And one evening I was in the Minster as evening fell; then it was wonderful to see how even in the shadows those golden windows radiated coloured light. Such an effect would not have been possible with thirteenth-century windows. The secret, of course, is in the silver stain. Nevertheless, these fourteenth-century windows, for all their aesthetic appeal, do not awaken the spiritual exaltation which the old Canterbury windows arouse. They play fine organ music, but not harmonies so solemn they seem to be the Voice of God Himself.

After the Minster come the parish churches of York, for fifteen of them have between them (or had, before the air-raids of the Second World War) seventy windows containing mediaeval glass. In some cases there are only a few jumbled fragments, but in others whole windows are virtually complete. So I began a happy pilgrimage to these humbler places of worship, where, the windows being as a rule lower than those of the Minster, I could in most cases see all they contained distinctly and come so close to them that the saints and prophets living in them became my familiar friends.

In St. Martin-cum-Gregory in Micklegate – a lonely church, where services are no longer held – there is in the north aisle a window with fourteenth-century 'illuminated manuscript' type of glass in it, showing figures in blue and pink and gold under yellow canopies standing against green or red patterned backgrounds. In the east window of the south aisle St. Martin divides his cloak with a beggar in the middle light, and two other saints, unidentified, stand in the lights on either side; when the sun shines through them it makes the ruby glow, and turns the silver stain canopies as gold as itself. In this church I discovered that some of the glass was of the fifteenth century. I soon found this to be the case with all the York parish churches, though it was a little while before I saw anything complete enough to show unmistakably what fifteenth-century characteristics in stained glass were.

St. Michael-le-Belfry, which stands in the shadow of the Minster, is a wide, light church. It has a high, eighteenth-century reredos adorned with gilded Corinthian columns, so that the lovely fourteenth-century glass in the east window was rather difficult to see properly. But it was 'illuminated manuscript' glass again, red, white, gold, blue and green, glowing like fire! St. Peter and St. Paul were there, the Coronation of the Virgin, the Resurrection, the Nativity, the Annunciation, and below knelt the donors. Large crocketed canopies filled all the lights above in a wide band. The rest of the glass here was very late mediaeval, moving fast into the orbit of the Renaissance.

In Holy Trinity, Goodramgate, standing embowered in trees far back from the street, the glass is also rather late; but the east window is still mediaeval in detail, though verging on the sixteenth-century 'pictorial' era in the mass. Craftsmen were even yet, in mediaeval wise, depicting St. Christopher, St. Mary, Cleopas, St. Anne, Salome, Zebedee and St. John the Evangelist; even yet, in pale green and yellow, they painted crowned virgins and mitred bishops; but the aura of sanctity has fled from them. They are all flourishing and personable, and probably, from the look of them, wealthy citizens.

I made my way to St. Denys, in one of the poorer quarters of the city, to see, at the east end of the north aisle, the jumbled remnants of a once magnificent fourteenth-century Jesse Tree, filling five lights. As a Jesse Tree it is now, in its mutilated state, rather disappointing, but its colours were very beautiful, chiefly blue, and light green where the branches twine to form symmetrical vesicae, and it is touched with spots of ruby. The most easterly window in the north wall of this aisle is, however, in its complete fourteenth-century state, tracery lights as well, and gives a good idea of what a mediaeval window really looked like when it was young. Once more the donors appear, kneeling in the lower panels of the windows; there is one especially attractive example in St. Denys, in a ruby robe and green cloak, and hair which can only be described as 'ginger', holding an upward floating scroll inscribed in blackletter, *Domine miserere mei* – 'Lord, have mercy upon me.' Lombardic lettering passed away with the thirteenth century, and inscriptions are now in blackletter. In this church, in the south aisle, a Victorian and a fifteenth-century stained glass window exist side by side. It is instructive to compare them.

St. Michael's, Spurriergate, had, however, rather more to offer the quester after mediaeval glass. Most of it – certainly the best – was late fifteenth century, and in the windows of the south aisle (always, of course, the best lit).

P

It was a little fragmentary, jostled and jumbled, but its effect was pale and delicately beautiful, blue and red and green of crystal clearness with touches of gold, the middle window in particular having that rather wistful fragility which is perhaps a reflection of the fifteenth-century *memento mori* outlook upon life.   Kings and prophets remain as fragments of a Jesse Tree, and God the Father with eight of the nine orders of angels who surround the Throne of God: Seraphim, Cherubim, Thrones, Principalities, Dominions, Virtues and Powers.

Finally, in a dingy back street behind Micklegate, I found the small, dark church of All Saints, North Street. Nothing about its exterior gives any hint of the glorious treasure of mediaeval glass it contains within, including two windows untouched by the hand of the destroyer.   Fourteen out of the sixteen windows have some mediaeval glass in them, eight of them are more or less complete.   Many of them, as is usual in these centuries, show saints under canopies, notably St. William of York, mitred and in full vestments, standing with his episcopal cross, all in gold and white, against a diapered ruby background, and to match him, in the same colours, St. John the Evangelist.

But most impressive of all the many mediaeval windows here were two in the north aisle farthest east: one representing six of the Seven Corporal Works of Mercy, and the other the 'Prykke of Conscience'.   Presumably these two windows remain (apart from a little judicious restoration) as their makers left them nearly 500 years ago because their subjects are such that no reformer, however Puritanic, could take exception to them.   The dominant colours of the nine panels of the Six Corporal Works of Mercy and the canopies above them are white, red, blue and gold; and the window is interesting not only because of its unusual (in stained glass) subject matter, but also because it illustrates contemporary dress and certain details of everyday life.   In all six of the panels showing the Merciful Works the same figure appears; a gentle, elderly man (rather like the 'Good Man' of the wall painting at Trotton Church) perhaps a king, with curly hair and beard and a kindly expression. First he feeds the hungry from a large basket full of bun-shaped loaves, then with his own hand pours drink into the out-stretched bowls of six thirsty beggars, one of whom, bald-headed, is drinking greedily from his bowl. He then entertains strangers, emerging from beneath a gabled doorway to clasp the hand of a weary looking figure and to usher him and his three companions within; after which, with a most commiserating gleam in his eyes, he holds out a long tunic to a naked man, while an attendant in the doorway behind carries another garment over his arm for a second naked man with the face of a rough peasant standing near the first. Not content with these charitable acts, the kingly benefactor next visits the sick man as he lies in bed – naked, as was the mediaeval custom – under an embroidered coverlet; a quaint and lovable little tubchair is on one side of the bed, and on the other sits a woman who, by the gesture of her hands, seems to be telling the visitor how very ill the patient is; the visitor, meanwhile, lays upon the bed several large coins – as large as biscuits. Lastly, he even penetrates into the prison and offers comfort to the prisoners chained in the stocks. Two of the lowest panels show kneeling donors and a priest in a blue robe before an altar, saying mass for them. The sun and seven stars shine in a blue sky over a stretch of water in the middle panel.

The 'Prykke of Conscience' window is unique. As far as I know its subject was never elsewhere treated in any mediaeval art that has survived. It was directly inspired by the poem, *The Agenbite of Inwit* of the early fourteenth-century writer, Richard Rolle of Hampole, or rather that part of it which describes the last fifteen days of the world as foretold by St. Jerome:

> Thus speaks the holy man St. Jerome
> Of fifteen tokens that shall come
> Before Christ's coming, as he says,
> The which shall fall in fifteen days.

In fifteen small panels these 'tokens' are presented. The sea rises up against a ruby background and subsides again before a blue one and again before a blue one the waters return to their former level, conventional yellow and green trees appearing in all these panels. Then great white fishes and sea monsters leap up from the white sea into a blue sky; on the fifth day the sea is on fire, and glowing red tongues of flame play before the deep blue; whereupon on the next day the trees catch fire – two are still green, but the third is turning red. The next day an earthquake brings toppling down houses, castles, towers and walls; they hurtle together against the same deep blue background. On the eighth day rocks and stones are consumed, while the sky glows red and the three trees, seemingly resuscitated, appear again amongst upheaved yellow boulders. On the ninth day mankind hides in variously coloured holes; on the terrible morrow of that day only a blood-red sky is visible above a white waste of uninhabited land – and the trees seem at last overpowered, for they have vanished. On the eleventh day men in red and pink and greyish blue, having come out of their holes, pray before the blood red sky; on the twelfth day, scattered about over the white waste under the glowing sky are yellow coffins and the bones of the dead. On the thirteenth day golden stars fall from heaven, in the fourteenth men lie dead in bed and a red-robed figure lifts up his arms in despair and lamentation. Lastly, raging fire in which appear tongues of blue consumes all: the Day of Doom has come and the world is at an end.

Unperturbed by these catastrophic events three little donors in red and blue appear in each of the lights, below the panels, meekly kneeling, with their hands lifted or clasped in prayer. Far up above the lurid scenes on earth, in the tracery lights, St. Peter, holding the great key with which he opens the doors of Paradise, welcomes the blessed into heaven; and the devil, with the 'fat stick wherewith he prods his unhappy victims' drives the damned down to hell. This is, then, another Doom; but represented like no other Doom in England or France, in sculpture, mosaic or wall-painting.

Seen from across the church this window presents a curious appearance, quite unlike that of any other medi-aeval stained glass window.*

The characteristics of fifteenth-century glass are now growing clearer. One obvious difference between the work of the fourteenth and fifteenth centuries lies in the canopies. One has only to look first at the canopies in the fourteenth-century window at the east end of the south aisle, and then at those in the fifteenth-century window above the high altar in All Saints, North Street (a better example still of a fifteenth-century canopy would be one in Cirencester Church) to see the change. In the fourteenth century there is one large, geometrical, crocketed central gable, and however bewildering the array of finials and pinnacles and gablets and towers above and behind it there is always a certain symmetry about them. In the fifteenth century the central gable has gone, and the turrets and pinnacles are in complete disarray, not always even perpendicular, making what has been called a 'froth of pinnacles';† moreover, while fourteenth-century canopies always soar ever up-wards, usually in a rather brassy silver stain, those of the fifteenth century are lower and flatter, and are often white only faintly touched with pale yellow, standing against a background of red or blue.

There is also a good deal of white in the figures in fifteenth-century work, and all the silver stain is more delicate. As the predominating colours of the fourteenth century were red, green and deep gold, so of the following century they are blue, red and white. The figures, too, have lost the S-bend, the willowy elegance and with it the mannered affectation of the fourteenth century; they are

* St. Martin's, Coney Street, formerly another treasure-house of ancient glass, was unfortunately a casualty of the Second World War.

† Arnold and Saint: *Stained Glass of the Middle Ages in England and France.*

shorter, less graceful, more stolid, though often much better drawn and more vital.

An interesting feature of fifteenth-century glass is its heads. They usually have curly hair, and in the case of elderly men, curly beards, and a curious and rather quaint tip-tilted nose; expressions are wide-eyed, innocent and naïve. Very rarely are the occupants of fifteenth-century windows sophisticated. Matt-shading is introduced upon garments, and the rich blues of the former century fade into a kind of bluish grey.

Finally, owing to the craftsmen's mastery, by this time, of the art of silver stain and his accomplished use of brown enamel he could now depict so many details on one piece of glass that it was no longer necessary to have scores of tiny pieces all leaded together as in days gone by. The result is at once apparent. The jewel-like mosaic glass of the thirteenth and early fourteenth century disappears, with all its wonder of mystical glowing colour. In fifteenth-century glass all that is left is a clearly stated picture – which often reminds one in the best preserved examples of scenes espied through the limpid waters of a crystal-clear pool pierced to its depths by strong sunlight.

One last difference – the alternating colour-panel and *grisaille* of the fourteenth century vanishes. I had only to go back into the Minster, look at the fourteenth-century nave windows and then walk eastwards to the St. William and St. Cuthbert windows of the choir transepts and to the great east window to see how the fifteenth century filled all its lights, as the thirteenth had done, with coloured glass – though with a totally different effect.

In the tracery of the huge east window there are 144 compartments, and in the lights below 117 panels, and the subjects are difficult if not impossible to decipher without field-glasses. This window is a representation above of scenes from the Old Testament, and below of the Apocalypse, with figures of ecclesiastics, kings and archbishops. Actually, however, one may be content to gaze on this wonderful window for its colours alone: blues and greens, golds and silvery whites, all sparkling with a translucent quality again reminiscent of jewels flashing their radiant hues through crystal-clear water.

My study of fifteenth-century glass took me also to Great Malvern Priory, in the shadow of those hills where Langland dreamt his dream 600 years ago and saw the 'field full of folk' and his vision of *Piers Plowman*. Here there is late glass of varying quality in windows of the north aisle, the clerestory, the north and south choir aisles, and – fragmentarily – in the east and west windows. Those in St. Anne's Chapel in the south choir aisle are especially attractive. They are low down and very easy to see, and in a glitter of white and gold, dark blue, green and red and pink, under moon and stars or the daylight blue of the sky, amid streams full of fish, birds in the trees and grass over which roam camels, deer, goats, oxen, porcupine and lions, one red ram and one small white pig, they tell the story of Creation, and the Fall of Man beside the Forbidden Tree in the Garden of Eden. In the first window a golden winged angel in a gold-bordered white robe banishes Adam and Eve, driving them forth with his brandished sword, and then we see Adam digging the earth and Eve with a mediaeval kerchief over her head – in fact, a mediaeval woman entirely – with the baby on her knee. The second window shows Noah and his family and the ark; his subsequent shame of nakedness and drunkenness; the building of a mediaeval-looking buttressed tower which can be none other than the Tower of Babel, and the story of God's Covenant with Abraham. The third window gives the Old Testament stories of the Sacrifice of Isaac, Jacob stealing Esau's birthright, Joseph and his brethren, and the whole life of Moses.

Saints and bishops, Apostles and Evangelists, and the nine orders of angels look down from the clerestories, where too, with the aid of glasses, the story of the foundation of the Priory in 1085 may be made out. Christ's Passion fills most of the east window, with donors and benefactors below (easily seen from the ambulatory) and Apostles and the Virgin in the tracery above. Some of this glass in the east window is lost, some damaged, some jumbled; once again it seems better to regard parts of it merely as pleasing kaleidoscopes of colour, without looking overmuch for details.

Malvern has in its glass several representations of angel musicians – chiefly in the east window and in the late one in the north transept, said to have been given by Henry VII, perhaps in the opening years of the sixteenth century. In dark blue and green, gold and purplish red, they pluck the strings of their lyres with a plecten, blow their recorders, manipulate the pipe and tabor, or finger the clarion; they play shawms, dulcimers and portative organs, viols and the organistrum – all the instruments so often illustrated in the illuminated manuscripts.

From one place to another I went, studying this fifteenth-sometimes verging on sixteenth-century glass; to the east window at St. Peter Mancroft in Norwich, the glittering red and blue and gold legacy of the Norwich School of Glasspainters, an inspiring sight early on a summer morning when the sun kindles its colour to fire; to Gloucester Cathedral, to the enormous 'Creçy' window at the east end; to the windows at Ludlow, at Cirencester, the Beauchamp Chapel at Warwick, or to humble parish churches where a window here and a quarry there, tracery lights alone in one, a single small panel in another, still existed to tell how much glory, not of the fifteenth century only, but of three centuries preceding, had been lost. Sad little fragments of an angel's wing, a yellow crowned head, a piece of deep blue with a fern-like pattern meandering over it, the Sacred Monogram, or M (for Maria) with a crown above it, the finial of a canopy, an irregular hexagon of glowing ruby, were sometimes jumbled all together without coherence into a 'museum' window – little broken pieces picked up after the iconoclastic storm which shattered them had passed by, and put in some corner where they were discovered long after and leaded into a window where one glowing panel after another makes a mockery of some Victorian monstrosity beside it.

The tale of all of them cannot here be told in full; but one further pilgrimage I must describe in detail before I have done.   That is to the church of Fairford, not far from Cirencester; for this church is unique in retaining the whole of its original set of stained glass windows almost intact.   It is also extremely interesting because it is on the verge of a new, non-mediaeval world, and its style is rather different from that of other fifteenth-century glass.

This gracious Perpendicular church standing in rural surroundings in a most picturesque Cotswold village was built right at the end of the fifteenth century, and the glass is that with which its windows were filled at that time. Here, then, is a complete scheme again: an exposition of the Christian faith.   There are single figures in the nave windows, the prophets on the north facing the Apostles on the south; each Apostle holds the sentence he is traditionally supposed to have contributed to the creed, the prophet opposite holds a corresponding verse from his Old Testament writings – all on curling scrolls which wind decoratively above the writers' heads.   Opposite the four Evangelists are the four Latin Fathers.   At the east end of the church the Fall of Man and other scenes from the Old Testament are in the north aisle, leading up to the Passion of Christ in the central east window.   At the east end of the south aisle we are shown Christ's Descent into Hell, His Resurrection, and subsequent events.   The Day of Judgement, so often painted upon the west wall of mediaeval churches, is here shown in the glass of the great west window (the tower of the church is central, so that there is space for an open window).   In the west windows of the aisles are David condemning the guilty Amalekite, type of the judgement upon the damned, and the Judgement of Solomon, type of the salvation of the elect.

Vivid hues are everywhere.   In the Temptation scene a green tree has bright red apples, and a blue serpent coiled around its trunk, and though Eve is colourless, except for her faint yellow hair, there are architectural canopies in brown outline above in front of a deep blue background; the background of the tree is pink.   Moses and the burning bush have red backgrounds behind the canopies; Gideon is a fifteenth-century knight praying by a very green tree the trunk whereof is purple; and near by is the Queen of Sheba in gold, who kneels before a Solomon resplendent in ruby. The Adoration of the Magi is a glory of gold and ruby.

The dominating colour in the east window of the south chapel is blue: here Christ meets the Holy Women leaving the Sepulchre.   There is a deep blue and green landscape background to the scene, reminiscent of Flemish illumination.   But this landscape background – and that Crucifixion – and the Doom in the west window, all of them spreading across the lights instead of each incident confining itself as hitherto, to one – what do these things portend? The beginning of the end, alas!   The first faint shadow falling before of that treatment of glass windows as if they were one stretch of canvas to paint a whole picture on: the approach to the 'pictorial' treatment which was to ruin the art till the dawn of the twentieth century.

But the end was not yet.   The Flemish-type prophets standing under their squat canopies in the north aisle, clad in matt-shaded red and blue and white, have a tender graciousness better felt than described.   Still the patched-up west windows (all the west windows were damaged in a storm in 1703) have the glowing reds and greens and gold of mediaeval pageantry.   Although there are those who do not agree with me I do not care much for even the mediaeval part of the west window – I think it gaudy.   The terrific flames of a glowing hell on the right, with blue and purple demons carrying the miserable souls of the damned, and a brilliantly golden heaven on the left are no doubt responsible for this.   The upper half of the window, with

Christ in Majesty, is a nineteenth-century copy of the original, destroyed in that eighteenth-century storm, and does not help matters in the least.

In the clerestory windows the Persecutors of the Church fill the north side, glaring across at the martyrs on the south. One can distinguish Herod, transfixing a Holy Innocent, Nero with St. Paul's head, and Judas with a halter round his neck and the thirty pieces of silver in a bag, between Annas and Caiaphas; and the persecuting Roman emperor Diocletian is there too. All these figures, being so high up, were not, of course, as easy to see as the others had been. I had to be content to sit and let them glimmer with all the rest of the windows around me. As I did so – if only the carved woodwork of the screens had been painted as they were long ago, if only those faint figures of angels and saints which hovered like faded phantoms upon the walls had retained the aspect they once had had, if those fragmentary indications of pattern by the chancel arch had sprung again to their former life – if, in short, the whole church had still worn throughout the mediaeval colours which its windows alone had kept – then I should at last have known that which no one to-day can now ever know: what a church of the Middle Ages really looked like to those who entered it in centuries gone by and found every part of it a glory of radiant, vivid colour.

16

'LIKE PAGEANTRY OF MIST ON
AN AUTUMNAL STREAM'

∽∽∽∽∽∽∽∽∽∽∽∽∽∽∽∽∽∽

Now surely it would seem that I have reached my journey's end. Yet have I? I remember the by-lanes, the little winding ways, the tracks that struck off the main highway to where

> Towers, and battlements it sees
> Bosom'd high in tufted trees.*

These by-ways, winding paths and tracks far afield I have in turn followed, one after the other, and I am still following them, I am ever finding fresh ones; and so I say my journey is for ever without an end.

Through a fairyland of pinnacles and finials of choir-stalls and canopies I find my way into the world in which it was the turn of the fifteenth century to be pre-eminent: the world of carved woodwork. All around are carved rood screens, carved timber roofs, lacey openwork tracery of roof spandrels, struts and braces and horizontal beams with all manner of devices wrought upon them. And angel roofs – a peculiarity of East Anglia – or at any rate, this is the region where they are seen at their best. In the Church of St. Wendreda on the outskirts of March, in the flat, poppy-encrimsoned fenlands of Cambridgeshire, there is a

* Milton: *L'Allegro*.
228

carved angelic host with outspread wings soaring upwards in the double hammer-beam roof as if to the ridge pole at its apex; one can almost hear the rush of ascending wings. How splendid a sight they must have been when they were all painted and gilt! Yet St. Wendreda's is only one of several such roofs, though all are not so overpoweringly glorious.

Then in cathedral after cathedral there are miserere seats, their undersides carved with grotesque or heraldic beasts, with mermen and mermaids, with birds and fabulous monsters – the griffin, dragon and the unicorn. They tell Biblical stories, as of Jonah and the Whale, the Beheading of John the Baptist, Samson carrying off the gates of Gaza, or Noah's ark; they laugh over Pilate trundling Judas Iscariot away in a wheelbarrow, or at two grotesque musicians, one of whom pretends to play the rebec with a pair of tongs and bellows. They illustrate fables like the Fox and the Grapes, or romances such as that of Tristran and Iseult or of Alexander, and the tale of the Swan Knight, Lohengrin. There are warnings against incontinence and pride, the latter represented by a knight tumbling from his horse; they illustrate sports and pastimes – footballers, and a game of backgammon. They depict the labours of the months – at the little church of Ripple, near Tewkesbury, there is a complete set of twelve, and the same subject is repeated at Great Malvern and Worcester Cathedral.

The saints, of course, are present; St. Martin dividing his cloak with a beggar, and the Murder of Thomas à Becket. But best of all are the genre scenes: the woman belabouring her husband with a besom or dragging him by the hair of his head, the housewife chasing off a fox who has one of her chickens in his mouth, the man warming his feet at the fire, with two sides of bacon hanging up behind him, the tippler filling a big mediaeval 'baluster' jug from the ale-cask, with a beatific expression on his face, or the apes robbing a sleeping pedlar. They even represent one of the wood-carving fraternity at work at his bench.

In many churches in East Anglia and the West Country the backs of the benches are carved; the bench-ends also, which often rise into carved 'topknots' known as 'poppy-heads'. Sometimes instead of ordinary poppyheads, figures of knights and musicians are represented, or animals snarling, or archers drawing their bows, or the personified Seven Deadly Sins, with demons attendant. On the bench-ends themselves are evangelists writing their gospels, ladies with hands clasped in prayer, merchants in long robes, an acolyte, perhaps, with a processional cross, St. Lawrence with his gridiron, the martyrdom of St. Agatha, and Christ holding the orb of the world. At Brent Knoll in Somerset there is a series representing the misdeeds and ultimate hanging of Reynard the Fox, and at Dennington in Suffolk the only carved-wood example I know of in England of a Sciapod: one of those men (so the old travellers used to say) who had only one foot, of enormous size, which they used as a parasol to shelter them from the sun.

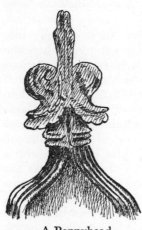

A Poppyhead

I seem now to walk along a path through dying autumn woods where leaves turn sere and yellow and fall sighing to the ground, and to come to a covert of dull, embossed gold and ancient red in the midst of olive green. Here are the faded remnants, damaged and often decayed, of the panel paintings on wood of the Middle Ages. Here, in those sombre, Time-darkened colours the saints and apostles stand, each in his patterned niche tracery-canopied, along the bases of East Anglian and West Country rood screens. This one holds his saltire cross, that one his sword, his key of heaven, a boat, a flaying-knife, a castle, a wheel, all

attributes to show his (or her) identity. The noblest array
is on the screen at Ranworth, in the midst of the Norfolk
Broads, but there are scores of others, and in some cases
where the saints have gone, the screen retains its mediaeval
colouring.

Here, in the eighties of last century, 'Hanging separately
on rusty nails in various parts of the church', neglected and
forgotten, but now cleaned and restored, and back in their
rightful place as a reredos for the high altar, are the wistful,
delicate panels of the Norwich church of St. Michael-at-
Plea, picturing an Annunciation, a Betrayal, a Crucifixion,
St. Margaret and St. Erasmus – all of that pathetic, fragile-
looking, fourteenth-century Norwich school type. Here,
for all to see at the west end of the nave of Westminster
Abbey, is the portrait of the child Richard II, holding orb
and sceptre and wearing England's crown: dark and
sombre in its dulled reds and gold; and here is another
portrait of the young Richard in the Wilton Diptych: now
in the National Gallery. On one side Richard is being
presented, kneeling, to the Virgin and Child by his patron
saints, St. John the Baptist, St. Edward the Confessor
(holding the legendary ring) and St. Edmund, bearing like
a sceptre in his left hand one of the arrows wherewith the
Danes slew him; on the other side, in a glory of intense blue,
the Virgin stands in a flowery mead thronged with angels,
holding in her arms the golden-nimbed Holy Child who
stretches out welcoming arms towards the suppliant – all
against a background of gold.

And here, in the south aisle of Norwich Cathedral, is the
mediaeval retable, with the same type of painted figures as
on the St. Michael-at-Plea panels. The top of the Crucifixion panel has at some time been cut off, but in the others
Christ suffers at the pillar, He almost faints under the
weight of the Cross, He steps out of His tomb, and in the
last panel ascends into heaven.* And here, in the rooms of

* In February, 1959, this panel, restored, was fixed as a reredos in
St. Luke's Chapel, off the south choir aisle of the Cathedral.

the Society of Antiquaries in London, hang four darkened
scenes from the Life of St. Etheldreda, and some of the
earliest portraits extant of mediaeval kings.

But one unique surviving series of panel paintings is the
Jesse Tree in the roof of the Lady Chapel at St. Helen's
Church in Abingdon. Here, on the branches of a painted
vine-trail, in pairs under crocketed ogee arches, with a
slender buttress terminating in a crocketed finial separating
each pair, stand prophets and kings. The kings are the
earthly ancestors of Christ, the prophets, who hold scrolls
inscribed with Messianic prophecies, are his spiritual for-
bears.* At the eastern end on the north side – for the
panels are found on the slope of the roof both north and
south – there is an Annunciation, with a 'Lily' Crucifix –
that is, a pot of lilies with the figure of the Crucified upon
a lily-stem. All the figures are of fourteenth-century type,
some of them slightly showing the S-bend, all courtly and
fine-featured, with the characteristic boneless fingers of
the century. Darkened scarlet, purple, green, blue, plum
and gold are the colours in which they are arrayed.

Such are some of the painted panels of the Middle Ages.
Faded, dimmed, many of them scratched and mutilated,
they are now but sad autumn's ghosts of the pageantry of
a summer that died long ago.

More often than I can say some thread-like path over
fields and beside streams and woods has led me onwards to
where I saw in the distance the tower or spire of an ancient
church. Mediaeval man said that one entered the Church
through Baptism; and so in every case where the mediaeval
order of things has not been disturbed by later centuries
one enters the church past the font, placed at, or very near,
the west end. They are mostly of stone; there are a very
few, in England, of lead. Round fonts, square fonts,
hexagonal and octagonal fonts, pudding-basin fonts – there
are all kinds, in two instances – at Trunch and at St. Peter

* See A. E. Preston, F.S.A.: *The Fourteenth-century Painted Ceiling at
St. Helen's Church, Abingdon.*

Mancroft – with their mediaeval closures still standing over them, in several cases – the very best I ever remember is at Ufford, in Suffolk – with their mediaeval covers still existing. At Salle, in Norfolk, there remains in working order the mediaeval painted font crane fixed to the front of the tower gallery and projecting over the font, for lifting off the cover when a baptism was about to take place.

At Brighton there is a font carved with a rather grim Romanesque Last Supper. There sit the stern-faced disciples at a table covered with a cloth, and round the other side an equally stern Romanesque St. Nicholas defeats the wiles of the devil. In Tournai marble at Winchester Cathedral St. Nicholas and his Romanesque miracles appear again, on the square basin of the font. At Walpole St. Peter, among many other churches in Norfolk, the Seven Sacraments are carved in canopied panels on each face of the octagonal font – Baptism, Confirmation, Eucharist, Matrimony, Ordination, Penance and Extreme Unction, a Crucifixion often appearing on the eighth side. Sometimes on fonts heraldic beasts and the evangelical symbols are carved; sometimes angels with scrolls, and often coats of arms. Norman fonts generally have arcades with bulbous capitals to their miniature columns, Saxon ones plaited strapwork or beasts in a coil of foliage showing the 'Saxon lock'; in one instance (this font is now only a museum piece, at York) crude, childishly executed figures with bows and arrows stand under equally crude arcading.

On the lead font at Walton-on-the-Hill in Surrey apostles sit under arcades, just as they do at Dorchester Abbey, in solemn Romanesque aloofness; but the font at Brookland, on Romney Marsh (the church with its 'candle-extinguisher' timber steeple standing on the ground beside it) has a double row of arcades on its lead font, with the signs of the zodiac on the upper row, and the labours of the months along the lower. These are executed just as primitively as another collection in the church at Burnham Deepdale in Norfolk, not very far from Holkham and Wells-next-the-Sea,

Q

only this time the font is a stone one, and square and Norman.

Another time a flower-decked footpath led me through fruiting trees over green, beflowered meads where the larks sang to battlemented walls and machicolated towers, and I saw the chief existing secular art of the Middle Ages in the tapestries, breathing the fresh air of the Touraine countryside. They hung once, many of them, in the castles which rise along the borders of the Loire, at Blois, Loches, Tours, Chinon and Fontainebleau, where the French court wandered from place to place during the fifteenth century, and a procession of illuminators, goldsmiths, sculptors, painters and tapestry-weavers followed it. The most famous set is the 'Lady with the Unicorn' – an allegory of the Five Senses – from the Castle of Boussac in the remote Auvergne, where George Sand saw it 100 years and more ago, and wrote in her diary,

Cette dame blonde et ténue est très mystérieuse et tout d'abord elle a presenté hier à ma petite-fille l'aspect d'une fée.

The whole set was exhibited a few years ago in London, and the poetry of it, the lyrical quality of its figures and colouring – dominated by a background of subtle, elusive red – wafted me straight back to the age which gave it birth.

Sometimes the French tapestries, in scenes set against a ground bestrewn with flowery plants – the *millefiori* or *mille-fleurs* backgrounds – depict the leisured delights of the 'Seignorial Life': here men prepare for the hunt or actually chase the quarry, here ladies in leisured grace take a bath or gaze at themselves in mirrors, or embroider. Or there are sets of 'Chamber Tapestries', with romantic subjects. One famous one is the 'Offering of the Heart', but the 'Tale of Troy' was woven also, and the 'History of Alexander' – with innumerable mediaeval accretions.

But the hand of the Church grasped tapestries also. I seemed to see them again as they were in centuries gone by, hung on festival days above the stalls in the choir, or sometimes from column to column along the nave arcades of great churches. The Apocalyptic Visions of St. John covered the walls of the private chapel of Louis, Duke of Anjou, at Angers, the woven scenes of the Legend of St. Stephen were in the choir at Auxerre, and the Life of the Virgin along the nave of the Cathedral of Rheims. Especially I could see, between the massy Norman piers of Bishop Odo's Cathedral at Bayeux, unfaded in its original splendour, the so-called *Bayeux Tapestry* (which of course is not a tapestry at all, but a long strip of embroidered linen). I saw its Norman knights with their kite-shaped shields, its Saxon lords and bishops, its ships and castles and thrones and the towers of the earliest Westminster Abbey whither Edward the Confessor was borne to be buried, all twinkling and flashing out then sinking into shadow again as the draughty wind in the dark nave set the sparkling points of light of all the candles wavering on some great feast day – Christmas, perhaps, or Candlemas.

Then, too, I saw the famous English embroideries, the *Opus Anglicanum*, mostly now in museums: the Syon Cope, and the Butler-Bowden Cope of crimson velvet with saints, kings and ecclesiastics standing under canopies, the Annunciation, the Adoration of the Magi and the Coronation of the Virgin all embroidered in coloured silks, gold and silver thread, pearls and beads. Both are in the Victoria and Albert Museum, and though there are perhaps no others so splendid as these, there are many beautiful embroideries in museums and in the houses of the great, worked undeniably by English hands five and six centuries ago.

Among silver censers and thuribles and incense, under vaulted roofs and through monastic choirs I seemed to walk to the up-piled treasures of the minor arts: *champlevé* and *cloisonné* enamels from Limoges and the region of the Moselle, crucifixes and reliquaries and portable altars for private devotions, purple and blue, 'mystic, wonderful', shining with a burning intensity of blue; or book covers gleaming with pearls and semi-precious stones set around the enamelled figure of Christ in Majesty. Or there are ivory triptychs and diptychs, minutely carved with Passion scenes and saints, still clinging to the last remnants of ancient greens and blues and reds in the corners of their tiny trefoil or cinquefoil headed arches, and their microscopic traceried windows; their Crucifixions are crowded with Lilliputian actors all with their hands and feet and features meticulously carved. Here again I touched secular life. Not infrequently I came upon mirror-cases and caskets carved with such romantic themes as the Siege of the Castle of Love, with ladies pelting the attacking knights with roses.

Through a less rarefied air, out into the light of common day, I followed the path to the English alabasters. Here in the fourteenth and fifteenth centuries was mass-production on a large scale, centring, it would seem, upon Nottingham, and doing export business to the Continent. The surviving alabasters are many. There is a great array of them at the Victoria and Albert Museum,* many of these, too, still clinging to the fading traces of their mediaeval colour. How difficult it is to think of these and the ivories as originally all brightly coloured!

Here again are Passion scenes, especially the Resurrection, and the Life of the Virgin, and scenes from the Lives of the Saints, with in many cases, their martyrdom. Some of them are considerably more skilfully carved than others. Some are overcrowded, repetitive and monotonous. But nearly all, even if they fail in general design, have details of considerable charm; a tiny figure of Nicodemus, for example, in a fifteenth-century hat and nondescript cowled garment, who, with a determined expression, armed with an enormous pair of pincers, is removing the nails from the feet of Christ on the Cross; or the uplifted hands of the onlookers, men and women, behind the donkey's head in the Entry into Jerusalem; but these are mere random examples.

---

* Collected over many years by the late Dr. W. Hildburgh, and presented by him to the Museum in 1946, on his seventieth birthday.

There are naïve and charming touches everywhere in the alabasters.

Along cypress-bordered paths, through still places where the very wind holds its breath, this path has led me to the silent aisles, where the candles burn upwards in long tongues of flame to arabesques of smoke winding under the vaulted roofs till they are lost.   Here lie upon their tombs the effigies of the dead: king and prince and knight and burgher.   Here in the Royal Chapel of Edward the Confessor at Westminster reposes, fashioned in gilt-bronze, Henry III, the artist-king, in the abbey he rebuilt; not far from him lies Eleanor, queen of Edward I, whose last funeral journey was marked where her body rested overnight by the Eleanor Crosses.   Here is Edward III, no longer the victor of Creçy and Poitiers, but an old, tired, long-bearded man in an undistinguished robe, close to his ill-starred grandson, Richard II, who still clasps the hand of his beloved Anne of Bohemia – all these, like Henry III, are fashioned in gilt-bronze.   And here, aloft in his chantry chapel, is the mutilated wooden core of the proud effigy, once covered in silver, of the victor of Agincourt – a sorry relic now.   The little weepers stand mourning under canopies around the bases of the tombs.   We could mourn too, not only at the sight where

> Sceptre and crown
> Must tumble down
> And in the dust be equal made
> With the poor crooked scythe and spade*

but at the manner of their passing – Edward III's, Richard II's, Henry V's.

Near the shrine of the martyred Becket at Canterbury lies 'that noble prince' under his splendid gilt effigy: the Black Prince, in full military array; his funeral achievements, helm and lordly crest, shield and emblazoned jupon, gauntlets and sword scabbard used to hang above.   For

* James Shirley (1596-1666).

600 years they hung there, till, affected like their lord by decaying Time, they had to be sealed away in a glass case on the other side of the choir: only replicas now hang above the tomb.* And here, in cathedral and abbey, and in countless parish churches up and down the land, are those who once were powerful and great, wealthy and prosperous: archbishop and bishop, abbot and priest, baron and knight, citizen and merchant, and barons' and knights' and citizens' and merchants' wives. In vestments and mitres, in the habit of their monastic order, in chain-mail and jupon or plate armour and surcoat, in kirtle and wimple, in coif and with rosary or chatelaine, they lie flat and at rest, holding pastoral staff or with sheathed sword by their sides, their feet on heraldic lions or favourite hounds or pet dogs, their hands pressed together in never-ending prayer, their pillows sometimes smoothed and guarded by little angels. In stone or latten, once painted, sometimes piously re-painted, they lie; occasionally as their makers left them, more often mutilated, headless, armless and legless. Under gabled canopies they repose in wall-recesses, or on table tombs in side chapels, in chantries or before the High Altar, grey shadows mostly asleep, but a few seeming to start from their slumbers and lay their hands upon their swords as at a dream of 'old unhappy far-off things, and battles long ago'.† Sometimes they are nameless, without inscriptions, bereft even of the tomb upon which they once lay; but always there stirs a whisper from their dead lips: *Orate pro animabus . . . Domine, miserere mei. . . .*

'Pray for me, for Christe's love pray for me, as I may not praye now, praye ye with a pater noster': it is like a sigh along the silent aisles as I step soundlessly around those memorials to the less affluent deceased or their more economical heirs – the Monumental Brasses. 1277 is the

---

* Presented 1954 by the Friends of Canterbury Cathedral.

† See, for instance, the effigy of the 'Unknown Warrior' at Dorchester Abbey, of whom it was recorded 400 years ago, 'His name is out of remembrance'.

date of the earliest in the land, and they go on into the
seventeenth century, far beyond mediaeval times. Sir
John D'Abernon in the church at Stoke D'Abernon is
remembered by that first great brass – great in size as well
as craftsmanship, for the lance he carries, with its pennon,
is six feet long.   There are the remains of blue enamel on
his shield.   Roger of Trumpington's brass is not much
later – 1289.   It lies in the shadows of the church of the
village which bears his name, a few miles away from
Cambridge; his mailed head rests on a helm for a pillow,
his mailed hands are joined in prayer, and all his military
accoutrements are plainly and finely incised upon the metal.
Indeed, his and other monumental brasses show such details
of apparel, military and civilian, male and female, ecclesiastical and lay, that they are invaluable for the study of
mediaeval dress and armour, and the changing fashions of
both as the centuries went by.

The aisles of some cathedrals and churches gleam with
brasses let into their floors – where they should be – and
others gleam upright upon the walls, where they should not;
but they are often put there to avoid damage to them from
the tramping back and forth of the living, heedless of the
long-forgotten dead.

For some may have gained glory in war or statecraft, on
thrones or in ecclesiastical councils or chancellories, and
are remembered in the annals of history; but others,
especially those commemorated by brasses, lived and loved,
worked and played – and then they died, and as far as we
are concerned are as if they had never been and as if they
had never been born.   Not always on tomb or on brass do
even their names survive; and even when they do, they are
but names, and what manner of men or women they were
we know not, and now will never know.   'Richard Adams,
died 1522, vicar and prebendary, East Malling, Kent':
'John Strete, rector, died 1405, Upper Hardres, Kent':
'Wool Merchant and wife (nameless) Northleach, Glouces-
tershire': 'Robert Page, Woolstapler of Cirencester 1434' –

there he stands upon his woolsack bearing his merchant's mark, in his long, full-skirted, fur-collared gown with the baggy sleeves drawn in at the wrist, his hands joined in prayer under an arched and crocketed canopy with buttress supports on either side, all incised in the brass: typical of hundreds like him, in scores of churches, whose one last vanity this was: to be remembered by a world which has long since completely forgotten.

Orate pro animabus. . . . 'Pray for me, as I may not praye now, for Christe's love praye for me. . . .'

> We are such stuff
> As dreams are made on, and our little life
> Is rounded with a sleep.*

So died the Middle Ages, in all their ignorance and wisdom, their squalor and pageantry, in all the glory of their wonderful artistry: how glorious and how wonderful we can only guess from the wreck left us after the iconoclastic storm. So let the exhortation of the artist monk Theophilus to one of his pupils be as it were an epitaph for them:

Thou hast in a manner shown forth to the beholders a vision of God's paradise, bright as springtide with flowers of every hue, fresh with green grass and flowers. . . . For man's eye knoweth not whereon first to gaze: if he look up at the vaults, they are as mantles embroidered with spring flowers; if he regard the walls, there is a manner of paradise; if he consider the light streaming through the windows he marvelleth at the priceless beauty of the glass and at the variety of this most precious work. . . . Work, therefore now good man, happy in this life before God's face and Man's, and happier still in the life to come, by whose labour and zeal so many burnt offerings are devoted to God!†

Orate pro animabus mortu'um praeclarissimorum et omnium creatorum pulchritudinis: 'Pray for the souls of the illustrious dead and of all creators of loveliness. . . . Amen.'

* Shakespeare: *The Tempest*, Act IV, Sc. I.
† Theophilus: Prologue to Book III, *Schedula Diversarum Artium*.

GLOSSARY

ACANTHUS: a conventional representation of curling lobed leaves, a common classical decorative motif.

AMBULATORY: a processional way round the east end of a cathedral or large church behind the high altar.

ANNULATED: banded with rings. (See page 115.)

APOCALYPSE: the Revelation of St. John the Divine, recorded in the last book of the New Testament; a mediaeval book containing an illustrated version of this.

APSE: the semi-circular east end of a church or cathedral.

ARCHIVOLT: the inner part of the curve of an arch, or the moulding surrounding the curve of it.

BALDACCHINO: a canopy of stone or marble supported on four pillars over a high altar.

BASILEUS: Greek name for an eastern king.

BASILICA: a long, oblong church with rows of columns, forming aisles, down its length. *Basilical*: having this form.

BENEDICTIONAL: a mediaeval service book containing episcopal benedictions for the great feasts of the Church year.

BLIND ARCADING: closed arcading decoratively attached to a wall.

BOOK OF HOURS: a book for private devotions containing the office in honour of the Virgin as recited at the canonical hours (Matins, Lauds, Prime, etc.).

BOSS: a stone or wooden rounded ornament, usually carved, set over the junction of the ribs of a vault.

BREVIARY: a service book containing offices for the canonical hours (Matins, Lauds, Prime, etc.).

CHAMPLEVÉ: in enamels, a process by which the metal ground is scooped out into hollows to receive the paste, leaving a metal bar outlining the design. cf. *Cloisonné*.

CHEVRON: a Norman decorative motif of repeated parallel zigzags. (See page 111.)

CHI-RHO: the initial letters of the Greek form of CHRISTOS: the sign adopted for his standards by Constantine the Great, and subsequently a symbol of Christianity. (See page 38.)

CINQUEFOIL: an ornament at the head of a panel or arch having five lobes. (See page 121.)

CLERESTORY: the uppermost storey in a church or cathedral, pierced with windows to give extra light to the interior.   (See page 103.)

CLOISONNÉ: in enamels, a process whereby the pastes are laid inside a pattern of upstanding gold wires (cloisons). cf. *Champlevé*.

CODEX: the modern form of bound book as distinct from the classical scroll form.

COLOBIUM: the long straight 'seamless' garment worn by the crucified Christ in representations made under eastern influence.

CORBEL: a projecting stone or piece of timber, generally carved, for supporting a superimposed weight, as of a shaft, etc.

CORONA: a 'crown' of chapels radiating from the ambulatory (q.v.) of a large church or cathedral.

CROCKETS: carvings projecting at regular intervals from the vertical or sloping sides of spires, canopies, etc.   (See page 123.)

CRUCIFORM: in the shape of a Latin or Greek cross.

CUSPS: projecting ornamental points, often carved with leaves at the ends, in arches, windows, tracery, etc.

DIAPER: decoration of a background surface with an all-over pattern in squares or lozenges.

DIPTYCH: a devotional painting having two hinged wings.

DOG TOOTH: an ornamental carving characteristic of the thirteenth century, consisting of a series of small pyramids in a moulding carved in leaf form.   (See page 116.)

ENGAGED SHAFT: a smaller half or three-quarter round shaft attached to a larger central pillar, or to a wall.   (See page 116.)

EVANGELICAL SYMBOLS: representations of the angel, lion, bull and eagle symbolizing respectively SS. Matthew, Mark, Luke and John.

FINIAL: a conventionalized bunch of carved foliage or flowers at the top of a gable, canopy or pinnacle.   (See page 123.)

FLORIATED: incised or carved with a (usually conventional) pattern of leaves.   Also *Foliated* (applied especially to a column capital).

FONT CLOSURE: the free-standing wooden or stone canopy on four pillars over a font.

GENRE SCENE: a scene of ordinary, everyday life, usually domestic.

GRISAILLE: term applied to stained glass or mural or manuscript painting which has an overall monochrome grey or silvery appearance.

GROTESQUE: a small, fantastic painted or carved figure: e.g. a body of a bird with the head of a man and legs of a lion.   (See page 12.)

HAGIOSCOPE: an opening in the wall between an aisle chapel and the chancel of a church through which a priest officiating at a side altar could see the high altar.   Popularly known as a *Squint*.

HOOD MOULD: projecting moulding on the face of a wall above a window or doorway to carry off rainwater.   Also called *Label* or *Dripstone*.

ICON: a sacred mosaic or painted portrait of Christ, the Virgin, saints or martyrs, common in the Orthodox Church in Greece and Russia.

JUPON: a tight-fitting male tunic, fashionable in the last quarter of the fourteenth century.

LABEL STOP: a small carved head at the end of a *Hood Mould* (q.v.) or *Label*.

LANCET WINDOW: a tall, narrow window, pointed at the top, typical of Early English architecture. (See page 116.)

LATTEN: made of an alloy of copper and zinc.

LIERNE VAULTING: a type of stone roof vaulting where the main ribs are non-functionally joined by short cross-ribs which do not spring from the wall supports. (See page 126.)

LIMBO: intermediate region between heaven and hell, the abode after death of unbaptized souls, e.g. of those born before Christ's Incarnation.

LUNETTE: the semi-circular area between the head of a round arch and a horizontal lintel.

MACHICOLATED: (of a projecting gallery at the top of a castle tower or other fortification): having openings in the floor between the supporting corbels of the gallery through which missiles might be hurled down upon attackers.

MANDORLA: the almond-shaped glory surrounding Christ or the Virgin Mary. (See page 173.)

MISERERE: a bracket on the underside of a hinged seat in the choir of a monastic or cathedral church, usually elaborately carved. Also *Misericord*.

MURREY: mediaeval name for mulberry colour, or dark purplish red.

NARTHEX: an arcaded porch at the west end of an Early Christian church.

NIMBUS: the halo (usually circular) originally behind the head of any important personage, as a king, emperor Pope, etc. afterwards exclusively of a holy person.

Cross-nimbus: cruciform nimbus, i.e. a nimbus containing a cross; found only behind the head of Christ.

Square Nimbus: a halo indicating that the person behind whose head it appears was still living when the painting or mosaic was executed.

OGEE: a compound curve of two parts, one convex, the other concave, at the head of an arch, etc. (See page 120.)

ORANT(E): a figure standing in the classical attitude of prayer, with head raised and arms outstretched to the sky.

PALLIUM: a white woollen Y-shaped band worn on the shoulders and falling in front and behind, with four purple crosses on it; a vestment of the Pope and Roman Catholic high ecclesiastical dignitaries.

PANTOCRATOR: a representation of the bust of Christ in the centre of a dome or the curve of an apse vaulting, as Lord and Ruler of all.

PENDENTIVE: an architectural device whereby when a dome was placed upon a square base a curved triangle was introduced at the angles to effect the transition. (See page 43.)

PEPPER-POT: in Early English architecture, a small conical-topped turret at the end of a gable, most common in East Anglia.   (See page 118.)

PHALERA: a Roman military decoration for meritorious conduct.

PILASTER: a flat, shallow pier against a wall, typical of Anglo-Saxon and Norman architecture.

PISCINA: a basin for washing the sacred vessels after Communion, set in the wall, often under a carved arch, on the south side of an altar.

POPPYHEAD: the fleur-de-lys-like ornament at the head of a bench or desk standard in a church; sometimes carved with figures or genre (q.v.) scenes. (See page 230.)

PSALTER: a service-book containing the psalms.

PULPITUM: the stone or wooden screen placed across the east end of the nave in a monastic church to separate the monks' part of the building from that used by the laity.

QUARRY: a small rectangular or diamond-shaped piece of stained glass in a window.

QUATREFOIL: a four-lobed carving often inside a square.   (See page 177.)

RELIQUARY: an object of wood or metal, enamelled or gilded, containing the relic of a saint.

REREDOS: a wooden or stone screen or woven hanging at the back of an altar.

RETABLE: a shelf behind and above the altar or which are placed the cross, lights and vases.

ROOD SCREEN: a wooden or stone carved screen set up under the chancel arch of a church to separate the choir and sanctuary from the nave, so called because in pre-Reformation days a Rood (a cross carrying the crucified Christ) stood on top of it.

ROTULUS: a book in the form of a roll.

RUNE: one of the angular, stroke-like characters of the alphabet used by ancient Germanic peoples.

SALTIRE CROSS: a cross in the shape of an ✕ – usually a symbol of St. Andrew.

SARCOPHAGUS: A classical stone chest-shaped tomb.

SAXON LOCK: a mannerism in Saxon carvings where an animal's leg is thrust out over and beyond the branches in which the creature is imprisoned.

SCRAMASAX: an Anglo-Saxon weapon: a short dagger with a knife-like blade.

SEDILE (plural – sedilia): the seat(s) for the officiating priests, recessed into the wall on the south side of the high altar in a church, usually having carved canopies.

SPANDREL: the area between the segment of a circle and an angle of its enclosing rectangle.

STAVE CHURCH: Norwegian church built entirely of timber.

STELE: a tall, narrow classical gravestone.

STRIATED: marked with narrow, near-parallel grooves.   (See page 170.)

TABERNACLE WORK: intricate carving in wood or stone forming a canopy over a niche for a statue, etc.

TESSERAE: the small stone or glass cubes used in mosaic.

THURIBLE: a censer.

TRANSOM: a horizontal bar of wood or stone across the upper part of a window opening or panel.

TRIFORIUM: the windowless gallery, having an open arcade on one side, immediately above the nave and transept arches of larger churches and cathedrals.   (See page 103.)

TRIPTYCH: a devotional painting on three hinged wings.

TROPER: a liturgical service book containing the musical interpolations (tropes).

TRUMEAU: the pillar in larger churches between the twin doors of an entrance; in France it usually carries a statue.

VESICA: a pointed oval frame enclosing a figure of Christ enthroned (cf. *mandorla*).

VEXILLUM: Roman military standard; name also given to the staff with pennant carried by Christ in His descent into Limbo.

VOLUTE: a spiral ornament; term applied especially to the scroll ornament at the two sides of a column capital, particularly the classical Ionic capital.

VOUSSOIRS: the wedge-shaped stones forming an arch.

BIBLIOGRAPHY

ILLUMINATED MANUSCRIPTS

Cockerell, S. C. *A Psalter and Hours executed before 1270.* Chiswick Press, 1905.

Dodwell, C. R. *The Canterbury School of Illumination.* Cambridge, 1954.

Herbert, J. A. *Illuminated Manuscripts.* Methuen, 1912.

James, M. R. *The Canterbury Psalter.* Lund Humphries, 1935.

Malo, Henri. *Les Très Riches Heures du Duc de Berry.* Verve, 1945.

Mathew, Rev. Gervase. *Byzantine Painting.* Faber and Faber, 1950.

Millar, Eric George. *The Luttrell Psalter.* British Museum, 1932.

—— *The Lindisfarne Gospels.* British Museum, 1923.

Oakeshott, Walter. *The Sequence of English Mediaeval Art.* Faber and Faber, 1953.

—— *The Artists of the Winchester Bible.* Faber and Faber, 1945.

Rickert, Margaret. *Painting in Britain: the Middle Ages.* Pelican History of Art, Penguin Books, 1954.

Robinson, Rev. Stanford F. H. *Celtic Illuminative Art.* Hodges, Figgis & Co. Dublin, 1908.

Saunders, O. Elfrida. *English Illumination.* Pantheon, Florence, 1928.

Sullivan, Sir Edward. *The Book of Kells.* Studio, 1914.

Swarzenski, Hans. *Early Mediaeval Illumination.* Batsford, 1951.

Warner, Sir George. *Queen Mary's Psalter.* British Museum, 1912.

Weitzmann, Kurt. *The Joshua Roll.* Princeton University Press, 1948.

—— *Greek Mythology in Byzantine Art.* Princeton University Press, 1951.

Wormald, Francis. *English Drawings of the Tenth and Eleventh Centuries.* Faber and Faber 1952.

MOSAICS

Bovini, Giuseppe. *I Monumenti Antichi di Ravenna.* Amilcare Pizzi. (N.D.)

Demus, Otto. *The Mosaics of Norman Sicily.* Routledge and Kegan Paul, 1949.

Grabar, André. *Byzantine Painting.* Skira, 1953.

—— and Nordenfalk, Carl. *Early Mediaeval Painting.* Skira, 1947.

Kollwitz, Johannes. *Mosaics*. Herder Art Series, 1954.

Meyer, Peter. *Byzantine Mosaics*. Batsford, 1952.

Weidlé, Wladimir. *Mosaici Paleocristiani e Bizantini*. Electa Editrice, 1954.

—— *Les Mosaiques Venitiennes*. Electa Editrice, 1956.

Volbach, W. F. *Early Christian Mosaics*. Batsford, 1943.

FRESCOES AND WALL AND PANEL PAINTINGS

Bazin, Germain. *L'Ecole Provençale, XIV, XV Siècles*. Skira, 1947.

—— *L'École Parisienne, XIV Siècle*. Skira, 1947.

Bell, Clive, and Gernsheim, Helmut. *Twelfth Century Paintings at Hardham and Clayton*. Millers Press, Lewes, 1947.

Borenius, Tancred, and Tristram, E. W. *English Mediaeval Painting*. Pantheon, Florence, 1927.

Constable, W. G. *Exhibition of British Primitive Paintings*. Oxford, 1924.

Grabar, André, and Nordenfalk, Carl. *Early Mediaeval Painting*. Skira, 1954.

Hauglid, Roar, and Grodecki, Louis. *Norway: Paintings from the Stave Churches*. Unesco, 1955.

James, M. R. *The Frescoes in the Chapel at Eton College*. Spottiswoode, 1907.

Maiuri, Amedeo. *Roman Painting*. Skira, 1953.

Michel, Paul-Henri (translated, Joan Evans). *Romanesque Wall Paintings in France*. Thames and Hudson, 1950.

Pallottino, Massimo. *Etruscan Painting*. Skira, 1952.

Radojčić, Svetozar. Frescoes of Sopoćani. Magazine *Jugoslavija*, 1953.

Rice, D. T., and Radojčić, Svetozar. *Yugoslavia: Mediaeval Frescoes*. Unesco, 1955

Tristram, E. W. *English Mediaeval Wall Painting in the Twelfth Century*. Oxford, 1944.

—— *English Mediaeval Wall Painting in the Thirteenth Century*. Oxford, 1950.

—— *English Mediaeval Wall Painting of the Fourteenth Century*. Routledge and Kegan Paul, 1955.

ARCHITECTURE

Batsford, Harry, and Fry, Charles. *The Greater English Church*. Batsford, 1945.

Budden, Charles W. *English Gothic Churches*. Oxford, 1927.

Cautley, H. Munro. *Norfolk Churches*. Adlard, 1949.

Clapham, A. W. *Romanesque Architecture in Western Europe*. Oxford, 1936.

Cook, G. H. *The English Mediaeval Parish Church.* Phoenix House, 1954.

Cox, J. Charles, and Ford, Charles Bradley. *The Parish Churches of England.* Batsford, 1943-4.

Crossley, F. H. *English Church Craftsmanship.* Batsford, 1941.

—— *English Church Design.* Batsford, 1945.

Delaporte, Y. R. J. 'La Cathédrale de Chartres.' *Encyclopédie Alpina*, Paris, 1947.

Deschamps, Paul. *Les Cathédrales et les Sanctuaires du Moyen Age: Vézelay.* Editions Tel, 1943.

Hutton, Graham, and Smith, Edwin. *English Parish Churches.* Thames and Hudson, 1952.

Lethaby, W. R. *Westminster Abbey and the King's Craftsmen.* Duckworth, 1906.

Shaw, Rev. Patrick J. *An Old York Church; All Hallows in North Street.* The Church Shop, York, 1934.

SCULPTURE

Anderson, M. D. *The Mediaeval Carver.* Cambridge, 1935.

Ashton, Leigh. *Style in Sculpture.* Oxford, 1947.

Beaulieu, Michèle. *La Sculpture Romane.* Braun, 1951.

Cave, C. J. P. *Roof Bosses in Mediaeval Churches.* Cambridge, 1948.

—— and Pevsner, Nikolaus. *Mediaeval Carvings in Exeter Cathedral.* King Penguin, 1953.

Gardner, Arthur. *English Mediaeval Sculpture.* Cambridge, 1951.

Marcousé, Renée. 'Figure Sculpture in St. Mary's Abbey, York'. *Yorkshire Museum Papers, No. 1,* 1951.

Molesworth, H. D. *Sculpture in England: Mediaeval.* Longmans, Green, 1951.

Pevsner, Nikolaus. *The Leaves of Southwell.* King Penguin, 1945.

Réau, Louis. *L'Art religieux du Moyen Age: La Sculpture.* Fernand Nathan, 1946.

Saxl, F. *English Sculpture of the Twelfth Century.* Faber and Faber, 1954.

Zarnecki, George. *English Romanesque Sculpture, 1066-1140.* Tiranti, 1951.

—— *Later English Romanesque Sculpture, 1140-1210.* Tiranti, 1953.

—— *English Romanesque Lead Sculpture.* Tiranti, 1957.

WOODWORK

Anderson, M. D. *Misericords.* King Penguin, 1954.

Howard, F. E., and Crossley, F. H. *English Church Woodwork.* Batsford, 1927.

Vallance, Aymer. *English Church Screens.* Batsford, 1936.

STAINED GLASS

Anonymous. *The Last Fifteen Days of the World*. The Church Shop, York. (N.D.)

Arnold, Hugh, and Saint, Lawrence B. *Stained Glass of the Middle Ages in England and France.* Black, 1939.

Aubert, Marcel. *Stained Glass of the Twelfth and Thirteenth Centuries from French Cathedrals*. Batsford, 1947.

Hamand, L. A. *The Ancient Windows of Great Malvern Priory Church*. Campfield Press, St. Alban's, 1947.

Harrison, F. *The Painted Glass of York*. S.P.C.K., 1927.

—— Stained Glass of York Minster, *Studio*. (N.D.)

Le Couteur, J. D. *English Mediaeval Painted Glass*. S.P.C.K., 1932.

Rackham, Bernard. *The Ancient Glass of Canterbury Cathedral*. Lund Humphries, 1949.

MISCELLANEOUS SUBJECTS

Digby, George Wingfield. *French Tapestries from the Fourteenth to the Eighteenth Century*. Batsford, 1951.

Mann, James. *Monumental Brasses*. King Penguin, 1957.

Natanson, Joseph. *Gothic Ivories of the Thirteenth and Fourteenth Centuries*. Tiranti, 1951.

Rice, David Talbot. *Russian Icons*. King Penguin, 1947.

Schweinfurth, Philipp. *Russian Icons*. Batsford, 1953.

Stenton, Sir Frank (Editor). *The Bayeux Tapestry*. Phaidon, 1957.

Wild, Doris. *Les Icônes*. Payot. (N.D.)

GENERAL

Anderson, M. D. *The Imagery of British Churches*. Murray, 1955.

Boase, T. S. R. *English Art, 1100-1216*. Oxford, 1953.

Brieger, Peter. *English Art, 1216-1307*. Oxford, 1957.

Coulton, G. G. *Art and the Reformation*. Cambridge, 1953.

Dupont, Jacques, and Gnudi, Cesare. *Gothic Painting*. Skira, 1954.

Evans, Joan. *English Art, 1307-1461*. Oxford, 1949.

—— *Art in Mediaeval France*. Oxford, 1948.

—— *Cluniac Art of the Romanesque Period*. Cambridge, 1950.

Gantner, Joseph
Pobé, Marcel ⎬*Romanesque Art in France*. Thames and Hudson, 1956.
Roubier, Jean

Hinks, Roger. *Carolingian Art*. Sidgwick and Jackson, 1935.

Hussey, J. M. *The Byzantine World*. Hutchinson, 1957.

Ingram, Rev. James (translator). *The Anglo-Saxon Chronicle*. Dent. (N.D.)

Keary, A. and E. *The Heroes of Asgard*. Macmillan, 1908.

Kendrick, T. D. *Anglo-Saxon Art to A.D. 900*. Methuen, 1938.
—— *Late Saxon and Viking Art*. Methuen, 1949.

Kitzinger, Ernst. *Early Mediaeval Art in the British Museum*. British Museum, 1940.

Lethaby, W. R. *Mediaeval Art, 312-1350*. Duckworth, 1912.

Lidell, Robert. *Byzantium and Istanbul*. Jonathan Cape, 1956.

Mâle, Emile. *Religious Art from the Twelfth to the Eighteenth Century*. Routledge and Kegan Paul, 1949.

Milburn, R. L. P. *Saints and their Emblems in English Churches*. Oxford, 1949.

Morey, Charles Rufus. *Mediaeval Art*. Norton & Co., New York, 1942.

Newton, Eric. *European Painting and Sculpture*. Penguin Books, 1950.

Prentice, Sartell. *The Voices of the Cathedral*. Harrap. (N.D.)

Previté-Orton, C. W. *The Shorter Cambridge Mediaeval History*. Cambridge, 1952.

Réau, Louis (Editor). *L'Art Gothique en France*. Guy le Prat, 1945.

Rice, David Talbot. *Byzantine Art*. Oxford, 1935.
—— *English Art, 871-1100*. Oxford, 1952.
—— *The Beginnings of Christian Art*. Hodder and Stoughton, 1957.

Sander, N. *Istanbul*. Editions Rhea, Paris, 1955.

Saunders, O. Elfrida. *English Art in the Middle Ages*. Oxford, 1932.

Saxl, F., and Wittkower, R. *British Art and the Mediterranean*. Oxford, 1948.

Tanner, Laurence E. *Unknown Westminster Abbey*. King Penguin, 1948.

Toynbee, Jocelyn, and Perkins, John Ward. *The Shrine of St. Peter*. Longmans, Green, 1956.

Venerable Bede (translated, T. Stapleton). *Ecclesiastical History of the English People*. Burns, Oates & Washbourne, 1955.

Waddell, Helen. *The Wandering Scholars*. Constable, 1944.

There are also many guides to cathedrals and churches which contain valuable information and sometimes good illustrations. These are too numerous to mention in detail.

INDEX